WHY
MANAGERS
MATTER

WHY
MANAGERS
MATTER

THE PERILS *of the*
BOSSLESS COMPANY

NICOLAI J. FOSS
& PETER G. KLEIN

PUBLICAFFAIRS

New York

PublicAffairs
Hachette Book Group
1290 Avenue of the Americas, New York, NY 10104
www.publicaffairsbooks.com
@Public_Affairs

Printed in the United States of America

First Edition: October 2022

Published by PublicAffairs, an imprint of Perseus Books, LLC, a subsidiary of Hachette Book Group, Inc. The PublicAffairs name and logo is a trademark of the Hachette Book Group.

The Hachette Speakers Bureau provides a wide range of authors for speaking events. To find out more, go to www.hachettespeakersbureau.com or call (866) 376-6591.

The publisher is not responsible for websites (or their content) that are not owned by the publisher.

Print book interior design by Amy Quinn

Library of Congress Cataloging-in-Publication Data
Names: Foss, Nicolai J., 1964– author. | Klein, Peter G., author.
Title: Why managers matter : the perils of the bossless company / Nicolai
    J. Foss and Peter G. Klein.
Description: First edition. | New York : PublicAffairs, [2022] | Includes
    bibliographical references and index. |
Identifiers: LCCN 2022006749 | ISBN 9781541751040 (hardcover) | ISBN
    9781541751033 (ebook)
Subjects: LCSH: Management. | Executives. | Organizational behavior. |
    Organizational effectiveness.
Classification: LCC HD31.2 .F67 2022 | DDC 658—dc23/eng/20220216
LC record available at https://lccn.loc.gov/2022006749

ISBNs: 9781541751040 (hardcover), 9781541751033 (ebook)

LSC-C

Printing 1, 2022

CONTENTS

1

FIRE ALL THE MANAGERS?

THE CLASSIC 1956 FILM *THE MAN IN THE GRAY FLANNEL SUIT* features Gregory Peck as Tom Rath, a junior executive struggling to rise to the top of the fictional United Broadcasting Corporation. Tom is a World War II veteran struggling to adjust to civilian life while balancing work and family demands. Tom doesn't like his job or his bosses and doesn't care about the business. But he wants the money, influence, and respect that come from being a corporate big shot. As he works his way up the corporate ladder, he starts to rebel against the bland conformity of office culture—represented by the clothing that gives the story its title—and of 1950s suburban life. Tom's struggle to retain his individuality and autonomy, as well as to keep his family together and supported, while navigating the corporate hierarchy makes for a compelling narrative.

The popular recent TV series *Mad Men* takes its inspiration from the corporate world of that era, with its cool hats, two-martini lunches, office politics, and family intrigue lurking beneath the quiet suburban landscape. Fans loved the retro look and sharply drawn characters, but few would want a return to the corporate hierarchy on display in *Mad Men* in their own jobs today.

By contrast, consider the workplace depicted in the 2010 blockbuster *The Social Network*. Voted number 27 among the 100 best films of the twenty-first century by 117 film critics from around the world, the movie deals with all-American themes like entrepreneurship and lawsuits, telling the story of the founding of Facebook and the controversies that followed. A striking feature of the culture of Facebook in the early days is its flatness—friends and fellow students working together without bosses, coming together in fluid groups to solve problems.

These two movies depict completely different ways of organizing and managing work. They are iconic exactly because in the popular imagination they represent different eras with all that implies about different tastes, work, and personal relationships. The flat, networked, team-based organization is juxtaposed against the traditional managerial hierarchy— or "the square versus the tower" in the words of the historian Niall Ferguson.[1] In the network organization you do things and make others follow—sometimes "moving fast and breaking things," as Facebook CEO Mark Zuckerberg described his philosophy—because you're better, smarter, or more charismatic. In the hierarchical organization things move when the person above you in the organizational chart allows you to move them.

THE BOSSLESS COMPANY NARRATIVE

An influential genre of business books, articles, lectures, and college and business school courses teach today that the classic managerial hierarchy is dead, or at least dying—and good riddance. They aren't just saying that reform, restructuring, and reimagining are often necessary. Indeed, some companies have excessive corporate fat: layers could often be cut, and empowering employees might increase productivity. This genre—which we call the bossless company narrative—has something far more radical to say. The title of one article, "First, Let's Fire All the Managers"— published in, of all places, the *Harvard Business Review*—may have been adopted for dramatic effect, but it also clearly communicates this genre's message.[2]

Humanocracy: Creating Organizations as Amazing as the People Inside Them by best-selling management writers Gary Hamel and Michele Zanini is the most recent in a decades-long string of books telling us that leaner, flatter, and more agile organizations are in and corporate dinosaurs are out.[3] The book and its message resonate with the intended audience: *Humanocracy* is a best-seller and comes complete with "Humanocracy: Hack My Org," an online course developed and run by the authors. Another recent example is Frederic Laloux's highly popular *Reinventing Organizations: A Guide to Creating Organizations Inspired by the Next Stage of Human Consciousness.*[4] The book has sold more than 400,000 copies worldwide and may well be the most influential management book of the decade. Reflecting its New Agey subtitle, this book offers a new "soulful" (yes, really) way of running a business—one with no performance targets or job descriptions and very little budgeting. Instead, it features "soulful practices" that, of course, make organizations extraordinarily productive and highly purposeful!

The basic thrust of the genre is that while bosses are still around, the less control they exercise the better. Their job is to preach corporate culture and values, balance the interests of competing stakeholders, and keep regulators and critics at bay, as when 181 top CEOs from the US Business Roundtable pledged in August 2019 to be good corporate citizens and not to privilege the interests of shareholders over other elements of society. What the Harvard historian Alfred D. Chandler Jr. called the "visible hand" of management should give way to worker autonomy, self-organizing teams, outsourcing, and an egalitarian office culture. Today this is the dominant business narrative. Countless blogs and articles in the *Harvard Business Review* either directly promote it or more indirectly reflect it. The narrative is sometimes used to advertise highly popular self-management approaches like "Agile" and "Holacracy."

To be sure, the workplace changed a lot between the time of *The Man in the Gray Flannel Suit* and that of *The Social Network.* In the corporate world, one traditional, hierarchical corporate giant after another fell, or at least became a smaller and less important player. Everyone knows the Kodak story, and other well-known examples include Xerox, Blockbuster, Nokia, JCPenney, Yahoo, Myspace, Macy's, Hitachi, Polaroid, Toshiba, RadioShack, Netscape, and Toys"R"Us. Most of these firms failed because they didn't notice deep-seated changes in technologies or, if they noticed, didn't act quickly enough. Unfortunately, the business press and the gurus alike have rather uniformly ascribed these failures to the hierarchical nature of these companies, indicting hierarchy in general, rather than the specific form it took in (some of) these companies.

We will detail many ways in which the workplace has changed in response to changes in society, culture, technology, and globalization. And yet we don't buy the new narrative. We think it is largely misguided, based on cherry-picked examples with little grounding in theory or evidence.

Of course, it is easy to criticize and much harder to create. What do we offer instead of the bossless company narrative? That one is easy: the real alternative to the bossless company, by and large, is the conventional managerial hierarchy. Writers like Hamel and Zanini and Laloux are fiercely critical of traditional hierarchy, but we think they exaggerate its problems and neglect its many benefits. The traditional hierarchy still plays an essential role in most companies and has continued to do so despite rapid technological change, the challenges of the information economy, and increased global competition, all of which supposedly have contributed to its demise. The near-bossless companies—and there aren't many of them—with their self-managing teams, empowered knowledge workers, and ultra-flat organizations are not generally or demonstrably better than traditionally organized ones. Bosses matter, not just as figureheads but as designers, organizers, encouragers, and enforcers.

With that said, and as we show in the coming pages, there are right and wrong ways to organize corporate hierarchies. Sometimes the right way is a steep hierarchy with many bosses; other times something flatter works better. More important, the role of the boss has changed in important ways. Smart bosses spend less time on day-to-day supervision of employees and more time thinking about the key strategic issues and designing the company by specifying the basic rules of the game: Who can do what with company resources? What are the overall goals each unit should meet? How are incentives best tailored to suit the organization? Good bosses also spend time managing uncertainty and adapting the company's strategy and structure by handling overall coordination between employees and units.

Before previewing the arguments in detail, consider the context in which the new narrative of the flattening hierarchy and the bossless company has emerged. The fluid world of *The Social Network* seems more familiar to today's audiences than the rigid hierarchy of *The Man in the Gray Flannel Suit* because the tech giants have replaced the manufacturing firms of the nineteenth century and the service companies of the twentieth as the dominant companies. Quarter after quarter Microsoft, Google, Apple, and Amazon are in the top five, with Meta (Facebook) just behind. These are the firms that generate the most press and that our students want to work for, not only because they are good companies, but also because they are sexy and cool with their open workspaces, casual dress codes, and horizontal structures. These companies are seen as the wave of the future, the harbingers of the flat, decentralized, worker-empowered, team-based, networked, even "bossless" company. (Still, most people recognize that these companies are often headed by autocratic leaders who can come across as almost as compulsive about control as the late Steve Jobs.)

To exemplify the new and increasingly influential trope for how people talk about companies—the bossless company narrative—imagine working for a company with no hierarchy or authority. On your first day at work you are given a *Handbook for New Employees*. It welcomes you to "Flatland," "our shorthand way of saying," the handbook explains, "that we don't have any management, and nobody 'reports to' anybody else. We do have a founder-president, but even he isn't your manager. This company is yours to steer—toward opportunities and away from risks. You have the power to green-light projects. You have the power to ship products." Oh, and if you don't like what you are working on, with whom you work, or where you work, you just move—that's why there are wheels on your desk!

"Flatland" is an actual company: Valve, the computer game developer behind games such as *Counter-Strike*. It became the poster child for the emerging bossless company narrative when its employee handbook was "leaked" in 2012. However, various insider accounts have told a different story about how it is organized. A former employee said that "there is actually a hidden layer of powerful management structure in the company" that made it feel "a lot like high school." Another insider described it as a company run by a cabal of "barons." A company, like any social system, abhors a power vacuum, and companies are no exception to what the sociologist Robert Michels called "the Iron Law of Oligarchy."[5] If there are no formal bosses, informal ones will emerge. Natural leaders arise to fill the gaps left by formal leadership structures. So if you look more closely at those ostensibly bossless companies, you see that they do have formal bosses. At Valve, he is Gabe Newell, the subject of countless fawning profiles. Right away, this suggests that perhaps the whole boss-less company narrative is a bit of a head-fake—a way to draw attention to the charismatic, influential leaders who create and promote flat structures. We will say more about Valve in the pages ahead as we show more generally how the bossless company narrative paints a misleading picture of the actual business landscape.

On the more positive side, our key claim in this book is that *The Man in the Gray Flannel Suit* is still in many ways a more useful guide to corporate life and workplace culture than *The Social Network*. Contrary to popular opinion, the world is not becoming dominated by flatter, even bossless, network organizations. Very flat organizations exist, but they are outliers, and likely to remain so. Measured by revenues, the top ten largest companies worldwide are Walmart, Sinopec, Royal Dutch Shell, China National Petroleum, State Grid, Saudi Aramco, BP, ExxonMobil, Volkswagen, and Toyota—one retailer, two carmakers, and a bunch of oil companies—and all are traditionally organized with conventional managerial hierarchies. Although traditional corporations may be changing as they move from manufacturing to services, become slightly smaller, and increase their levels of delayering and delegation, they are far from the near-bossless companies that are supposedly the wave of the future.

Moreover, many of the poster children for the flat, networked, decentralized company story are not as special as they seem. Consider Spotify, one of Europe's few big tech firms, often seen as a stereotypical knowledge economy company that empowers employees in freely forming teams. On closer inspection, however, Spotify turns out to be a fairly

[Handwritten margin notes: "bosses always arise" and "if bosses so great why aren't they at the top?"]

ordinary company, although its wall colors are a bit brighter, its sofas cozier, and the names it gives its organizational units hipper than what you see in ordinary companies.

China's Haier Group, one of the world's largest appliance manufacturers, touts its RenDanHeYi model in which every employee "acts as a CEO." As the actual CEO, Zhang Ruimin explains: "With the RenDan-HeYi model we move away from being like an empire (with a traditional, closed pyramid) to be more like a rain forest (with an open networked platform). Every empire will eventually collapse. A rain forest, on the other hand, can be sustained." Haier delegates most decision authority to its four thousand micro-enterprises, which are bundled into three hundred "ecosystem microcommunities."[6] This is a highly decentralized model, to be sure, but not a radical departure from the decentralized multidivisional structure pioneered in the 1920s and discussed in Chapter 6.

An even more salient example is the ultimate bossless organization, Wikipedia, the world's most popular encyclopedia. This open-source, open-access, crowdsourced lexicon contains (at the time of this writing) almost six million articles on topics ranging from Aa! (a Japanese pop group) to Z.O.W.I.E. (a fictional spy outfit)—an astonishing achievement that would be inconceivable in the world of conventional, hierarchical, curated encyclopedias. The latest print version (2013) of the *Encyclopedia Britannica* had approximately 40,000 articles, and the online version had 120,000—an impressive number, but still short of Wikipedia by a factor of 50. Wikipedia looks like a slap in the face to the traditional model of top-down design. In fact, it looks like the quintessential example of what Nobel laureate F. A. Hayek called the "spontaneous order" of undesigned interaction that mobilizes and leverages bottom-up initiative and knowledge in the absence of any central direction.

But Wikipedia was in key respects designed; it didn't just emerge in an entirely spontaneous manner. Articles are written and edited by the crowd, but the structure of Wikipedia—the underlying code, the rules of format and content, the processes by which articles are created and revised—was created by Jimmy Wales, who established the project in January 2001, wrote most of the code, and currently presides as head of the Wikipedia Foundation. Wales read Hayek's "The Use of Knowledge in Society" in an economics class at Auburn University and became convinced that bottom-up, crowdsourced designs were the future for directories, guidebooks, and other information resources. He set out to create an online, open-source encyclopedia. But the "order" he created was at best "semi-spontaneous."

The Wikipedia case is interesting, not because of the usual interpretation, but because of what most accounts leave out—the importance of a founding organizational architect and the framework he designed. It raises the crucial questions that we are concerned with in this book: What are the limits of management in an increasingly knowledge-based, networked, and dynamic world? Even in a case of entirely knowledge-based production based on loose networks of people who are mostly entirely anonymous to each other, there is a need for management to define and enforce the basic rules of the game. What are the broader implications of that requirement? That is, what is the role of management in more traditional organizations, even if it needs to source the knowledge from outside their boundaries, hire specialists and knowledge workers, and delegate much decision initiative down the hierarchy?

The way we approach and answer these questions matters in practice. It matters for what we tell our prospective employees, it matters for the management style and rhetoric we endorse, and it matters for how we organize, manage, and lead our companies. For example, if the way we communicate to our employees is mostly along the lines of *The Social Network* but our actual management practice is more like *The Man in the Gray Flannel Suit* (or, less likely, the opposite), such corporate hypocrisy is going to cause trouble. Later we will see how such a mismatch between espoused and actual management practices created difficulties at Oticon, one of the first organizations to experiment with radical decentralization. How we answer these questions also matters to whether we find experimenting with implementing "holacratic" or "teal" organization worthwhile. And at the most fundamental level it matters to whether we adopt an organizational and management approach that fits the productive activities we engage in to create value for our various stakeholder groups. There may be activities for which a radically decentralized management model with very little of the traditional hierarchy functions well. But most companies are not engaged in such activities. And if goods and services really can be produced without any managerial intervention at all, then we have no need for companies in the first place—individuals and groups will just come together spontaneously in the marketplace.

THE TRADITIONAL BUSINESS FIRM

So what is a company? Here is our take: the traditionally structured business, with its owners, executives, middle managers, and employees, is the most salient of what Nobel laureate Oliver Williamson called the "economic institutions of capitalism." Of course, a market economy is characterized by . . . markets. Still, in a complex, modern, industrial economy, nearly all production takes place inside business firms, and much of what we call the "market" is firms competing or cooperating with each other. Entrepreneurs bring firms into existence, and employees acquire, combine, and assemble resources into an ever-increasing variety of consumer goods and services, all under the watchful supervision of the managerial hierarchy, itself reporting to a board of directors representing investors.

In the late twentieth century, the popular perception of management was shaped by cinematic hits like *The Man in the Gray Flannel Suit*. In fact, "office movies" is a distinct cinematic category. Films such as *Office Space* (1999), *Brazil* (1985), *The Devil Wears Prada* (2006), and *Up in the Air* (2009) and TV shows like *The Office*—or, outside the Anglosphere, movies like *Meraty Modeer A'aam* (1966) and *Ard El-Nefaq* (1968)—have certain main themes: employees hating their dreary, predictable jobs; the hierarchy turning employees into corporate-tamed dogs; the arbitrary, even cruel power of top executives; and the liberation of joining an informal start-up or abandoning corporate docility. Books such as William Whyte's *The Organization Man* (1956) had a similar message: the large, hierarchical enterprise may be highly efficient, but it is also a bland and dehumanizing machine.

Of course, this machine also comes with a lot of benefits: it lowers costs, reduces the variability of the quality of the goods and services it

delivers to the marketplace, and guarantees relatively stable employment—including a regular paycheck. This explains its longevity.

In the academic literature, the business historian Alfred Chandler's
landmark studies of managerial hierarchy, *Strategy and Structure* (1962)
and *The Visible Hand* (1977), showed how the large enterprise had displaced its smaller predecessors through its superior efficiency and productivity. Businesses grow by bringing transactions and activities inside their
boundaries, and the managerial function organized in a formal hierarchy is central for the understanding of what firms are and do and for the
functioning of the economy.

Interestingly, while the traditionally organized business firm may not
have been viewed favorably in popular culture, until recently most scholars, journalists, policymakers, and businesspeople saw it as an important
source of dynamism, wealth creation, and growth. Even critics like John
Kenneth Galbraith and Ralph Nader, who wanted the corporation regulated heavily to avoid mischief, could not imagine an industrial economy
without large companies. Developing countries and rural areas have recruited factories, distribution centers, and other big firms to generate employment and kick-start their economies. Adam Smith's division of labor
has gradually been brought from the market into the modern industrial
enterprise.

THE DEATH OF HIERARCHY?

This narrative about the benefits of the way companies have traditionally
been organized has been foundational for most thinking about management. It has informed the way economists, sociologists, historians, and
other scholars think about firms, hierarchies, and managers. It is central
to the thinking of most academics, consultants, and managers, and it in-
forms almost everything taught in business schools. And yet, paradoxically, according to the new and increasingly influential bossless company
narrative, the standard account is wrong! The managerial hierarchy—in
some understandings, management itself—once served a useful purpose but is now becoming outdated. Just as the old-fashioned workplace
famously described by Frederick Winslow Taylor (and hence dubbed

"Taylorite"), with its army of worker-drones, was replaced by highly educated, strongly motivated, independent, and creative "knowledge workers," the traditional firm is now being replaced by flatter organizations,
peer-to-peer networks, distributed leadership, platforms, extreme decentralization, worker empowerment, independent contracting, and entrepreneurship. As *Sloan Management Review* editor Paul Michelman
declares, we are entering "a time of disintermediation both within and
between organizations. Layers of management will fall; the need for centralized systems and trusted go-betweens will dissipate, if not disappear."[7]

Note the future tense in many of these kinds of pronouncements! The
scholars, pundits, and consultants who promote the new narrative engage in more prophesying than analyzing. They bolster their predictions
by pointing to a few companies that broke down hierarchies and implemented flatter structures. Besides Valve, another highly touted example is
the online retailer Zappos, now an Amazon subsidiary, which embraced
the "Holacracy" model purported to replace traditional job titles and reporting lines with flexible, emergent, self-organizing teams. As we will
see in our discussion of Holacracy in Chapter 5, this model led to a series
of problems at Zappos (including, ironically, an increase in bureaucracy
resulting from endless meetings and negotiations) and was quietly abandoned, although this history doesn't seem to have tempered the enthusiasm of bossless company advocates.

The bossless company narrative is typically justified by pointing to two
overall trends. One is technological: transactions between firms or between workers can be handled seamlessly through electronic interfaces
and managed by the blockchain. The other is psychological, ranging from
Laloux's claims of a radical shift in human awareness—remember that
his book's subtitle invokes "the Next Stage of Human Consciousness"—
to more cautious (and verifiable) claims that empowered and intrinsically
motivated millennial and Gen Z workers cannot function under the rigid,
stuffy bureaucracy of the traditional large firm.

The result of these two trends, we are told, is that just as the top-down,
hierarchical, and conventional *Encyclopedia Britannica* was displaced by
the bottom-up, flat, and flexible Wikipedia, so traditionally organized

companies are being displaced by the "wikified" firms of the knowledge-based, networked economy with its flat structures, self-organizing teams, employee ownership, worker democracy, and mobilization of the spontaneous forces of the market inside hierarchies.

Allegedly, the management model of the future is one that combines extreme delegation and continuous learning supported by IT. As we will show, there are many benefits to decentralization, as well as costs, and these vary widely with context and circumstance. Our book separates the wheat from the chaff in the many claims about "bossless" and "wikified" organizations to show when the benefits of delegation exceed the costs— and vice versa.

Unfortunately, strong decentralization is being pushed as a one-size-fits-all solution. Consultants promote Holacracy and Agile Scrum as self-managing replacements for the top-down exercise of authority, and even as ways to eliminate authority altogether (although, as we will argue, these tools don't actually do this). Agile has been implemented by Barclays, Cerner, C. H. Robinson, Microsoft, Ericsson, Riot Games, Google, and Spotify. Overstock uses internal voting systems to decide company priorities. In other words, the new narrative on firm organization is not just a set of abstract academic theories or fluffy consultant talk with no serious implications for business. On the contrary, these are ideas that truly *matter*—and they are already reshaping business.

The claims that are made on behalf of the new narrative range from heavy-handed extrapolations of real trends from a few cherry-picked examples to wild speculation. Many of these claims are flatly wrong at worst. There is little real evidence behind them, despite many colorful anecdotes. We are worried that the ideas associated with the new narrative are misleading to journalists and students and potentially harmful to practitioners who may be too eager to jettison their existing management structures in pursuit of the latest fad.

While the internet, cheap and reliable wireless communication, Moore's law, miniaturization, information markets, and other technological miracles have induced sweeping changes in manufacturing, retail, transportation, and communication, the laws of economics are still the laws of economics, human nature hasn't changed, and the basic problem of management and business—how to assemble, organize, and motivate groups of people and resources to produce the goods and services consumers want—is the same as it ever was. Since the industrial revolution, entrepreneurs have been organizing extremely complex activities in firms that are neither completely centralized nor completely flat. Imagine the complexity involved in operating a national railroad, a steel mill, or an automobile assembly plant in the nineteenth and early twentieth centuries. These were all "knowledge-based activities" conducted in teams organized in various structures. The historical work of Alfred Chandler showed that the emergence of large-scale enterprise depended not only on investments in production and distribution but also on innovative management structures that delegated decision authority throughout the corporate hierarchy. Are things different today?

OUR ARGUMENT IN A NUTSHELL

This book is both critical and constructive. First, we assess the bossless company narrative with a skeptical eye. We show that the narrative gets important tendencies in business wrong. It is true that many companies have been delayering by cutting middle management roles and delegating decisions to lower levels of the corporate hierarchy. This trend was greatly accelerated by the Covid-19 pandemic. Travel restrictions kept multinational corporations from sending managers abroad, so local subsidiaries had to assume more responsibility. Governments made companies send their employees home, where they worked with less formal supervision.

The lesson of the pandemic, according to the tech writer Ed Zitron, is that "America has too many managers." He thinks that the United States, "more than anywhere else in the world, is addicted to the *concept* of management," that management is a "title rather than a discipline," and that it "is focused more on taking credit and placing blame rather than actually managing people."[8] This view of management as a drain on productivity is increasingly common. But it is wrong. Management is essential for coordinating people, resources, and tasks, especially during unprecedented disruptions like the pandemic, when decisions had to be made about moving to remote work, delegating decisions, and reconfiguring supply chains (a point that Zitron, paradoxically, admits).

Our book summarizes key thinking and evidence about the nature and purpose of the managerial hierarchy to show what good managers do and how the managerial role has changed. We tell the story of the transformation of managerial authority and corporate hierarchy. While some gurus and the fads they promote argue for scaling back or eliminating hierarchy, even promoting the fully bossless company, we will show, echoing Mark Twain, that the death of hierarchy has been greatly exaggerated and that its bad reputation is largely undeserved. Authority and hierarchy—rightly exercised—are useful and necessary for companies to thrive. But to see this we need to provide a clear understanding of the crucial role that hierarchy and authority play in a modern, knowledge-based economy. In a nutshell, we present the positive side of hierarchy in the twenty-first century.

Here is how we tell this story:

We critically discuss the new narrative about management. We evaluate claims about the death of hierarchy from a theoretical and historical point of view. Throughout the book we examine the usual cases invoked as examples in the new narrative—not only Valve and Zappos but also the textile and clothing company W. L. Gore, the tomato producer Morning Star, and the hearing aid company Oticon, all of which have been important poster companies for those developing a myth about the bossless company.[9]

This myth has two parts: first, that today's most exciting and innovative companies are bossless (or almost bossless), and second, that all other companies should embrace the bossless company model. As Tim Kastelle, an innovation management expert at the University of Queensland Business School, put it: "It's time to start reimagining management. Making everyone a chief is a good place to start."[10] Laloux sees his flat (and humanistic) organization (which he calls "teal") as the model, not for just a few companies in a few industries but for "every kind of organization." As he explains in a 2018 interview:

I've heard from a number of manufacturing businesses that have flourished with these new practices. Same thing with a number of retailers. There are tech start-ups. Nonprofits. Hospitals. Schools. Retreat centers. There are truck drivers who self-manage, cleaning companies that adopt these practices. . . . You name it. In the last few months, I've also suddenly heard from a number of municipalities and local government agencies.

What's been most surprising to me is that a handful of CEOs of very large organizations (tens of thousands of employees, multinational or global) are really getting the ideas of the book and are inviting their organizations to move in this direction. That's really hopeful to me! Of course, reinventing such large organizations takes more time, but the first signs are very promising.[11]

Other writers are more cautious, admitting that the bossless model may not work for all companies in all situations. However, the more bombastic statements are typically not so nuanced.

As we will show in this book, this myth is based on a basic misunderstanding of what companies do and how companies work. Basic economic theory suggests that there's no point in organizing a firm without someone to do the organizing and to run the operation—otherwise everyone would be an independent contractor. Even partnerships normally feature some kind of hierarchy, with one partner assuming more leadership responsibility than others. To be sure, there are potential benefits from delegating responsibility, empowering workers, and adopting a more decentralized structure. But flattening the hierarchy also brings costs: for example, coordinating people and activities is harder, particularly when tasks are highly interdependent. Decentralization makes sense when its benefits outweigh the costs, as they sometimes do—but not all the time!

Failing to recognize these contingencies and embracing flatness without regard to the circumstances is dangerous. This kind of thinking encourages firms to jump on the bandwagon, following the latest fashion without thinking carefully about whether it works for their own company. It favors razzle-dazzle—clever slogans, fancy jargon, social media attention—over thoughtful, careful deliberation about how to manage well. The new narrative that "bosslessness is always best" ignores what we call the "perils of the bossless company": inefficiency, lack of agility, and stagnation—exactly the outcomes the narrative claims you can avoid!

These perils result from the lack of structure, transparency, supervision, and leadership. Without well-defined roles and responsibilities, it is hard to coordinate people and tasks quickly and smoothly. Without formal rules and procedures, everything gets politicized and decision-making becomes messy and prone to conflict. In the absence of skilled managers, opportunities to coach and monitor for effective talent development are lost, disagreements cannot be settled without endless meetings and arguments, and the company becomes unable to adapt to outside changes caused by competitors, regulators, or technology.[12]

The bossless company model, as we will see, often comes with a personality cult, lacks clear mission and focus, and results in an overall lack of employee satisfaction—despite loud claims to the contrary. Paradoxically, management and hierarchy can help companies become agile and adaptive.

To be fair, a few companies have adopted nearly bossless structures while avoiding these perils. Businesses that use simple technologies and processes have little need to coordinate people and processes. For example, single employees of Safelite Autoglass can replace broken windshields in cars and trucks. An employee carrying out a self-contained task doesn't depend directly on what another employee is doing. A boss isn't needed to sort out how tasks are connected in the production process. Still, there may be a need for a boss to define the tasks and provide incentives. Even when tasks are simple, complete bosslessness is unlikely to be the most successful model.

For most companies, however, the perils of the bossless company structure are roadblocks to profitability and growth. People, tasks, and processes are normally *interdependent* and can't always organize themselves from the bottom up. These perils are costly! We spell them out using examples and logic and show you how to avoid them.

There is another big problem with the new narrative: the evidence doesn't match the exaggerated claims made by the gurus. Just look at the poster companies for the bossless company narrative. Although firms such as Oticon and Morning Star experimented with strongly decentralized models, managers played important roles at every stage. Moreover, their flat structures worked (or seemed to work) only because they already had in place a technology that made decentralization easy. Valve, for example, relies on heavily modularized software development that can easily be delegated to self-managing teams. In other cases, the hand of management was actually quite heavy; Zappos, for example, faced the problem of dominant, even overpowering, top managers, as we will see. This suggests that either the cases are cherry-picked or the claims are directly misleading.

Finally, we show that even seemingly successful examples of flat organization, like Gore and Morning Star, are special cases. They are fun to read about but don't provide general lessons for managers. The Gore and Morning Star models don't scale, aren't easily replicable, and owe their success as much to luck and special circumstances as to a carefully worked-out philosophy of management. For every media darling like Zappos, there are firms like Blinkist, a German company that produces short summaries of important books (hopefully including ours!). Blinkist tried replacing its traditional management structure with Holacracy only to discover, after two years, that

> the bold experiment that had promised freedom had turned into a straitjacket. "Instead of solving problems, we were spending all our time asking how do we solve them Holacratically?" [cofounder Niklas] Jansen says. Blinkist concluded that being ruled by the book was as onerous as being ruled by a boss. "One thing we really underestimated was the step-by-step explaining required to familiarize new people with a completely different way of working. It's so many words that you need to learn to get the whole system."[13]

We argue that, in the knowledge-based economy, *management is becoming more important, not less.* Contrary to the new narrative, meeting the demands of the current environment has made managerial authority even more essential than it was in earlier periods. In knowledge-based, networked economies, the conditions are far less predictable. Part of the function of management has always been to adapt the company to uncertainty. When something out of the ordinary happens that cannot easily be handled by the company's existing procedures, managers step in to handle the situation. When conditions become less predictable, the need for managers to handle uncertainty becomes even more important.

In fact, many companies that have survived major shocks to technology, regulation, and global competition have had strong, charismatic leaders with highly authoritative styles. In what is arguably the greatest corporate comeback of all time, Steve Jobs, faced with a major restructuring, rescued Apple by making tough decisions (cutting the Newton project, setting up a partnership with Microsoft) against considerable resistance. It is no coincidence that many of the best-known successful corporate turnarounds are pinned to single individuals, such as Jobs at Apple, Lou Gerstner at IBM, Carly Fiorina at HP, Howard Schultz at Starbucks, and Peter Cuneo at Marvel. The lesson is that centralizing decision authority can often reduce the delays resulting from more collaborative and consensus-driven approaches.

Also, research suggests that corporations that delayer their hierarchy are often not decentralizing—quite the contrary. For example, Lego, the Danish toy company, has recently moved to a more centralized business model. As Lego reduced the number of its management layers in recent years, it expanded the layer of top management, bringing in functional specialists and moving senior managers much closer to operations. Lego's moves may be part of a broader trend. In a study of management hierarchies and compensation at three hundred Fortune 500 companies over fourteen years, researchers found that even though companies were delayering, the size of their executive team (defined as the number of positions reporting directly to the CEO) doubled from an average of five to ten. What's more, executives were intervening more frequently in operating decisions. The result is counterintuitive: flat management structures can have more micro-management than vertical hierarchies.

We explain how management meets essential needs. The basic message of thinkers from Max Weber to Chester Barnard, Ronald Coase, Alfred

Chandler, Herbert Simon, and Oliver Williamson is still the best way to understand hierarchy and what it does: management can often coordinate activities in organizations and make people work together better than can be accomplished with any other known method, including unstructured, bottom-up, spontaneous coordination. Our own research and that of colleagues in our field finds that management (and hence executive authority) is essential where decisions are time-sensitive, key knowledge is concentrated within the management team, and there are strong complementarities among actions or tasks. Such conditions are hallmarks of our networked, knowledge-intensive, and hypercompetitive economy. Indeed, we argue that these conditions and the consequent greater time-sensitivity, need for expert decision-making, and focus on internal alignment are exactly why we have seen top management teams expanding at the same time companies have been delayering.

We compare different kinds of executive authority and hierarchy. The kernel of truth in the new narrative is this: for many everyday business activities, employees no longer need a boss to direct them to tasks or to monitor their progress. In fact, such involvement can be demotivating. In a networked economy characterized by dispersed knowledge residing inside the heads of highly qualified specialists, leaders need to let go of the notion that things should be managed from the top. This means that the definition of "authority" needs to change. Managers need to move away from specifying methods and processes, in favor of defining the principles they want people to apply or the goals they want people to meet. In other words, they can design the rules of the game without specifying the actions of the players, as in the case noted earlier of Wikipedia founder Jimmy Wales, who doesn't control the content of Wikipedia entries but who designed the structure for the format of the entries, the process for revising them, and the procedures for resolving disputes.

Besides establishing guidelines for rewards, instruction, rules, and communication, something else is needed to help employees react to changes and act in the face of unexpected events, like the Covid-19 pandemic. For example, in emergency situations, employees don't want to have to wait for permission from the boss to respond—they need a general understanding of "how things are done here." Effective leaders excel at defining such frameworks. Letting culture emerge and percolate on its own, without deliberate structure and design, can lead to several problems—not the least of which is a rough-and-tumble culture that favors certain employees at the expense of others.

We agree that the new environment suggests the need for a redefinition of the traditional managerial role. Despite all the changes that have occurred, there is a strong need for someone to define the framework. In the knowledge economy, the main task for top management is to define and implement the organizational rules of the game.

THE PARADOX OF THE BOSSLESS COMPANY

The popular narrative that radically decentralized, effectively bossless companies are better than traditionally organized, hierarchical ones is strikingly paradoxical. It goes against our deeply ingrained instincts and experiences: although we applaud autonomy, individualism, and freedom (especially from tyrannical government), humans are a remarkably hierarchical species!

We are born into a family. We grow up with parents or guardians who guide and direct us. The theory of attachment developed by the British psychologist John Bowlby suggests that the presence or absence of "secure ties" to our parents or caregivers is a major contributor to future life satisfaction. As we get older, we gain more freedom, but adults are making the rules. In school, we follow the cool kids or the star football player, and we try to avoid the schoolyard bully. All these people hold authority over us, formal or informal. We (mostly) listen to and obey our teachers, and after we graduate we work for a boss, who commands respect (or not). Some of us strike out on our own, leaving the nest as soon as possible or starting our own company. But even a start-up has key stakeholders, regulators, lawyers, and other authority figures who must be answered to. Most of our relationships are hierarchical to some degree.

Hierarchy can be unpleasant. Whether in a dysfunctional family, an oppressive boarding school, the rigidly disciplined military life, you name it, hierarchy may feel wrong and run counter to our interests. History is full of hierarchies behaving badly. Everyone knows the crucial role played by hierarchy in the wars, genocides, and other horrors of the twentieth century.

But hierarchies have benefits as well. Familial bonds, cultural and social ties, religion, and well-functioning businesses have layers, lines of authority, and rules. Indeed, we couldn't cooperate and coordinate our efforts without institutions, what the Nobel Prize–winning economist Douglass North calls the "humanly devised constraints that structure political, economic and social interaction." By constraints he means policies or rules that tell us what we can and can't do. These constraints can be informal (customs, taboos, traditions) or formal (constitutions, laws). As North puts it, these constraints "create order and reduce uncertainty in exchange."[14] Without institutions—rules that tell us what we can and cannot do, and how we relate to each other—society would fall apart. We literally need rules of the game. Hierarchies provide such rules. In a sense, they *are* the key rules in a modern economy.

So here is the paradox. On the one hand, we have a highly popular genre of thinking on management that is fundamentally skeptical of, sometimes even hostile to, bosses and hierarchies. On the other hand, common sense and much evidence (which we detail later) tell us that hierarchy and bosses are natural, even essential. This paradox calls for explanation—as does another paradox. If hierarchy is such a big thing, how do we explain a company like Valve, often described as the ultimate, nonhierarchical, bossless company?

In the pages that follow, we flesh out these arguments in greater detail with plenty of examples and illustrations along the way. We hope to convince you that, while decentralizing and delegating are important parts of the manager's tool kit, they are just that—strategies and practices that can make managers more effective when the conditions are right. In other words, decentralizing and delegating are not synonymous with bosslessness or the death of hierarchy.

Summary

> transition from traditional managerial cooperation to one that is bossless

> Decentralized organizations not always successful

> leadership reduces many problems and promotes greater efficiency

Part I

THE BOSSLESS COMPANY

Most ostensibly "bossless" companies aren't. Flat structures work in a few cases, but there are perils to radical decentralization, including how hard it becomes to coordinate people and tasks when things must come together in a certain way. As management thinkers have known for a long time, all ways of organizing business have pros and cons.

2

WELCOME TO FLATLAND

Video game developer and distributor Valve, introduced in the last chapter, is one of the best-known modern examples of a radically decentralized, almost bossless company. How is Valve actually organized? How well does its structure work? Is the company really bossless? Let's take a closer look.

WHAT REALLY HAPPENED AT VALVE

You're probably familiar with Valve's products even if you don't know the company itself. Valve produced some of the most popular video game titles of the last two decades including *Counter-Strike*, *Portal*, *Day of Defeat*, *Team Fortress*, *Left 4 Dead*, and *Dota*. Big hits like *Half-Life*, launched in 1998, and the next year's *Counter-Strike* have made Valve extremely profitable, with more than $4 billion in 2017 revenues—a huge number for a company with only four hundred employees. (In fact, in 2012 Valve was the most profitable US company by headcount.) In 2016, Valve's Steam platform accounted for almost 40 percent of all games released.[1] As of this writing, it handles around 80 percent of all digital distribution of PC games.

Founded in 1996 by two former Microsoft employees, Gabe Newell and Mike Harrington, Valve is one of the most prominent poster children for the bossless company narrative. This is not surprising. Valve has skill-fully marketed its organizational structure. As the BBC noted in 2013, "The video games developer caused a stir when a handbook detailing its unusual structure leaked onto the web last year." One writer described the handbook as "a deeply seductive re-imagining of the workplace that enraptured the tech world." And word got around. In a 2014 study, more than 2,200 game developers ranked Valve as the most desirable place to work, ranking it above even "my own company."[2]

Valve also received media attention when Yannis Varoufakis, the Greek finance minister who fought the European Union plans to control the Greek macro-economy (to no effect), became a central figure in European politics in 2015. Varoufakis had been "economist-in-residence" at Valve, overseeing the virtual economics in Valve games.[3] In a strangely schizo-phrenic article, the UK magazine *New Statesman*, not exactly a friend of private business, swooned over Valve, calling it "the first anti-cap soft-ware company" on account of its organization as "the perfect anarchist collective"—that is, a place where freedom-loving individuals could freely associate and pursue projects of their own choosing. (There were limits. As the article notes, "If 'projects of your own choice' means spending every working hour laying down slap bass grooves for your funk garage band, you'll probably be asked to find employment elsewhere.") But then, learning from Varoufakis that Valve may be thought of as "the exact op-posite: a rare entry of free market ideals inside the corporation," the *New Statesman* concludes that we don't really know if Valve is the "free marke-teer's dream, or nightmare."[4]

While Valve is best known as a game developer, it is increasingly in-volved in its digital storefront and delivery platform, Steam. Launched in 2002, Steam emerged as Valve had a hard time maintaining the patches for its games that allow players to be up to date. When Valve couldn't find a supplier or developer for a platform that could deliver this functionality, the company developed and built Steam itself. Other companies now offer their games on Steam, which accounts for the majority of all digital sales in the online games industry. Steam's success has prompted Valve to turn more toward providing services for the industry than developing games.

This change has not gone over well with some critics, who would prefer that Valve focus on game design. "What happened?" asked an angry journalist in 2019. "In a word: capitalism. Valve has mutated from a game developer into a ruthless financial middleman through its platform Steam, which has become the largest platform for digital game distribution—allowing them to make huge amounts of money while creating virtually nothing original themselves."[5] Of course, developing and maintaining a distribution platform is just as "creative" as making the products distributed on that platform. (Would anybody say Amazon is not a creative, innovative, outside-the-box company?)[6]

The particular organizational design of Valve is described in the aforementioned *Handbook for New Employees*, subtitled *A Fearless Adventure in Knowing What to Do When No One's There Telling You What to Do*. The do-away-with-hierarchy, bossless theme is struck right at the beginning of the handbook:

> Hierarchy is great for maintaining predictability and repeatability. It simplifies planning and makes it easier to control a large group of people from the top down, which is why military organizations rely on it so heavily. But when you're an entertainment company that's spent the last decade going out of its way to recruit the most intelligent, innovative, talented people on Earth, telling them to sit at a desk and do what they're told obliterates 99 percent of their value. We want innovators, and that means maintaining an environment where they'll flourish. That's why Valve is flat. It's our shorthand way of saying that we don't have any management, and nobody "reports to" anybody else.[7]

Let us quote more from the handbook. It is a lively document, fun and somewhat cynical—appealing to the millennial and Gen Z ironic style. As an example of frankness, the handbook lists what Valve is not good at, such as formal knowledge-sharing, making long-term predictions, and mentoring people. A knowledge-based company that isn't good at sharing knowledge and mentoring! Valve tries to compensate for this with its recruitment policies. It values "T-shaped" people—people who are "both generalists (highly skilled at a broad set of valuable things, representing the top of the T) and experts (among the best in their field within a narrow discipline, representing the vertical leg of the T)."[8] The handbook repeatedly emphasizes the importance of hiring the right people—those who can find interesting things to work on through their own initiative, are not afraid of approaching others with new ideas, can navigate the occasionally chaotic environment that is "Flatland," and may even, because they appreciate being empowered and trusted, "thrive on chaos," to borrow a phrase.

The idea is that the "right" people will not only be motivated to search for the knowledge they need but will also know where to look. With such employees, the company has little need for formal knowledge management systems with their huge databases and their requirement that employees place new knowledge in the system and retrieve existing knowledge from it (which too often they don't). With highly competent and driven employees, there is also less of a need for job descriptions—employees can figure out what to do by themselves. Hence the handbook's glossary entry for "manager": "The kind of people we don't have any of. So if you see one, tell somebody, because it's probably the ghost of whoever was in this building before us. Whatever you do, don't let him give you a presentation on paradigms in spectral proactivity." (A nice dig at presentations and paradigms!)

Or, at least, that is the idea. Even highly competent employees are sometimes motivated to pursue their own interests rather than the company's (what the academic literature calls a "principal-agent problem"). To alleviate this problem, companies implement performance management systems to align employee motivation with company goals. Valve uses a "360-degree system" in which everybody evaluates everybody else and all employees are ranked by performance outcomes. To construct these rankings, Valve uses a special team that interviews employees, asking who they work with and what their experiences were working with that employee. The team anonymizes the feedback and then presents it to employees.

The outcome of this review—the specific scores and ranks—affects the employees' share of the yearly bonus. Because the bonus pool is large, a bad review can lead to quite a bit of lost income. As Yannis Varoufakis explained, "Bonuses can end up being 5, 6, 10 times the level of the basic wage."[9] Catch that? Valve employees do not receive the usual tech-sector bonuses of 10, 20, or 30 percent of base pay, but up to *ten times* their annual salary. Falling in the rankings means losing big money!

Valve also makes heavy use of norms. As Varoufakis put it, using the "spontaneous order" terminology of F. A. Hayek, the Austrian-English-American economist and classical liberal thinker who inspired Jimmy Wales,

> It is important to understand that such spontaneous order–based enterprises rely to a large extent on individuals that believe in the social norms that govern their existence. So by the very nature of the beast, you don't have people there who try to hide and who try to somehow create a smokescreen around the fact that they're not very good at what they do.[10]

FLATTER, LOOSER, MORE NETWORKED

Valve has become a poster company for the bossless company narrative for a number of reasons. It is a tech company that produces something that is youthful and hip. Its organization serves as exhibit A of the key ideas of the bossless company writers—extreme delegation, self-organization, powerful incentives, and norms of good behavior that serve to keep things together. (We will later see that things are a bit different in real life.)

The bossless company narrative, remember, is the genre reflected in business books, programs pushed by consulting firms, and college courses that preach the death of authority and hierarchy and its supersession by flat, self-organizing, tech-supported, bossless organizations. *The Social Network* depicts the workplace of the future, while the office culture in *The Man in the Gray Flannel Suit* or *Mad Men* is as dead as its gender stereotyping would suggest.

Certainly, workplace behavior has changed on the surface. But the deeper message is that the *Social Network* workplace is much *better* than its predecessors. The flatter, looser, networked office liberates humans and their creative energies. It is democratic and egalitarian. It empowers educated workers, using their access to nearly unlimited information at their desktops and in their pockets, to apply their knowledge and skills. A looser, more flexible office culture is adaptive and allows for better work-life balance. If you've sampled business books on organization and strategy in recent years, you've come across titles such as *Wikinomics: How Mass Collaboration Changes Everything, The Starfish and the Spider: The Unstoppable Power of Leaderless Organizations, Here Comes Everybody: The Power of Organizing Without Organizations, Unboss,* and *Humanocracy: Creating Organizations as Amazing as the People Inside Them.*[11] They all tell us that leaner, flatter, and more agile organizations are in and corporate dinosaurs are out.

At first glance, these books seem to capture fundamental changes in our economy and society. When we want to look something up, we use the crowdsourced Wikipedia, not the old-school *Encyclopedia Britannica.* We increasingly arrange to have our cab rides, our overnight stays, our food deliveries, and various professional services delivered not by employees of large companies but by people just like us who are working a "gig" on the side, all coordinated through an app. We feel comfortable with loosely structured, decentralized, bottom-up ways of doing things. And yet the bossless company narrative grossly exaggerates their benefits.

When you have a radical message, it helps your selling effort to be able to point to real examples that seem to work. Political radicals have often struggled to show how their ideas work in practice. "Defund the police" appealed to many during the social justice protests of 2020, but as it turned out, nobody actually wanted to eliminate policing altogether, and few had any concrete ideas about how to make it better. This also seems true of radicals in management thought. Proponents of the bossless company narrative don't have that many examples to point to (hence the dozens of articles, blog posts, and book chapters about the same companies, mostly Valve, Morning Star, and Zappos).

Neither the bossless company narrative nor the attack on hierarchy is that new. Management gurus, business consultants, management professors, and a number of business leaders have peddled it for what seems like ages. (We will provide more detail throughout this book.) Among the major management gurus, Tom Peters has been arguing for decades that hierarchies stifle creativity, empower autocratic managers, and hold back human potential. Gary Hamel and Frederic Laloux (and their many epigones) echo the message nowadays. Both urge us to break down corporate hierarchies and get rid of bosses—or at least to keep the bosses from doing too much harm. Dramatically flattening the hierarchy has become a mantra in many parts of the business world, not just among gurus and consultants.

Mike Sharkey, CEO of Autopilot HQ, which analyzes customer data for client companies, told *Fast Company*: "I think anytime I've seen failure in decision making or getting things done, it's been because there are multiple layers to that decision being made."[12] Tesla and SpaceX CEO Elon Musk noted that in traditional hierarchies employees in one unit wanting to engage employees in other units "are forced to talk to their manager, who talks to their manager, who talks to the manager in the other dept, who talks to someone on his team. Then the info has to flow back the other way again. This is incredibly dumb." He warned that any Tesla manager "who allows this to happen, let alone encourages it, will soon find themselves working at another company. No kidding."[13]

Many managers have been listening, and many have been persuaded. While few have stepped to the side entirely, we have witnessed a trend over the last several decades toward decentralization, delegation, worker empowerment, and managers designing structures and processes more than monitoring daily activities (although we will argue that the trend is weaker than advertised). For example, two decades ago Unilever allegedly operated with no less than thirty-six tiers of management but later reduced that number to six.[14]

In our networked, knowledge-based economy, these changes make sense. When work is organized around temporary projects and relies on peer-to-peer software tools, the job of the traditional middle manager, primarily a monitor and director of work, gets more complicated. It is difficult for her to direct and monitor the details of a project she may not understand or to stay on top of what goes on inside the team. However,

employees working in peer-based teams may be able to direct and monitor themselves. This is not a universal fix, as such teams have their own
problems. But the kernel of truth in the bossless company narrative is
that sometimes peer organization and peer monitoring beats supervision
by middle managers.

The underlying message in the growing literature on the bossless company has very old roots. Decentralization, flatness, and empowerment
have for decades been part of the lexicon of consultants, professors, gurus,
and even CEOs. Alfred P. Sloan of General Motors—GM's CEO from
the 1920s through the 1950s and one of the most important business executives of the twentieth century—probably started the trend. Although
GM was one of the biggest US industrial companies and is usually seen
(along with IBM and US Steel) as the most traditional of the traditional
hierarchical organizations, it was not actually managed as a conventional
hierarchy. Instead, as Sloan explains in his autobiography, *My Years with
General Motors*, he adopted a highly decentralized organizational structure for General Motors and managed the firm as a consultant, favoring
persuasion over direct orders.[15] This sounds much nicer than authoritarian order-giving. And with Sloan as a spokesman for such an approach, it
is perhaps not surprising that the flat, decentralized, lean, etc., message is
powerful and often resonates strongly with managers. Not surprisingly, it
is still being promoted, even more than ever.

However, despite decades of calls for flatter, leaner, more empowered
management structures, the corporate dinosaurs haven't gone extinct.
They may never go away completely. But as Frederic Laloux's wildly influential manifesto insists, they may need to be "reinvented."[16] Again, leading management gurus such as Tom Peters and Gary Hamel have been
saying the same thing since the 1980s. Still, the message has changed in
two key respects that make the bossless company narrative appear fresh
despite its solid historical roots.

First, the message has been made more operational and practical.
Tom Peters's books, such as *Thriving on Chaos* and *The Pursuit of Wow!*,
are preachy and over the top.[17] Laloux's book, by comparison, is more
practical, offering hands-on advice and realistic examples. It shows the

reader how to make decisions, resolve conflicts, promote culture and values, and (of course) embrace the softer things like safe spaces and mood management.

Second, the message has become more sweeping and ambitious. The most explicit example comes, again, from Laloux. He calls the company of the future the "teal organization." Employees will self-manage, and the organization will be highly adaptive in the presence of change. (We will have more to say about the content of his book later.) But this organizational form also somehow reflects the "next stage of human consciousness." It is based on the three "pillars" of wholeness, self-management, and evolutionary purpose. Other writers may support their claims with less New Agey ideas, but arguments about breaking down hierarchies and empowering employees are in sync with the zeitgeist. The unstated implication is that these changes are good not only for companies but for humanity.

So, is the bossless company really the wave of the future? Did the gurus finally get it right? Or are they combining flashy and sweeping claims with a few cherry-picked examples? And do they even get the examples right? Let's take another look at Valve.

BACK TO VALVE: NO HIERARCHY IN FLATLAND?

Valve claims to have no formal hierarchy. But it turns out that those self-organizing projects actually have project leaders. That is already a kind of hierarchy. But there is more. At the end of the handbook is a glossary. One of the entries reads: "Gabe Newell—Of all the people at this company who aren't your boss, Gabe is the MOST not your boss, if you get what we're saying." Of course, this is a tongue-in-cheek way of saying that Gabe Newell is in fact *very much* the boss around Valve.

Still, apart from Gabe being the boss, there is no *formal* hierarchy at Valve; there are no job designs, departments, business units, or defined chains of command and reporting. But there is "informal" organization—the networks of advice, information, friendship, and gossip that form at any organization. Organizations are collections of people and activities. They need some measure of coordination. And to some extent people need to be kept in line. Norms of behavior, citizenship, and work effort emerge. When an organization is very flat, such informal structure may fill the void left by the absence of formal structure. For example, informal power positions may be held by actors who are brokers in networks, such as employees who are better at connecting different projects.

Valve's notion of "flatland" may have come from *Flatland: A Romance of Many Dimensions*, an 1884 novella by Edwin Abbott, an English school-master.[18] You may remember *Flatland* from high school math class. Abbott wrote under the pseudonym "A Square," which, with the book's title, directs our focus to geometry. (There is also an animated 2007 movie based on the book.) The story is a quirky exploration of life in a two-dimensional world in which women are line segments and men are many-sided polygons.

On New Year's Eve, the narrator (the Square) has a dream about a visit to a one-dimensional world. This is Lineland, which is inhabited by "lustrous points." The Square is later visited by a three-dimensional sphere and eventually visits Spaceland. The sphere turns out to be an envoy from Spaceland who is tasked with explaining the existence of a third dimension to the people of Flatland (who cannot really grasp it, just as we Earthlings cannot really grasp a fourth or fifth dimension). The leaders of Flatland secretly acknowledge the existence of the third dimension but crack down on those who proclaim its existence. Flatland turns out to be highly hierarchical and intolerant of dissenting opinions!

A former Valve employee who confessed that Valve "felt a lot like high school" elaborated: "It is a pseudo-flat structure where, at least in small groups, you're all peers and make decisions together. But the one thing I found out the hard way is that there is actually a hidden layer of powerful management structure in the company and it felt a lot like high school. There are popular kids that have acquired power in the company, then there's the trouble makers, and everyone in between."[19] Other former employees tell similar tales of informal power hierarchies in Valve. "To succeed at Valve you need to belong to the group that has more decisional power and, even when you succeed temporarily, be certain that you have an expiration date. No matter how hard you work, no matter how original and productive you are, if your bosses and the people who count don't like you, you will be fired soon or you will be managed out."[20]

THE INEVITABILITY OF HIERARCHY

Nature abhors a vacuum, and groups of people tend to abhor a power vacuum. In the absence of formal hierarchy, other authority relations—like the informal social hierarchies of the cool kids and nerds—emerge to fill the void. This is an example of what Michels calls the "Iron Law of Oligarchy," the notion that all organizations, even if founded on completely egalitarian principles, will develop rule by an elite (i.e., an oligarchy).[21] Not only does the ostensibly bossless Valve have a boss, but it also has a ruling elite!

As we noted earlier, even highly decentralized projects like Wikipedia have founders, designers, coordinators, and referees. Wikipedia's operations are governed by a complex, multilayered system of roles—stewards, overseers, administrators, editors, reviewers, and more—responsibilities, policies, guidelines, and principles. These are not fixed rules, and they're subject to discussion, negotiation, and revision by consensus, but they are rules nonetheless. Wikipedia has a structure and processes that govern its operation.

Wikipedia illustrates another aspect of the Iron Law of Oligarchy, namely, that even without a formal hierarchical structure, a kind of hierarchy inevitably emerges. In a 2016 paper, two Indiana University researchers analyzed millions of Wikipedia pages and users over a fifteen-year period to study the emergence of informal norms and practices, such as the use of copyrighted materials, rules on spelling and grammar, and means by which disputes among users were resolved. They found that the majority of norms were established early on by a small set of initial users; contrary to the usual assumption about decentralized peer production, these norms did not evolve as the network grew. "The evolution of this network is a remarkably conservative process. Early features are maintained, and in some cases even amplified, over the course of the network's development. Our findings are consistent with the 'iron law' of oligarchy in peer-production systems."[22]

On closer inspection, many of the main examples of decentralized, flat, and bossless organizations such as Valve turn out to be far from bossless. Before examining more of these companies in detail, let's look more broadly at the origins of the new narrative of the bossless company. Are these ideas really new? If not, why are they attracting so much attention today?

3

BOSSLESSNESS AND OUR CHANGING CULTURE

THE BOSSLESS COMPANY NARRATIVE CAN BE SEEN AS PART OF A broader cultural story, one that stresses liberation, autonomy, and empowerment. That helps to explain its appeal: bosslessness is hip and cool, while the traditional theories and models taught in business schools and associated with the big companies of yesteryear are stodgy and square.

The traditional corporation was once seen as capable of "delivering the goods"—job security and a paycheck. That attitude changed as some traditional companies declined and once-dynamic industries like steel, shipbuilding, oil and gas extraction, and textiles were disrupted. The US steel industry, once dominated by titans of industry such as Andrew Carnegie, employed 650,000 workers in 1953; by 2015 that number was 142,000.[1] Some of those jobs went overseas, but much of the decline resulted from technological improvements that allowed more steel production per worker, as well as from the rise of "minimills" that recycled scrap metal into new materials and often operated on a much smaller scale than traditional steel mills. Even in Japan, where lifetime employment has long been offered for a variety of workers and executives, traditional operations have gradually been replaced by a more flexible system that lowers firms' costs at the expense of social and cultural stability.

Still, even before many traditional corporations began to decline and stopped honoring what was seen by many employees as an implicit social contract, the corporation, with its managerial hierarchy, had been under regular attack in popular culture and by critics of excessive bureaucracy.

THE COUNTERCULTURE AND THE CRITIQUE OF SCIENTIFIC MANAGEMENT

Jack Kerouac's *On the Road* appeared in 1957. Its protagonist, Sal Paradise, takes a very different approach to finding a way to live, and generations of readers have found this way much more sympathetic, compelling, honest, and "modern" than Tom Rath's acceptance of the soulless way of life symbolized by the traditional company in *The Man in the Gray Flannel Suit*. The contrast is familiar: the bourgeois (petty or not) and his traditions, daily routines, and obligations versus the free, creative spirit of the romantic. This trope is reflected in much of the critique of hierarchy and authority in our contemporary culture.

Skepticism about the planning and authority embedded in hierarchy goes back a long time in other ways too. Donaldson Brown was one of the architects of GM's famous planning system in the 1920s, but also an early critic of the stifling tendencies of corporate bureaucracies.[2] However, he and other critics (such as the political theorist James Burnham, author of a famous 1941 book called *The Managerial Revolution*) were lone voices in the wilderness. The seeming successes of wartime planning in World War II in directing the US industrial base toward the war effort, the expanding welfare state, the rise of the philosophy of "scientific management," and the continuing growth and intrusion of the large corporate hierarchy in virtually all industries made the critique of planning and authority seem almost eccentric.

The 1960s changed all this. A decisive event was the US failure in Vietnam. Secretary of Defense Robert McNamara had honed his planning skills (and ambitions) in his rise to the presidency of the Ford Motor Company, a position he left when he was hired by the Kennedy administration in 1961. The massive deployment of troops (first 16,000 "advisers" and ultimately more than 500,000 combat troops by the late 1960s), backed up by a massive planning and resource allocation effort by the military bureaucracy, clashed with the realities of combat. The American war machine was frustrated by an enemy that was more agile and adaptive. An organizational structure based on deliberate, forward-looking planning and an authoritarian chain of command was being beaten by a looser, seemingly self-organizing structure. McNamara's growing realization of this led him to quit as defense secretary in 1967, the year of the Summer of Love—and the official start of the counterculture.

COUNTERCULTURAL MANAGEMENT THINKING

The year after the Summer of Love is often taken to be the emblematic year of the counterculture. Indeed, perhaps particularly in Europe, the generation that was shaped by the counterculture is sometimes referred to as the "nineteen-sixty-eighters." In that year, the management consultant and leadership guru Warren Bennis published *The Temporary Society*.[3] The book emerged from Bennis's previous work on group dynamics, but it arguably also reflected the organization of his employer in the 1960s, MIT, as well as the lesson learned from the Vietnam War concerning the potential superiority of a loosely organized, agile form of organization. *The Temporary Society* introduces the notion of the "adhocary," which was later systematized and made influential by the leading management thinker Henry Mintzberg.[4]

The term was also used by Alvin Toffler in *Future Shock*, the 1970s best-seller that popularized futurology and became a counter- and popular culture classic.[5] (Inspired by the book, Curtis Mayfield wrote a song titled "Future Shock"—later picked up by pianist Herbie Hancock—and the rock group Gillian titled a 1983 album *Future Shock*.) The key idea in Toffler's book was that the dramatic change in society (meaning mostly the United States) from an industrial to a "super-industrial" society would result in massive information overload and basically stress everyone out, in particular as they stuck to existing, obviously old-fashioned ways of thinking and organizing.

Adhocracies—defined by Bennis, Toffler, and Mintzberg as flexible and informal forms of organization that would allow for adaptive, creative, and flexible integrative behaviors—could help the inhabitants of "super-industrial" society cope. Critics might observe that this early new narrative might have been shaped by the academic backgrounds (Bennis, Mintzberg) or affiliations (Toffler) of these influential writers, who generalized the model of the university (already quite idealized) as a loosely organized collective of adaptive and creative knowledge workers as a universal mode of organizing for the future. Indeed, as we shall argue repeatedly throughout this book, the tendency to generalize in an unwarranted way from a few organizations, or from organizations dedicated to one specific activity, to the rest of the economy is a general feature of the bossless company narrative.

"TEAR DOWN THE WALLS": EMBRACING THE COUNTERCULTURE

The counterculture is often taken as an anticapitalist revolt, but that is largely a misunderstanding: although parts of the counterculture morphed into Marxism in the 1970s (particularly in Europe), its primary targets were conformity and authority, in politics and society as well as in business. Few people symbolize the counterculture as much as the psychologist and champion of psychedelic drugs Timothy Leary. Reflecting on the 1960s, Leary proposed that

> counterculture blooms wherever and whenever a few members of a society choose lifestyles, artistic expressions, and ways of thinking and being that wholeheartedly embrace the ancient axiom that the only true constant is change itself. The mark of counterculture is not a particular social form or structure, but rather the evanescence of forms and structures, the dazzling rapidity and flexibility with which they appear, mutate, and morph into one another and disappear.[6]

Embracing the ancient philosophy of Heraclitus that the "only constant is change" is the true hallmark of counterculture, according to Leary. The emphasis on constant change and the idea that organizations, as well as people, should be flexible, resilient, and adaptable is, of course, a hallmark of the bossless company narrative.

There is nothing anticapitalist about change, whether disruptive shocks or continuous innovation. On the contrary, inspired by the great Austrian economist Joseph Schumpeter, who coined the term "creative destruction," many writers have seen evolution and constant change as the hallmark of a modern capitalist economy. For example, in *The Future and Its Enemies*, the procapitalist writer Virginia Postrel paints an almost Manichean picture of a world riven in a clash between (bad) "stasis" and (good) "dynamism."[7]

Capitalism was in any case extremely quick to embrace the counterculture. Remember the much-discussed final scenes of *Mad Men*? Don Draper goes on a California retreat to seek self-awareness and enlightenment after his lifelong and endless string of lies have caused considerable damage to the people in his life. He hugs a stranger and meditates with the hippies. But then, strikingly, the episode cuts to the advertising classic, the 1971 Coca-Cola "Hilltop" commercial featuring a multicultural group of (mostly) teenagers on top of a hill singing "I'd Like to Teach the World to Sing." The implication is that, after the retreat, Don returns to McCann-Erickson to create the Hilltop ad.[8] Symbolically, the sequence shows how the counterculture insinuated itself into the modern corporation despite its anti-establishment, anticorporate rhetoric.

More recent movements framed as challenges to the status quo—such as the various "resistance" movements that emerged following the 2016 election of Donald Trump and the "racial reckoning" of 2020 sparked by the death of George Floyd—have the same character. They feature anti-establishment, anticorporate, anticapitalist language and imagery borrowed from the civil rights movement and even older revolutionary periods, such as twentieth-century Marxism, yet these movements were embraced by virtually every major corporation in the United States and around the world. Capitalism is often quick to incorporate supposed challenges to capitalism!

UNLEASHING HUMAN POTENTIAL

While "feel-good" ideas often tap into real issues and concerns, they often lack concreteness and practicality. As Professor Robert Grant, author of one of the most widely used business strategy textbooks, has observed: "From the outset of the industrial revolution, humanists, social reformers, religious leaders and political revolutionaries have sought to design productive organizations where individual liberties, personal fulfilment and caring social relationships can coexist with the demands of technology and productivity. Robert Owen's New Lanark Mills in Scotland and New Harmony in Indiana were early examples."[9]

Grant goes on to observe that these early experiments with participative humanitarian management didn't pass the survival test; he points to the troubled history of the cooperative movement as further evidence of how hard it is to combine participative decision-making with efficiency in production and a customer orientation. He ironically observes that what is remarkable about the Mondragón cooperative (discussed in more detail in the next chapter), which has often been invoked in discussions of industrial democracy, isn't that it seems to have achieved commercial success with a high level of employee participation in decision-making, but "that it is so rare an example of a large industrial cooperative with long term endurance."[10]

And yet these ideas keep making their influence felt. One reason is that they cater to commonly held political views. While the bossless company narrative may seem to fit with a "left-wing" understanding of business (and capitalism), it taps into moral values held by most people, namely, universal standards of treating people with respect and as equals and promoting structures that allow us to make the most of our human capabilities. Of course, the question is whether adopting a near-bossless structure will realize such universal moral values or instead create hidden power structures, promote factionalism, and ultimately lead to more conflict, as egalitarian models often do.

An early example of the humanistic values that the proponents of the bossless company narrative often hail was the "human potential movement," which became influential in the early 1960s, particularly in

California. Its main prophet, Abraham Maslow, created his "hierarchy of needs" triangle, with basic physiological needs at the bottom and "self-actualization" at the top. The human potential movement pushed the idea that companies could help their employees move to the top of the triangle. Fortunately for employees whose companies took up this challenge, one way to do it was arranging paid trips to the Esalen Institute in Big Sur, California, where they could engage with the Esalen "network of seekers who look beyond dogma to explore deeper spiritual possibilities, forge new understandings of self and society, and pioneer new paths for change."[11]

An outgrowth of the human potential movement, the Erhard Seminars Training, was started by Werner Erhard (nee John Paul Rosenberg) in 1971. The seminars consisted of two weekend-long workshops. At these boot camps participants were introduced to Erhard's take on Zen Buddhism, which would free them from the past and allow them to discard the baggage of the past (notably broken agreements) and embrace compassion.

Erhard's ideas had a substantial effect on business thinking. His seminars were followed by many businesspeople, and he delivered a keynote address to gurus and scholars at the Academy of Management's annual conference in San Francisco in 1990. Thought leaders from the leadership guru Warren Bennis to Michael Jensen, a Harvard finance professor, endorsed his thinking. The *Financial Times* noted that his influence "extends far beyond the couple of million people who have done his courses; there is hardly a self-help book or a management training program that does not borrow some of his principles."[12] The *Harvard Business Review on Change* gushed: "We are indebted to numerous philosophers, scholars, and thinkers who have inquired into the nature of being, especially Werner Erhard."[13] So did Paul Fireman: when he was CEO of Reebok, he made all his managers take EST training. "I believe in anything that allows you to look at yourself and see what's possible."[14]

Not surprisingly, then, individual empowerment and self-actualization increasingly came to be seen as something that could take place not just at the Esalen Institute or during an Erhard seminar, but also in the workplace. Unfortunately, the embrace of EST caused friction at Reebok, and the company became divided "between those who buy into the EST message and those who don't. Key employees, even top managers, at times seem to be kept out of the loop, denied crucial new research or excluded from strategy meetings unless they accept the EST outlook and methods."[15]

The technology sector was an early adopter of counterculture ideas, particularly its California representatives. In his 2005 Stanford commencement address, Steve Jobs waxed lyrical about Stewart Brand's influential magazine, the *Whole Earth Catalog*, which popularized ideas for better, more ecologically oriented living and promoted technology as a liberating force. "One of the bibles of my generation," Jobs said, "sort of like Google in paperback form, 35 years before Google came along."[16] And of course, the famous Macintosh commercial that was themed after *1984*, George Orwell's dystopian novel, and aired nationally for the first time during the 1984 Superbowl not only made fun of then-dominant IBM but also alluded to the anti-establishment, liberating culture of the new tech start-ups. Directed by Ridley Scott, the commercial pits an unnamed heroine in a white tank top (with a drawing of the Macintosh computer on it), armed with a sledgehammer, taking on Big Brother (of *1984* fame). Basically, the ad tells us that the coming of the Macintosh will save humanity from conformity (Big Brother).

Jobs (like other tech gurus) was not exactly a champion of delegation and decentralization himself. As Adam Lashinsky puts it in a 2011 profile: "To Apple's legion of admirers, the company is like a tech version of Wonka's factory, an enigmatic but enchanted place that produces wonderful items they can't get enough of. That characterization is true, but Apple also is a brutal and unforgiving place, where accountability is strictly enforced, decisions are swift, and communication is articulated clearly from the top."[17]

At the top, of course, was Jobs, Apple's cofounder and CEO through most of its existence until his death in 2011. Jobs was known to the public as the charismatic, creative visionary, clad in his trademark jeans and black turtleneck. Insiders knew him as the ultimate control freak, one who maintained tight control over a company with fifty thousand employees. Notes Lashinsky:

> Every conversation with insiders about Apple, even if it doesn't start out being about Jobs, eventually comes around to him. The creative process at Apple is one of constantly preparing someone—be it one's boss, one's boss's boss, or oneself—for a presentation to Jobs. He's a corporate dictator who makes every critical decision—and oodles of seemingly noncritical calls too, from the design of the shuttle buses that ferry employees to and from San Francisco to what food will be served in the cafeteria.[18]

That sounds like a flannel-suit culture, not a jeans-and-T-shirt culture! Indeed, as we will discuss in more detail in later chapters, appearances can be deceiving: some ostensibly flat, loose, and bottom-up companies and systems turn out to be quite different upon a closer look.

Still, counterculture rhetoric is often used to package and justify new management approaches that espouse these ideas. The case for delegation and decentralization is framed as enabling diversity and unleashing creativity with a classic 1960s "let a thousand flowers bloom" vibe. Sometimes that case is made in distinctly spiritual terms. The subtitle to Frederic Laloux's *Reinventing Organizations* is *A Guide to Creating Organizations Inspired by the Next Stage of Human Consciousness*. It could have been written at the corner of Haight and Ashbury, ground zero of the counterculture in San Francisco.

The counterculture introduced a new mindset with general ramifications for how people think about the organizations that employ them (or that they manage). The "tear down the walls" chorus from Jefferson Airplane's 1969 song "We Can Be Together" became a guide for reorganizing the corporate hierarchy.

More broadly, top-down models now seem to be out, and bottom-up ones are in. The mighty US war machine was basically defeated by the much more loosely organized Vietcong. The successes of the Al-Qaeda organization against an ostensibly well organized, hierarchical US intelligence community and military were widely interpreted as a triumph of the loosely organized network over hierarchy. (As we will argue later, the problem may have been the opposite: the US intelligence community, distributed as it was across more than a dozen competing agencies, wasn't *sufficiently* hierarchical to handle the threat from Al-Qaeda.)

COUNTERCULTURAL COMPANIES

Proponents of the bossless company narrative say that the managerial hierarchy—maybe even management itself—once served a useful purpose but is now outdated. Just as the traditional armies of worker-drones were replaced by highly educated, strongly motivated, independent, and creative "knowledge workers," the traditional firm will be replaced by flatter organizations, peer-to-peer networks, distributed leadership, platforms, extreme decentralization, worker empowerment, independent contracting, and entrepreneurship. The future tense used in many of these pronouncements is more prophesy than analysis.

Frederic Laloux's influential book *Reinventing Organizations* is even more speculative than most in an already speculative genre, but its central message about the organizations of the future is representative. Laloux calls them "teal" organizations (based on a color-coding system that describes different stages of human consciousness: red represents impulsiveness, amber conformism, orange achievement, green pluralism, and teal evolution). In his foreword, Ken Wilber explains that teal organizations "no longer work with dominator hierarchies, the boss-subordinate relationships that are pervasive in organizations today."[19] If this sounds confusing, we agree. Like a lot of New Age philosophies, pronouncements, and slogans, it seems to mean whatever the reader wants it to mean.

WHAT MILLENNIALS AND GEN-ZS WANT

The Age of Aquarius is long behind us, but its ideas about individual autonomy and empowerment, doing something for the greater good, and freedom from convention and tradition have made a sharp comeback in the last couple of decades. Indeed, we have personally witnessed a sea change in the mentalities of our students. When we both started our academic careers some thirty years ago, most of our students sought secure, well-paying jobs and career paths at established companies. Business schools offered plenty of courses in accounting, finance, marketing, and general management. Now one of the hottest majors on US and European college campuses is entrepreneurship. Students watch *Shark Tank* and dream of working for a start-up or founding their own firm. Often this ambition is combined with a desire to do something "responsible" and "sustainable." Who wants to work for "the man" when you can be your own boss—and do good for society at the same time?

Of course, we are generalizing. Plenty of students, just like plenty of working-age adults, are perfectly comfortable in conventional, hierarchical settings. But a substantial number want autonomy and independence. Fortunately for them, a new kind of work environment is emerging—at least, according to their textbooks and some of their professors. Although tech firms and other hipper, flatter companies are certainly not bossless—indeed, leaders like Amazon's Jeff Bezos and Meta's Mark Zuckerberg are very visible bosses who have become household names—they serve as colorful and visible challenges to the traditional, *Flannel Suit*–style workplace, at least in the public eye. They reinforce the idea that nobody wants to work for an old-fashioned company.

Before we explore in detail more examples of companies that have adopted flatter structures, we need to say more about the origins of the bossless company narrative. It turns out that most of the seemingly novel and exciting practices put in place at companies like Valve and Zappos were introduced in the 1970s and 1980s, with mixed success. Today's "bossless" companies took these business models, added new terminology, and advertised their structures as radical departures from the status quo. In doing so, they missed the key lesson from those earlier experiments, which is that successful organizational design is *contingent* on features of the product, market, and environment. In the following chapters, we look at some of these earlier experiments, show where they succeeded (and where they failed), and draw out some general principles about when flatter structures can work. We start with Semco and Gore, two older companies that were among the first to embrace the near-bossless model.

4

ANTICIPATING FLATLAND

Early Calls for Flatter Hierarchy

THE APPEAL OF THE BOSSLESS COMPANY NARRATIVE STEMS FROM ITS presentation as fresh and new. And therein lies its peril. After all, who wants to be cut off from this newer, greater world? Who would embrace the boring, obsolete, old-fashioned model of producing things inside a traditional factory, office, or workshop? Go with what's hip and cool, not with what's square and out-of-date. Who doesn't want the newest model? Roll over Beethoven and tell Tchaikovsky the news!

The peril of uncritically embracing the bossless company model is that flatter hierarchies work only in a few cases under certain conditions, such as simple technology, a stable industry, and a collaborative culture. And though the narrative is presented as new and revolutionary, it's really not; people have been searching for and experimenting with alternative ways of managing work for a long time. Some of the key ideas about empowering people, unleashing creativity, freeing workers from the shackles of micro-management, and letting leaders emerge from the bottom up have been around for almost two hundred years.

Some of the resulting experiments succeeded, but many failed. Searching for new ways to organize work makes sense. Technological

improvements in communications and information processing have enabled changes in the workplace that were not obvious when the internet
and mobile telephony took off in the business world in the mid-1990s.
Similarly, the Covid-19 pandemic forced massive experimentation in
remote working and collaboration, and some of those changes—fewer
in-person meetings, reduced business travel, more flexible hours, greater
accommodation of health and family concerns—are likely here to stay.

Experimenting with the organization of work is an inherent feature of
a free society and a dynamic marketplace. However, as in the scientific
laboratory, such experiments should be designed and conducted in light
of sound theory and prior experience. So we will investigate whether this
new narrative is informed by what we know about earlier experiments
with near-bossless organizations.[1]

THE ORIGINS OF THE NEW NARRATIVE:
SEMLER AND SEMCO

The "bossless" company idea didn't emerge with the advent of the internet
or the systematic digitalization of business processes that has increasingly
taken place over the last decade. The Danish hearing-aid producer Oticon tried out a much-hyped and very flat structure called the "spaghetti
organization" thirty years ago, when the internet consisted of a few thousand connections between mainly government and university computers
and long before "digitalization" entered the business lexicon. (We discuss
Oticon in detail in Chapter 6.)

A decade earlier, Johnsonville Sausage, a Wisconsin company, slashed
managerial oversight and put quality control, personnel management,
customer relations, and even business expansion in the hands of worker-
managed teams. As CEO Ralph Stayer declared, "My job was to put
myself out of a job."[2] Stayer's approach to worker empowerment earned
plaudits from Tom Peters, who credited worker education and self-
improvement as the key to the firm's success: "Continuous learning, with
the sky the limit, is almost a religion at Johnsonville."[3] Indeed, the firm
grew rapidly and remains profitable, although it's hard to say whether empowerment and continuous learning or strict performance measurement

and rewards based solely on merit are responsible for the firm's success. (It's worth noting that, when Stayer retired as chairman of the privately held Johnsonville in 2019, he appointed his wife Shelly as his successor— not exactly standard procedure in a meritocracy!)

Similar examples popped up from time to time but did not seem to herald a sea change in management style. Around the same time of Johnsonville's success, however, another executive articulated a vision of a radically decentralized organization that caught the attention of the business world. Ricardo Semler published an influential *Harvard Business Review* article, "Managing Without Managers," in 1989.[4] Semler, who was just a twenty-one-year-old law student when in 1980 he became CEO of Semco, a Brazilian manufacturer of cement mixers and industrial agitators, made a splash in the following decade. Semler rejected the autocratic leadership style of his predecessor (his father Antonio Curt Semler) and adopted a radical form of industrial democracy.

Semler started by firing 60 percent of the top managers and engaging in a massive exercise in delegation. The essence of this model was what Semler called the "organizational circle" (actually three concentric circles), which replaced the conventional pyramid. (Semco had no formal organizational chart.) The innermost circle included the top five executives, who at Semco were called "counselors." The next ring consisted of the eight division heads, or "partners." Everyone else was in the third circle of "associates," among whom were managers, line workers, and a few team leaders who held the title of "coordinator." So, instead of bosses and workers, Semco had counselors, partners, coordinators, and associates.

These sound like hipster labels for conventional employment roles. And Semler is a typical salesman: "At Semco, we don't play by the rules. We are unabashedly, unapologetically different, and we're proud of it. In fact, we revel in it. We've changed the way work works and improved the quality of our lives, and so can you."[5]

These are the words of a guru, not a CEO (although, admittedly, many CEOs have bought into the guru role). And yet Semler put his money where his mouth is, developing a system that really is different, and that got results: the company grew from ninety employees when Semler took over to three thousand in 2004, around the time he stepped away. Annual revenue grew over that period from $4 million to $212 million.[6] Semler became a global celebrity, winning multiple awards and authoring *Virando a Própria Mesa* (*Turning the Table on Yourself*), which became the best-selling nonfiction book in Brazilian history.

What makes Semco unusual is the single layer within the outermost circle: associates report to a coordinator, but no coordinator reports to another coordinator. Like other decentralized firms, Semco features profit-sharing, employee voting on major decisions, flexible work hours, job rotation, and substantial worker and team autonomy. But Semco goes further. There are no formal job descriptions. Employees set their own work hours, working in teams that establish production requirements and whose members, much like independent contractors, decide how and when to meet team goals. Salaries are determined largely by peer reviews. There is no dress code.[7]

Like other apostles of radical decentralization, Semler waxes poetic about human dignity, freedom, and democracy. "Most of our programs are based on the notion of giving employees control over their own lives. In a word, we hire adults, and then we treat them like adults."

> Outside the factory, workers are men and women who elect governments, serve in the army, lead community projects, raise and educate families, and make decisions every day about the future. Friends solicit their advice. Salespeople court them. Children and grandchildren look up to them for their wisdom and experience. But the moment they walk into the factory, the company transforms them into adolescents. They have to wear badges and name tags, arrive at a certain time, stand in line to punch the clock or eat their lunch, get permission to go to the bathroom, give lengthy explanations every time they're five minutes late, and follow instructions without asking a lot of questions.[8]

The assumption here is that following formal procedures, coordinating closely with others, keeping careful track of individuals' activities, and otherwise sticking to routines is suitable for children, but not for adults.

One wonders what Semler thinks about professional orchestras, sports teams, and military units, all of which prioritize tight coordination over spontaneity and autonomy! Indeed, Semler claims to have eliminated most monitoring programs, such as internal audits and locks on storerooms, to convey trust. Employee resistance to company procedures is described as "civil disobedience." "We had to free the Thoreaus and the Tom Paines in the factory." But it appears there is little to disobey: "One of my first moves when I took control of Semco was to abolish norms, manuals, rules, and regulations."[9]

Ultimately, Semler's style may have been too New Agey even for fans of radical decentralization. His 2004 book *The Seven-Day Weekend* challenged the distinction between work and play, office time and free time:

> Drop the traditional notions of a workweek and a weekend, and divide the
> seven days among company time, personal time, and idleness (free time).
> Rearrange your schedule to work when most other people don't. Arrange
> a workweek to sleep according to biorhythms rather than a time clock,
> and enjoy a sunny Monday on the beach after working through a chilly
> Sunday.[10]

We're not quite at the point of replacing time clocks with biorhythms, though smart watches and other tools (designed and manufactured by more traditionally structured companies like Apple) can help with our sleep.

Semco became an early poster child for the bossless company narrative partly because of its pioneer status and impressive financial results and partly because of the showmanship of Ricardo Semler. Literally hundreds of magazine and newspapers articles have been written about the company, with titles such as "Semco: Insanity That Works," "Managing Without Managers," and "Who's in Charge Here? No One." However, as the journalist Pim de Morree noted, most accounts of Semco's story stop around the time Semler left the company in 2003.[11] Semler began selling his shares in 2001 and gradually shifted his interests to other ventures. Although de Morree doesn't detail what happened, it appears that

Semco in a sense was Semler. When Semler effectively left (he maintains a financial interest in the company), Semco declined. In its heyday, it had three thousand employees. Now it has fifty.

While Semler and his company are less well known today than in the early 2000s, when Semler was a more visible public figure, some of his principles have been embraced by newer firms, such as Netflix, where CEO and cofounder Reed Hastings has adopted the "no-rules" approach to dress codes, vacations, and expense reports. His 2020 book (with Erin Meyer), *No Rules Rules*, explains his philosophy: "If you give employees more freedom instead of developing processes to prevent them from exercising their own judgment, they will make better decisions and it's easier to hold them accountable." According to Hastings, if you hire only the most talented employees and encourage a culture of absolute candor—one that ditches "the normal polite human protocols" for speaking and interacting—you can eliminate all or most controls.[12]

Netflix's financial performance has been impressive, with rapid subscriber and revenue growth over the last decade; the company has continued to maintain its strong position despite robust competition from Amazon Prime, Hulu, Disney+, and other streaming services (all of which did well during the Covid-19 pandemic). Still, the Netflix work environment is not for everybody. A 2018 *Wall Street Journal* investigation, based on interviews with a large number of current and former employees, revealed a high-performance culture that, "at its worst, can also be ruthless, demoralizing and transparent to the point of dysfunctional." For example, Hastings encourages Netflix managers to apply a "keeper test" in evaluating employees: Would they fight to keep the employee from leaving? And yet, "many employees say they see the keeper test as a guise for ordinary workplace politics while some managers say they feel pressure to fire people or risk looking soft. Postmortem emails and meetings explaining why people got fired are viewed by some employees as awkward and theatrical when the audiences can be dozens or even hundreds of people."[13]

In any case, Netflix has not embraced the Semler philosophy in its entirety. Instead, it has stuck with a traditional hierarchical structure rather than the flatter model championed at Semco. Netflix is a conventionally organized firm that relaxes many of the kind of reporting and control systems used by other firms and gives employees considerable latitude, while imposing a strong performance-based culture and rigid performance evaluation criteria. In hindsight, Netflix did the wise thing by not adopting the Semler approach in its entirety. Semler's approach seemed to work for a while, but after he left the company things began to fall apart, and Semco is now a tiny company compared to its size in the glory days under Semler. This is not an unusual outcome of experiments with supposedly bossless organizing: these experiments, paradoxically, are initiated and kept together by powerful leaders. When they leave, the "bossless" organization collapses.

THE GORE LATTICE ORGANIZATION

Before Ricardo Semler, another businessman, Bill Gore, promoted what he called the "lattice organization," an organizational design that he implemented at W. L. Gore and Associates in the late 1960s. Gore is best known for Gore-Tex, the waterproof, breathable fabric it invented in 1969, and for other consumer products like Glide dental floss. The company offers more than a thousand products, is present in about thirty countries, and has more than eleven thousand employees (or, in typical bossless lingo, "associates").

Gary Hamel calls W. L. Gore the "original" bossless company and gushes that Bill Gore "was bent on creating an entirely new kind of company—one that unleashed and inspired every person in it, one that put as much energy into finding the next big thing as milking the last big thing, one that was robustly profitable and uniquely human."[14] (When you read a company analysis that sounds like a press release, be wary.)

Like bossless organizations in general, the lattice organization emphasizes decentralized decision-making and lateral coordination. In a memo from 1975, Gore describes the lattice organization as

one that involves direct transactions, self-commitment, natural leadership, and lacks assigned or assumed authority. . . . Every successful organization

people work better w/o someone up their ass

has a lattice organization that underlies the facade of authoritarian hierarchy. It is through these lattice organizations that things get done, and most of us delight in going around the formal procedures and doing things the straightforward and easy way.[15]

What Gore describes here is what organization theorists call "informal organization"—the unofficial networks of advice, help, friendship, and influence through which employees communicate horizontally and vertically in parallel with the official, formal communication channels.[16] Informal communication is often faster, can more easily reach those who are really in the know, and has more bandwidth. (We all know how an informal conversation can communicate much more than a written memo.) Research by one of us on information-sharing in major knowledge-based firms (engineering consultancies, pharmaceutical firms, and medical devices producers) found that employees much preferred informal ways of sharing knowledge and saw them as more effective.[17] Even in manufacturing, knowledge tends to diffuse most effectively through informal networks, which act in concert with formal structures such as cross-functional teams.[18]

Although the lattice organization is not a fully "bossless" structure, Bill Gore wanted a structure that prioritized side-to-side communication and coordination over top-down control, to make effective use of informal channels. Like Semler, he largely eliminated management titles and called everyone an "associate." In his model, leaders are chosen by consensus, with associates deciding which leaders to follow. Associate performance is determined by peer review. Associates communicate directly with other associates. To make this system work, plants are necessarily small. With no more than 150 workers per plant, W. L. Gore illustrates what Malcolm Gladwell calls the "Rule of 150," the idea that effective consensus-based, group decision-making is limited to groups of that size. "Gore doesn't need formal management structures in its small plants," he writes, "because in groups that small, informal personal relationships are more effective."[19]

This is an important point: decentralized structures tend to be most effective in particular circumstances, such as where groups and tasks can be broken down into smaller independent units. These small units work well at Gore, in part because they're based on a principle of cross-functional collaboration: salespeople, chemists, R&D specialists, engineers, and machinists work in the same plant on specific projects. Having employees cooperate directly within the same unit is usually more effective than having functional units collaborate on projects. Siloing, turf wars, and the like are more easily avoided when teams are organized around projects—say, building a bridge or developing a specific piece of software—rather than on business functions such as marketing, sales, or finance.

ORGANIC STRUCTURES AND HUMANISTIC MANAGEMENT

Other early ideas on flattening hierarchies, delegation, and empowerment include the famous "organic structure" described in 1961 by Tom Burns and G. M. Stalker.[20] Looking at a sample of British electronics firms that had been government contractors during World War II but had to adjust in the 1950s to a postwar environment featuring rapid technological change and increased consumer and private industrial demand for electronics, Burns and Stalker argued that the firms best able to make this transition were those that largely ditched the traditional hierarchy. In contrast to the "mechanistic" form of organization, characterized by a formal hierarchy, a high level of specialization with fixed roles and responsibilities, and vertical lines of communication, they identified a superior, more adaptable structure that they called "organic." The organic structure features flexible roles and tasks, lateral rather than vertical coordination, and peer assessment of performance. The organic structure, according to Burns and Stalker, adapted better to environmental shocks and was well suited for firms operating under dynamic, innovative conditions.

Burns and Stalker's work has been hugely influential in research on organizational structure and innovation and still shapes much of what is taught in the business schools. Much of the follow-on work building on the Burns-Stalker thesis is consistent with their insights from the original case studies, but there is also evidence that more formal structures work better for start-ups. Formal structures help start-ups overcome what the influential organizational sociologist Arthur Stinchcombe famously called the "liability of newness"—the increased risk faced by fledging ventures.[21]

Even better known is the psychologist Douglas MacGregor's distinction between "authoritarian" and "participative" management, outlined in his 1960 book *The Human Side of Enterprise*, which seems to have been the original inspiration for Bill Gore.[22] MacGregor's work grew out of what is sometimes called the "human relations school," or, nowadays, "humanist management thinking." Thinkers in this movement include one of the very first management theorists, Mary Parker Follett, who is often called the "Mother of Modern Management"; Elton Mayo, a founder of organizational psychology, or what business schools call "organizational behavior"; and Abraham Maslow, who created the famous "hierarchy of needs" triangle. Gary Hamel may be seen as a modern representative of this line of thinking, which argues that workplace organization needs to start from a fundamentally respectful stance toward employees as human beings who best flourish in self-organizing, collaborative teams.[23]

MacGregor argued that authoritarian management is based on a particular understanding of workers, what he calls "Theory X," which holds that people dislike their jobs, are motivated primarily by financial rewards and punishments, and must be given explicit directions. Participative management, or "Theory Y," maintains that people enjoy their work, are self-motivated, and need only general guidance, inspiration, and the resources to succeed. The Theory Y model is "liberating and developmental" and achieves improvement "by empowering and giving responsibility," treating employees as partners or participants in the managerial process. A Theory Y organization thus replaces the traditional managerial hierarchy with a flatter, more collaborative structure.

Burns and Stalker's organic model and MacGregor's Theory Y proved highly influential in theory but had an ambiguous effect on practice. A host of books and articles in the business and popular press have praised these decentralized, flatter forms of organization, but practitioners recognized early on that every management model has benefits and costs and that no single model provides the best performance in all circumstances.

MacGregor himself, for example, acknowledged that the authoritarian approach can work with novice employees or in crisis situations where quick decisions are needed—a circumstance we will revisit in Chapters 6 and 7.

Management scholars and writers have subsequently embraced the idea that the "optimal" organization structure varies with conditions—what has come to be called "contingency theory."[24] This theory holds that there are no universally best solutions when it comes to the design of a company. Instead, contingency theory directs our attention to the fit between tasks, organizational structure, and people and how this fit is influenced by various contingencies, internal and external to the company, such as technology, the intensity of competition, the degree of uncertainty, and resource availability. As summarized by John Morse and Jay Lorsch in a 1970 article in the *Harvard Business Review*:

> Enterprises with highly predictable tasks perform better with organizations characterized by the highly formalized procedures and management hierarchies of the classical approach. With highly uncertain tasks that require more extensive problem solving, on the other hand, organizations that are less formalized and emphasize self-control and member participation in decision making are more effective. In essence . . . managers must design and develop organizations so that the organizational characteristics fit the nature of the task to be done.[25]

That, indeed, is a core message of this book: when it comes to organizational structure, there are no one-size-fits-all solutions. In particular, bosslessness at best works for a handful of companies operating under special conditions, such as small companies that carry out simple tasks.

The point may seem obvious, but many managers miss it in their search for a universal recipe or "secret sauce" that, once discovered, can fix almost any company problem. Indeed, the bossless company narrative presumes that contingencies don't matter when it comes to flattening the hierarchy: because all people yearn for freedom, because the world is rapidly changing, and so on, we need to get rid of the managers—no matter the circumstances.

One main reason there is no secret sauce is what economists call "complementarities." Championed by Nobel laureate Paul Milgrom and John Roberts, complementarities theory holds that certain organizational practices work best only in the presence of other practices.[26] Worker discretion, for example, complements job flexibility, strong performance measurements, and technologies that need frequent adjustments. Consider the typical sales job: salespeople usually have better information about their territories and clients than the front office, and the most effective sales strategies and techniques often change rapidly with market conditions. It thus makes sense for salespeople to have a lot of discretion about how they target their clients. To give them strong incentives, they are typically paid by commission—the more they sell, the more they earn. Their supervisors may not care particularly what strategies the salespeople use, as long as they deliver.

Workers in other jobs, however, may have little discretion, and hence little ability to perform better; for them, performance-based pay doesn't make sense. Or they may have a lot of discretion, but their supervisors have no way to measure performance. Safety inspectors, for example, are usually paid by the hour or by the month. If they were paid per inspection, they would have strong incentives to cut corners!

A favorite example of organizational complementarities in MBA classrooms is the Ohio manufacturer Lincoln Electric, famous for its extensive use of performance-based pay, or "piece rates." Piece rates make sense only when workers have a certain amount of autonomy—that is, when they have some control over the number of "pieces" they produce. Lincoln offers not only piece rates but several complementary elements: near-permanent employment, promotion from within, flexible work rules, extensive firm-specific training, and so on. For Lincoln, these elements work well together. Having just some of these elements without the others, however, could be a recipe for disaster.

COOPERATIVES AND WORKER-OWNED FIRMS

Although it isn't always recognized in the bossless company literature, the employee-led, flat, almost bossless company has roots in an even earlier tradition: the cooperative movement of the nineteenth and early twentieth centuries. Back then, the term wasn't "employee" but "worker." Worker-owned firms, worker-led management, worker cooperatives, and "industrial democracy" anticipated many decades ago many of the ideas that are popular now. The "utopian" socialist writers Robert Owen and Charles Fourier organized worker-owned cooperatives in the 1820s in Scotland and in the United States, designing them as self-contained communities with mainly horizontal structures. All workers had an equal stake in the venture and an equal say in how it was run.[27] The cooperative movement dominated US agriculture in the early twentieth century as groups of farmers formed their own marketing and distribution associations to combat what they perceived as unfairly high railroad shipping rates.

At the time, the cooperative movement was justified primarily on ethical rather than efficiency grounds. As recounted in the 2012 movie *The Rochdale Pioneers*, the world's first successful cooperative retail store was founded in 1844 in the UK town of Rochdale by the working-class members of the Rochdale Society of Equitable Pioneers. It emerged in the aftermath of the Napoleonic wars in Europe, which brought declining wages, unemployment, and even famine. The idea was to end "exploitation" by monopolist merchants, promote the use of "honest weights and measures," and share surpluses from the store with the local community.

Writers such as the American economist John Kenneth Galbraith argued that cooperatives allowed workers or farmers to band together to exercise "countervailing power" against large industrial firms that sought to exploit their labor. For example, if large railroads or grain storage facilities were abusing their "market power" to keep commodity prices low, farmers could form a cooperative to fight back, using their joint bargaining power to push prices up. Likewise, industrial workers, artisans, and other laborers could form cooperatives to keep more of the value of their own labor (which would otherwise be "exploited" by bosses).

Cooperatives played an important role in some sectors; in agriculture they continue to exercise influence even today. In general, however, cooperatives have not been a hugely successful model in industry. An exception is the Mondragón Corporation, a federation of worker cooperatives located in the Basque region of Spain. Founded in 1956, Mondragón employs more than eighty thousand people. These cooperatives are united by a strong philosophy of participation and a shared business culture that stresses "Open Admission, Democratic Organization, the Sovereignty of Labor, Instrumental and Subordinate Nature of Capital, Participatory Management, Payment Solidarity, Inter-cooperation, Social Transformation, Universality and Education."[28] Mondragón is involved in a variety of manufacturing and service activities and is one of the most important employers in the region. As a recent profile put it, "The concept of the cooperative may conjure notions of hippie socialism, limiting its value as a model for the global economy, but Mondragón stands out as a genuinely large enterprise."[29] The unique social and cultural aspects of the Basque region may play a role in explaining its longevity. And yet, the model may be neither fully scalable nor sustainable. As the cooperative has expanded, it has added contract and temporary workers who are regular employees, not member-owners, as well as overseas subsidiaries that are organized as traditional companies, not cooperatives.

Cooperatives usually face several disadvantages over investor-owned companies.[30] The distinguishing feature of a cooperative is that the owners also have another relationship with the firm—as workers, customers, or suppliers. On the one hand, these relationships can increase motivation, promote loyalty, and build strong social and psychological ties. I want the firm to do well because I work here; I not only own the grocery store, but I shop there! (Older readers may recall the American entrepreneur Viktor Kiam, who bought the consumer goods maker Remington Products in a leveraged buyout and became the TV spokesperson for one of its most prominent products: "I liked the shaver so much, I bought the company!")

On the other hand, people with multiple ties to an organization can experience role conflict. In my capacity as a worker, I want the profits of the firm distributed in the form of higher wages. As an investor, I may also want profits invested in R&D or equipment maintenance or acquisitions, even at the expense of wages. A farmer who sells to a processing facility wants the highest price for his products, but if he is also a part owner of the facility, he may prefer lower prices or alternative suppliers. More important, while investor-owners are united in their desire for higher profits, worker-owners or supplier-owners can disagree among themselves on strategy, objectives, and priorities. Younger workers might prefer that the firm make long-term investments in innovation that will result in higher wages in the future, while workers just short of retirement want the money paid out in wages now.

NOTHING NEW UNDER THE SUN?

A few years ago, when we were writing the blog "Organizations and Markets"—a mix of serious and lighthearted commentaries on management that attracted academic readers and business professionals alike— we had a recurring feature called "Nothing New Under the Sun." There we pointed out that most of the fashionably new forms of organization and management have been tried before and that continuity, rather than radical innovation, is the norm. For example, decentralized, arm's-length networking goes back to the Victorian age, as detailed in Tom Standage's delightful book *The Victorian Internet*.[31] What is now called "open innovation," in which groups of firms share new ideas within horizontal clusters, was pioneered in the late nineteenth century.[32]

Ancient societies employed a variety of administrative structures, with greater or lesser degrees of central control. The modern term "decentralization" probably came into use in France (*décentralisation*) in the 1820s, when it referred to the French national administration.[33]

Academic interest in organizational structure goes back at least to the famous German sociologist Max Weber, whose 1922 book *Economy and Society* outlined a theory of bureaucracy. Weber defined bureaucratic management as a system featuring a formal hierarchy with defined and fixed roles and responsibilities, written rules and procedures, professionally trained managers, and performance evaluation and promotion according to neutral, objective principles. While praising bureaucratic management as the most "rational" form of organization in a market economy, Weber recognized its possibly stifling effect on spontaneity and creativity. (We return to Weber in Chapter 12.)

The Austrian economist Ludwig von Mises, a friend of Weber's, went further, arguing in his 1944 book *Bureaucracy* that while bureaucratic management was effective in static environments—in particular, in organizations like government agencies that do not sell their output on markets and are insulated from the profit-and-loss system—a more decentralized structure with employee autonomy made more sense for profit-seeking entrepreneurs.

In short, the core ideas behind the bossless company narrative—worker empowerment, flexibility, autonomy, flatness, and so on—have been part of the conversation on organization and management for a very long time. They have also been present in popular culture. There is a famous anecdote (we cannot verify its authenticity) about President John F. Kennedy visiting NASA in the aftermath of his dramatic expansion of the US space program. After the obligatory meetings with the astronauts in training, the chief engineers, and various NASA scientists, Kennedy bumped into a cleaner as he was leaving the building. The president asked the cleaner what his job was. The cleaner replied: "Sir, it's my job to help put a man on the moon." The longevity of this anecdote demonstrates that there has long been a basic appreciation of empowerment's ability to make all employees feel that they are an important part of the mission of the company.

In general, the ideas behind the bossless company narrative are well known to scholars and often used by practitioners—when they make sense. Take the notion of "flexibility," one of the supposed advantages of the bossless company. More employee discretion often means more flexibility with respect to choosing work hours. For example, Spotify increasingly lets its employees choose where and when they want to work as part of its new "Work from Anywhere" program.[34]

Most people intuitively agree that such flexibility is good. (We certainly value it as employees.) However, until recently it was hard to say how much it is actually valued. To get a sense of this, a recent study looked at Uber drivers.[35] They are not employees, but they're not standalone entrepreneurs either. (Legally they are classified as independent contractors.) Uber drivers have tremendous flexibility, being free to work whenever they choose (and to work concurrently for competing companies). The researchers estimated the value of flexibility by seeing how much drivers adjust their hours to the expected wage, which changes in real time: if a driver doesn't work more hours even when the expected wage goes up, we can conclude that he has better things to do—and that he places a high value on flexibility. Compared to a hypothetical "normal" job with inflexible hours, the average Uber driver gains a lot from setting his own hours—as much value as driving an extra 6.7 hours per week!

Likewise, a famous study of entrepreneurs found that, on average, self-employed people earn 35 percent less over their career than they would have earned as paid employees.[36] Why, then, do so many people choose self-employment? Because they value the flexibility, autonomy, sense of fulfillment, and other nonmonetary benefits.

In other words, flexibility and autonomy are worth a lot. No wonder the idea of self-management has been around for a long time. As Peter Drucker observed in 1954, however, the flexible workplace with high levels of worker autonomy works only in particular circumstances, with particular people, and with a new approach to human resources.[37] We discuss this further in Chapter 14.

Like other fashionable topics, the bossless company narrative resuscitates and repackages older ideas and is less radical than it seems. The problem isn't the repackaging and the over-the-top claims on behalf of the ideas; if the ideas are good, they are of course worth repackaging and pushing to have adopted in modern times. The problem is that too much is claimed on their behalf. Radical decentralization or a "bossless" organization may work for some companies some of the time, but they don't work universally—that is, for all companies at all times. Quite the contrary.

5

OLD WINE IN NEW BOTTLES?

The story of Valve shows that flat structures can work in specific circumstances or at certain times. Valve is highly profitable and dominant in its industry. W. L. Gore has been a consistently successful company, and Semco did well under the leadership of Ricardo Semler.

Our closer look at these companies, however, showed that, like all successful companies, they have prospered owing to strong management and visionary leadership. They do employ hierarchy, and they are certainly not bossless! Still, companies like Valve and Semco push the decentralized, organic, loosely structured model of organization about as far as it can go—and perhaps beyond. Other poster children of the bossless company narrative turn out, however, to be more style than substance. Many of their core "bossless" features are not too different from those found in traditional companies, just given a few tweaks perhaps, and clever new labels. This is what we will see with the world leader in music streaming, Sweden's Spotify, and then in the story of the Las Vegas–based and Amazon-owned online shoe and apparel retailer Zappos.

The Spotify and Zappos cases bring to life one of the key perils of the bossless company narrative—its faddishness.

Management can be faddish. Terms and concepts like "total quality management," "reengineering," "activity-based costing," "quality circles," "just-in-time-inventory," and "economic value added" suddenly appear in the business periodicals and then disappear almost as quickly.[1] Embracing a new idea just because your competitors have adopted it can be a recipe for disaster. The danger of the cheerleading style of the bossless company narrative is that it persuades managers to adopt a structure that doesn't work for their technology, industry, or workforce.

Spotify is the first of two Scandinavian companies (Oticon will be the second) that we use to illustrate this problem. Scandinavian managers were among the earliest supporters of the criticisms of the traditional corporate hierarchy that took off in the 1970s. Given the history of the Scandinavian countries, this is perhaps not that surprising. Despite some differences between them, they are all highly egalitarian and have long histories of cooperative movements and organizations. They have the world's highest levels of generalized trust, that is, the extent to which people trust other members of society, as distinct from the kind of trust they have in family and friends. These countries are low in so-called power distance (although Denmark is a great deal lower than Sweden and Norway), an anthropological concept used in studies of cultural differences between countries.[2] It measures the acceptance of power that exists between people with the most power and those with the least. In a society low in power distance, subordinates are less willing to accept their place, and they are typically skeptical of those at the top of the hierarchy.

The Scandinavian countries are also high in individualism, which is typically measured as the extent to which people prefer loosely knit social arrangements. Rather than expecting unquestioning loyalty from a large collective, the expectation of those with individualistic values is that individuals will take care of only themselves and their immediate families. It is easy to see that ideas about self-management and bossless organization will resonate in societies with such values.

One of the first Scandinavian businesspeople to promote these ideas was the Swede Jan Carlzon, CEO of Scandinavian Airline Systems (SAS Group) from 1981 to 1994. Carlzon published his own anti-hierarchy manifesto in 1985.[3] The Swedish title, translated as "Tear Down the

Pyramids: A Book About the New Man, Manager, and Leader," underscores our earlier point that the bossless company narrative is often linked to broader themes of personal renewal, empowerment, and self-actualization. When he became CEO in 1981, Carlzon implemented a training program called "Putting People First," which had been developed by the Dane Claus Møller. The idea was to execute a turnaround at SAS, which was widely seen as a rigid and stodgy organization, by delegating responsibility to people working in frontline, customer-facing jobs, empowering them to resolve issues on the spot.

The organizational redesign worked, attracting substantial media interest. "It may be that Jan Carlzon could level more than Sweden's pyramids," gushed *Industry Week*. "With his record, he might shake the foundations of tradition-bound business far beyond Scandinavia."[4] Warren Bennis, widely considered the founder of the modern field of leadership studies, opined, "I have long argued that organizations can and must encourage their executives to take chances, to see problems as opportunities, and to attempt big victories rather than settle for small wins. I have also urged leaders to listen—to everyone. Happily, Jan Carlzon's practices prove the validity of my preaching."[5] The lesson for businesspeople in Scandinavia and beyond was clear: organizational changes are good publicity and good for building a brand.

Carlzon knew how to attract media attention. So do the people running Spotify, the music streaming provider that has been a main disruptor of the music business.[6] Spotify is praised in the business press for its flat and flexible "N-form" structure, which promotes internal knowledge-sharing and employee recognition.[7] Spotify is consistently rated as one of Sweden's most desirable companies to work for. It is a prominent example of the approach called "Agile," which was originally designed for software development but is now increasingly used as a more general approach to organizing teams in dynamic environments. Spotify organizes teams in a seemingly innovative way, with a variety of links within and across people, tasks, and functions. Upon closer inspection, however, it turns out that this structure has been around for decades; Spotify just gave it a new name.

SPOTIFY: MUSIC ON DEMAND

Spotify (formally Spotify Technology SA) has built a so-called freemium business model, which is one that gives users the basic product—access to its music streaming platform—for free. But the free version is frequently interrupted by ads and lacks features found in the paid, ad-free, deluxe version, such as downloading and family accounts.

Spotify provides access to more than 70 million tracks for 365 million active users (of whom 180 million are paying subscribers).[8] Founded in 2006 by Daniel Ek and Martin Lorentzon, Spotify has tapped into what many see as a basic internet ethos, namely, that "information should be free." Of course, digitalized music is also information and hence "should" be free for everyone to enjoy—as long as they're willing to put up with the basic, limited-functionality version of the product.

Spotify has also benefited from Sweden being among the earliest countries to have the fast broadband that enables music streaming. The notion that information should be free, combined with fast broadband, can also enable piracy; the infamous Pirate Bay, a platform that facilitated illegal sharing of copyrighted software and media products, was started in Stockholm in the early 2000s. Ek and Lorentzon's basic business idea of making file-sharing legal was a response to the impending crackdown on illegal sharing, which would make users eager for alternatives. A third enabling factor was Spotify's bundling of its services with the mobile phone services of Telia, a major Scandinavian operator. Spotify has skillfully exploited the partnership tactic, allying with Facebook, for example, before entering the US market.

Currently the undisputed king of music streaming, Spotify is in many ways a success story. It has achieved huge growth in a short time doing something that many companies find extremely difficult: not only has it coordinated many product development units (groups of employees working on a particular piece of software), but it has also scaled the number of such units rapidly, all in the context of a completely globalized, high-velocity environment. With 180 million paying customers, Spotify, strikingly, has more than twice the number of customers of Apple Music! (And it has many more paying customers than smaller competitors such as YouTube Music, Tidal, Deezer, and Napster.) Many other technology start-ups have applied the Spotify digital freemium model (giving away the basic product for free, but hoping to attract users to the paid premium product) in other media—the arts, movies, journalism—but few have succeeded.[9]

THE N-FORM COMPANY

Spotify is almost the stereotypical knowledge economy company. Like Google and Microsoft, its product is software and services. Like Facebook and Netflix, it relies heavily on user-generated content—Spotify doesn't create or produce music, but rather distributes products made by others, and it relies on its community of users to rate and share music (thus also giving the platform information that can be used for targeted ads). Like all the tech giants, its key employees are coders sitting in cubicles, not assembly-line workers or sales agents. (The company also has plenty of lawyers, marketing people, and public relations experts.) If data is the new oil, as they say, then Spotify is sitting on a gold mine.

The music files that its platform lets users listen to are Spotify's key product. Of course, there is a technical infrastructure, but Spotify moved most of its data from its own servers to the cloud back in 2016. Its key inputs are the work efforts of its employees, most of whom are machine learning engineers, software engineers, data engineers—well, fifty shades of engineers—and a few designers, developers, and product managers thrown in for good measure. A quintessential knowledge economy company!

Also, Spotify competes or partners with the big and leading knowledge-based companies in the modern global economy—Apple, Facebook, and Google. Not surprisingly, it effectively adopts and uses the lingo associated with a hip, youthful, knowledge-based company. Its Stockholm company headquarters features brightly colored walls and furniture, a penthouse bar, and, of course, a game room.

Business commentators have swooned over Spotify's organizational structure, the secret sauce that allows Spotify to meet the classic challenge for almost all companies: combining agility with the ability to expand.[10] "The Spotify model," goes one typical comment, "is a people-driven, autonomous approach for scaling agile that emphasizes the importance of culture and network. It has helped Spotify and other organizations increase innovation and productivity by focusing on autonomy, communication, accountability, and quality."[11] (This sounds great, but most companies would describe themselves as "people-driven," and communication, accountability, and quality—and even autonomy—are part of many corporate cultures.)

Spotify is a great company. From its start in 2008, it has grown to a position where it now controls about one-third of the global music streaming market. It is the market leader. It has controlled costs while engaging in substantial product development (a big problem for many companies). To be sure, a big part of Spotify's recent success is attributable to its organizational setup (not to mention the business acumen and entrepreneurial judgment of its founders and leadership). Is Spotify an example of how a flat and "bossless" structure can drive superior performance? Actually, no.

Spotify's organizational structure is built around Agile software development, a technique designed to support the sharing of knowledge between teams. The structure is referred to as an "N-form," a play on Alfred Chandler's use of the term "M-form" to describe companies, such as General Motors or DuPont Chemical, that have multiple business units ("divisions") that typically are relatively autonomous and that specialize in producing a product or service (or a range of closely related products or services).

The N-form is the brainchild, appropriately, of a Swedish business academic, the late Gunnar Hedlund. He coined the term to describe a new kind of hierarchy that he observed emerging in the 1980s and 1990s, primarily in major Japanese industrial companies. The classic hierarchy— Hedlund would say, classic *Western* hierarchy—siloes activities and knowledge in business units and divisions, which can be functional units, such as production, sales, marketing, and R&D, or product-line units, such as consumer electronics and industrial devices. Although the conventional structure features cross-functional and cross-divisional teams, these are mainly used for temporary projects; the business units or divisions are the basic building blocks of the organization. Communication largely goes up and down the hierarchy, rather than laterally between employees in different units, and there is a clear and stable distribution of authority across the hierarchy.

When Hedlund looked at companies such as the Japanese cosmetics and chemicals producer Kao, he saw different organizing principles at work. Those companies still had business units, but temporary projects were the basic organizational building block. Employees communicated directly with employees in other functions and projects. There was still a managerial hierarchy, but it was fluid and looser than in the traditional company, based on which project the company was currently pursuing.[12]

The N-form company derives its agility from a combination of frequent lateral communication and a flexible authority structure. Spotify is largely organized along this model. But like the Japanese companies studied by Hedlund, it is hardly bossless or flat.

SQUADS, TRIBES, CHAPTERS, AND GUILDS

As the N-form example illustrates, all companies are structured around basic units, the building blocks of the organization. In a small engineering consultancy, the relevant unit may be the individual employee-consultant. After all, it is she who talks to clients, bills them, is reviewed by the owner or partners for her efforts, and so on. In a functionally organized manufacturing company, the relevant units are production, R&D, sales, and so on. In a multidivisional company, the product divisions are the building blocks.

At Spotify, the basic building blocks are "squads," which are teams of mainly developers, what other companies call "development teams." Squads usually have fewer than ten members and are given the task of developing a piece of software—for example, developing or maintaining the iOS or Android client, or designing a radio interface—or some kind of service, such as handling payments or solving a problem in one of these areas. As with many modern software products, these chunks of code can be treated as stand-alone modules because the system respects a lot of "interface standards," that is, protocols for connecting bits of code. For these reasons, the teams can be relatively autonomous and self-organizing.[13]

The specific development approach used by these teams is called "scrum." The word derives from a *Harvard Business Review* article by the Japanese innovation and management thinkers Hirotaka Takeuchi and Ikujiro Nonaka. The authors compare high-performing, cross-functional product development teams to rugby teams using the scrum formation when they restart play: rugby players pack closely together with their heads down and attempt to gain possession of the ball.[14] Successful development teams should be similarly committed and bound tightly together.

As an approach to development, the scrum approach starts by recognizing that circumstances often change in the middle of projects—for example, customers may change their minds during development. Linear, planning-based approaches that start with a clear definition of the problem don't work when the problem itself is vague or flexible. Instead, scrum teams break their work into smaller goals that can be met within short iterations ("sprints") that usually last only for about two weeks. This structure enables the team to quickly reorient its development effort in response to unforeseen events, such as changes in the requirements of the code, the composition of the team, or the overall company strategy. The team has a dedicated "product owner" who oversees the work. To increase adaptability, progress is tracked daily in fifteen-minute meetings. Each sprint ends with a sprint review that summarizes the work that has been done and pinpoints what went wrong (and what didn't) in order to fold this learning into future behaviors.

Lots of software companies and divisions use this approach. Its wildly enthusiastic adherents speak in a strange language of "artifacts," "user stories," and "ceremonies." Critics find Agile Scrum a bit cultish, and some have also criticized it for constraining employees, unintentionally killing employee learning and initiative.[15] The key here is that scrum techniques make sense for small, focused teams, such as Spotify's squads. A commitment to the scrum approach aligns well with the use of something like squads as a company's basic organizational unit.

How, then, do the efforts of the various squads fit together? Spotify features "tribes," defined as collections of squads that work on similar kinds of problems in related software areas. So, while Spotify seeks to make development work self-contained, there are still interdependencies between projects, and sometimes solutions developed by one squad are shared with another squad. These kinds of interactions are managed by "tribe leaders."

And wait, there's more. "Chapters" cut across tribes, organizing people with similar competencies. For example, many squads have database administrators. A "database chapter" then organizes all database admins across the squads, allowing them to exchange ideas and solve problems together. Of course, there is a manager handling the chapters—the "chapter lead"—who is essentially an HR manager for the employees in the chapter. Finally, there are "guilds," which are like interest groups for Spotify employees with particular interests in, say, Agile management or web technologies. Guilds help with the sharing of knowledge inside the company.

So what initially looks like a bunch of autonomous work teams is really a dense network of interlocking teams with management layers and specialized units that cut across the teams (the tribes, chapters, and guilds). Guess what? You have almost certainly seen something like this before, especially if you have worked for more than a day in any organization that uses terms like "divisions," "departments," and "cross-functional teams."

Indeed, Spotify's organizational chart is a version of the well-known "matrix" structure, only with cute labels for the various organizational units. The matrix structure has been around since at least the 1950s, when it was used for handling major complex projects in the emerging US aerospace industry. Matrix structures can take many different forms, but all feature employees reporting to more than one manager as well as cross-functional units. In the academic world, for example, professors typically report to a department chair for their research work but also to a program coordinator for their teaching duties. All matrix structures break with the model of strict vertical business units defined by function, product, or geography. However, they can be configured quite differently.

Some matrix structures are patched-up versions of the traditional siloed company with permanent cross-functional units. In others, often called "project matrix forms," employees from different functions and departments within functions are assigned to temporary projects. Once these projects are completed, employees revert to those functions, ready to be assigned to new temporary projects. Spotify is like these project matrix organizations. Its temporary projects are the scrum teams, or "squads," and their "chapters" are equivalent to functions. Like other companies with a matrix structure, Spotify recognizes that it would be impractical to have the organizational building blocks, the projects or squads, be in charge of everything. Chunks of software need to be defined for the squads to work on. Even though the scrum approach structures the work and makes sure that deadlines are met, the efforts of the individual squads must be assessed. Interdependencies need to be handled. It is often advantageous to share knowledge across squads and by people with the same competencies. All these needs call for . . . hierarchy.

Spotify hasn't really embraced a radically new, strongly decentralized structure. To be sure, the company features substantial autonomy and self-organizing, all happening within the confines of the (rather constraining) scrum approach, but apparently there is no more of this at Spotify than what is usual for any firm that adopts that approach.[16] And yes, there is organized knowledge-sharing and beneficial lateral communication. But plenty of firms have this! At the end of the day, Spotify is a relatively traditional, project-based company mixing a proven organizational structure with Agile development ideas—but one that uses hipster language to sound attractive to its industry, its employees (current and prospective), and its stakeholders.

This is a recurring theme in the bossless company narrative. Ideas about empowerment, employee initiative, and bottom-up organization resonate today, especially with younger workers, so it's not surprising that companies use this language when explaining what they are all about. But these firms really aren't all that different from conventional ones.

ZAPPOS: KING OF HOLACRACY

CEOs are obviously important, but there is no unique management or leadership style, temperament, or professional background that characterizes a successful top executive. How much does the CEO matter, really? Over the last decades, CEO tenure has decreased quite dramatically, suggesting that products, workers, reputation, and resources matter more than top-level leadership. Moreover, the power of shareholders (particularly institutional investors) has grown substantially, making it easier to oust badly performing CEOs. At the same time, and possibly in response, CEOs have become generalists with skills that are more readily transferable across industries.[17] A Price-Waterhouse-Coopers study found that total CEO turnover in 2018 was 17 percent and that over the past two decades the median tenure of a CEO has declined to a mere five years.[18] CEOs come and go.

However, the same study also found that a minority of CEOs stay in their job for a long time. Thus, almost 20 percent of US CEOs remain in their position for ten years or more. (The median for this group of longer-serving CEOs is fourteen years.) These are CEOs who matter—not least because, according to the study, they make their companies financially successful. They also matter because they are likely to "imprint" their companies.

To understand what imprinting is about, think of the engineer, business magnate, and apostle of the assembly line Henry Ford; the French fashion designer and businesswoman Gabrielle Bonheur "Coco" Chanel; the founder of the Playboy empire, playboy Hugh Hefner; or, closer to our time, the prankster, serial entrepreneur, and surfer Nick Woodman, the founder and CEO of GoPro, the action camera brand.

These owner-founder-managers all dramatically imprinted their businesses by shaping their cultures and identities and by making decisive early decisions on what would nowadays be called the "business model": the basic value proposition, key resources and processes, revenue model, and so on. Such imprinting is why company histories are often basically biographies of founders. Moreover, we can gain insight into companies and partly predict how they will behave if we observe and understand the characteristics of their top managers. Few contemporary companies and owner-managers illustrate this as well as Tony Hsieh and the online retailer Zappos. In many ways, Zappos *is* Tony Hsieh, even though Hsieh retired not long ago (August 2020), having headed Zappos for twenty-one years, and then passed away in November 2020.

Born in 1973 in Urbana-Champaign, Illinois, to Taiwanese immigrant parents, Hsieh graduated with a computer science degree from Harvard. He started early as an entrepreneur, partly financing his college education by buying frozen McDonald's burgers for $1 and preparing and selling them to other students for $3 (he later switched to pizzas). After a brief stint at Oracle, Hsieh started LinkExchange with a college friend. The company got funding from Sequoia Capital, was an instant success, and was sold to Microsoft for $265 million, making Hsieh a multimillionaire at twenty-four.

Like other successful entrepreneurs who successfully exit from the firm they created, Hsieh created a venture fund, Venture Frogs, and began reflecting on his LinkExchange experience and the kind of company he would ideally work for—and the kind he would start.[19] As a model for Zappos, Hsieh chose the friendship network, with its combination of fun, depth in personal relations, reciprocity, coherence, and, importantly, informality. In a move that indicated how seriously Zappos took this, as Hsieh explained it, the company began tracking employee relationships.

> When employees log in to their computers, we ask them to look at a picture of a random employee and then ask them how well they know that person—the options include "say hi in the halls," "hang out outside of work," and "we're going to be longtime friends." We're starting to keep track of the number and strength of cross-departmental relationships—and we're planning a class on the topic. My hope is that we can have more employees who plan to be close friends.[20]

As Hsieh explained in his 2010 autobiography (published at the advanced age of thirty-seven), he had tried out this model with LinkExchange, whose recruitment and hiring model was to hire friends and friends of friends. But LinkExchange had quickly morphed into a traditional firm with a hierarchy, a company where employees were motivated by careers and money and where politics and jockeying for internal power raised its ugly head. Hsieh asked himself: Was this a natural process? Or was it something that could be avoided in the right kind of company?

ENTER ZAPPOS

The opportunity came when Venture Frogs invested $500,000 in an idea for an online shoe retailing business. Zappos (a play on the Spanish word for "shoes," *zapatos*) launched in October 1999. After a relatively slow start, Venture Frogs made a second investment in Zappos, and Hsieh eventually joined the company in May 2001 as co-CEO, becoming sole CEO in 2003. Because Hsieh valued informality so highly, he deliberately shied away from formulating explicit company values for Zappos, deeming this too "corporate." As he later noted, most corporate core values or guiding principles were "very lofty sounding" or "read like a press release" from the marketing department.[21] However, the success of Zappos made such an exercise necessary—not as a way of keeping Zappos coherent under the impact of its expansion, but because an explicit list of values would be useful in recruitment and hiring. A yearlong process led to ten (of course!) core values:

1. Deliver WOW Through Service
2. Embrace and Drive Change
3. Create Fun and a Little Weirdness
4. Be Adventurous, Creative, and Open-Minded
5. Pursue Growth and Learning
6. Build Open and Honest Relationships with Communication
7. Build a Positive Team and Family Spirit
8. Do More with Less
9. Be Passionate and Determined
10. Be Humble.[22]

As usual with lists like this one, some of the items are obvious, even banal (and not a guide to coherent action). But many of the listed items here are actually different. Few companies deliberately try to "Create Fun and a Little Weirdness"—and quite frankly, many would be ill advised to do so. You probably would not want your bank or the company holding your 401(k) account to be even a little weird.[23] Few companies will thrive with headquarters designed to look like the Zappos Las Vegas headquarters, which features not only an open floor plan but also wacky decorations, bright colors, maximum casual dress, and a general atmosphere of sensory overload.[24]

In Hsieh's own assessment, the last item on the list, "Be Humble," is the most important value at Zappos. He reasoned that, without humility, prima donnas and egotistical employees will set the tone and building a friendly culture will be impossible. Humble employees are needed to meet the overall goal of creating a truly customer-centric organization. Thus, first on the list is still "Deliver WOW Through Service," a position that keeps the emphasis on consumers and vendors. That value is supported through 24/7 availability, no phone trees, no scripts, extremely generous return policies, and friendly reps.[25] As Hsieh explained, the basic principle is that "better service would translate into lots of repeat customers, which would mean low marketing expenses, long-term profits, and fast growth."[26]

The media swooned over Zappos's customer orientation, and many stories were published about the extreme lengths that Zappos employees will go to in helping customers.[27] Most calls are complaints, which customers want to have handled quickly. But one call in 2012 was different. He or she (the gender is unknown) wanted a chat. And a chat it was, clocking in at ten hours and twenty-nine minutes. In the end, the customer purchased a pair of boots, but that wasn't why the salesperson stayed with the call. As a Zappos representative explained: "Sometimes people just need to call and talk. . . . We don't judge, we just want to help."

In another anecdote, the mother of a customer had a swollen foot caused by a medical treatment. The customer bought no less than six pairs of shoes to figure out if one of the pairs would accommodate her mother's needs. Unfortunately, none of the shoes fit because of the mother's condition. The customer was allowed to return them all. Two days later, the customer's mother received a get-well-soon message attached to a bouquet of flowers—and the mother and daughter got an upgrade of their

Zappos accounts to VIP status (which includes no shipping charges on all orders).[28]

This unusually high level of customer service is reportedly enabled by heavily empowering Zappos employees, called "members" (as are employees of Morning Star, whose story we tell in Chapter 10). Employees who handle customers directly are not evaluated on how many customers they handle per hour or by similar efficiency metrics. Hsieh was explicit that the only relevant metric is customer satisfaction, or "happiness." That requires allowing reps to use substantial time and other resources (for example, letting reps determine what they will allow customers to return) to make customers happy. Delegation drives this. Also, all employees are empowered to speak freely to the media.[29]

Does it work? Zappos certainly has a reputation for excellent service. Some of these anecdotes, however, may be too good to be true. For years a story circulated about Nordstrom, the Seattle-based retailer also known for outstanding customer relations. The story held that a customer was unhappy with a pair of snow tires and brought them in for a refund, which was happily granted. The punch line: Nordstrom doesn't even sell tires! The story always gets a good laugh in a lecture or speech. Apparently this actually happened, but key details are omitted from the story. This particular Nordstrom was in Fairbanks, Alaska, in a building that formerly housed a tire dealer, from which this customer had bought the tires.[30] Still, good customer service! And good copy for retailers such as Nordstrom and Zappos.

HANDLING DELEGATION

When employees have so much discretion in how they use corporate resources, including their own work time, internal coordination may suffer. If left to their own devices, some employees may not honor the trust that is placed in them. They may shirk their responsibilities or misuse funds or other company resources, creating what economists call "moral hazard." Chaos seems latent in an organization that is heavily decentralized and whose employees have many rights delegated to them. It is because we know this instinctively that we tend to make hierarchy the default. But sometimes these latent problems can be controlled through shared culture and values, without the need for centralization.

Culture plays an important role at Zappos. It's reflected in the company's practice of vetting job candidates intensively and giving every new hire the same basic training as call center reps (perhaps in line with the Zappos value of humility). Recognizing that some hires will eventually realize that they aren't a good fit with Zappos, the company offers every employee a quitting bonus after the first training period. The bonus starts at $2,000 and increases yearly by $1,000, capping out at $5,000.

However, challenges emerged when Zappos began to grow and it became apparent that culture wouldn't be enough to keep things together in a business and management model built around empowering employees.

When Zappos began to break even in 2005, it was approached by Amazon. Hsieh felt that Amazon looked at Zappos as just another shoe seller, rather than as a potentially global brand with a unique culture. Tensions emerged between Hsieh and some board members who wanted to pursue profitability more aggressively (and to tone down "Tony's social experiments").[31] As Hsieh effectively controlled the majority of shares, the board couldn't force a sale, but Hsieh and his sidekick, Zappos CFO and COO Alfred Lin, were the only board members committed to those "experiments."

When Amazon approached Zappos again, Hsieh had come around to feeling that Amazon was willing to allow Zappos to continue as an independent business unit. The acquisition closed on November 1, 2009, with Zappos being valued at $1.2 billion. It helped break the stalemate between Hsieh and the board and gave Zappos access to important Amazon resources. Sales and profitability increased. However, the problems with scaling a model that emphasized playfulness, creativity, and delegation persisted.

ENTER HOLACRACY

Up to this point, Zappos had a fairly conventional management structure. In 2013, that structure was abandoned in favor of what was called "Holacracy." This system, designed by the software developer turned consultant Brian Robertson, is explained in the 2015 best-seller *Holacracy: The Revolutionary Management System That Abolishes Hierarchy*.[32] The subtitle is misleading, because Holacracy doesn't really "abolish hierarchy." Here is what it does instead.

The strange name of this method of governing companies derives from the notion of a "holarchy," defined as a set of connections between "holons," a term coined by the writer Arthur Koestler to refer to something that is both a part and a whole.[33] So the idea is that a holacratic company consists of units that are both self-contained wholes and dependent parts.

Here's how it works. In a Holacracy, employees don't hold the usual job titles of a conventional hierarchy; Holacracy claims to do away with job descriptions. Instead, employees are "members" who have "roles" that encompass a set of tasks, activities, or responsibilities. Each member is assigned to one or more roles. Roles are bundled into "circles," which can be combined into larger circles; for example, a "leadership circle" or a "board circle" supersedes a "design circle." So far, this doesn't sound that different from a conventional workplace, with "roles" functioning as job descriptions, "circles" being equivalent to teams, and the larger circles looking like departments and divisions.

What's different about Holacracy is how much freedom the members and circles have to organize themselves. The company sets goals, then leaves it to members to organize themselves into circles and decide how each circle will be run. Circles decide which circle members will fill each role. Decision-making within circles follows a set structure (designed by the company). Circles are connected by two roles, the lead link and the rep link; these members participate in relevant meetings and make sure organizational goals are translated into actions by the relevant circles. There are no formal managers and no formal job titles, only roles, which can be filled by different members at different times.

A 2016 *Harvard Business Review* article on Holacracy describes the process, using an example from ARCA, a global manufacturing and services company based in North Carolina that implemented Holacracy in 2015:

Take Karl, who came to ARCA before it implemented holacracy. A recent law school graduate, he had little business experience but showed great potential with his legal and analytical skills. His versatility allowed him to take on multiple roles at the growing company, in sales, legal services, and operations. However, as he worked across functional groups, he felt his contributions were getting lost in the organizational structure. When the company adopted holacracy, Karl's many roles across multiple circles became explicit and visible. He thought his value was more clearly recognized, which gave him even more confidence to initiate changes and make decisions. Karl said, "Pre-holacracy, I felt pretty empowered but always ran stuff by people. I think an org implementing holacracy is saying, 'You don't have to run stuff by us anymore.' I've taken the opportunity to exercise more judgment and discretion."

How did Karl fit all this work in? Holacracy let him jettison roles that weren't a good use of his time. For instance, he used the structuring process to carve out some administrative responsibilities and pitch them as a separate role, which the lead link filled with an enthusiastic new hire. The upside of designing roles in this way is straightforward: because employees are driving the process, they have a greater sense of making real progress on meaningful work.[34]

Assigning individuals to tasks, giving them flexible roles, and letting them work across teams and projects—calling them "circles" if you like— sounds great. But that is more or less what the conventional hierarchy already does. Indeed, Holacracy's more thoughtful proponents admit that it's one take on hierarchy. (Its less thoughtful proponents still peddle it as a "bossless" approach.)

What's different is the emphasis on breaking problems down into subproblems that can be assigned to circles and then to roles (or, for narrowly enough defined tasks, "micro-roles") and letting these structures emerge organically. Holacracy empowers employees handling a particular role to figure out how best to fulfill the purpose associated with the role. Employees in a holacratic company don't need permission to engage in a particular action that meets the purpose associated with their role (though, of course, using corporate resources beyond what is associated with the role requires asking permission). The default is autonomy.

This is really not that different from the decentralized model used by many conventionally organized firms, even if they don't use this language. However, Holacracy lends considerably more structure to the decentralized model. For example, Holacracy specifies particular protocols for team decision processes (for example, how to regulate roles).

This last point is critical. Remember Wikipedia? As we pointed out in Chapter 1, the content of a Wikipedia entry isn't written by a boss, but the system by which entries are solicited, written, edited, and revised was designed by the founders of the Wikipedia project. *Good bosses design systems and structures*, even those bosses who locate decision-making at lower levels of the organization. Holacracy is flexible and adaptable and allows for a great deal of autonomy, but within an overall structure that is very much designed—by the managers of a firm adopting Holacracy and ultimately by the originators of the concept itself.

In countries with limited government and the rule of law, these processes and procedures are made explicit in a constitution, either a written one like the US Constitution or a set of unwritten principles that are broadly understood by all, as with the British Constitution. Holacracy also features a constitution, which its originator describes as the "rulebook" of Holacracy.[35] Robertson explains that the first step in transforming a company into the holacratic form is for the CEO to formally adopt the constitution—and thus cede his power to the rule system embodied in the constitution. As he puts it, "By heroically releasing authority into the system's embrace, the leader paves the way for an authentic distribution of power through every level of the organization."[36]

This is good thinking! It is basically an attempt to deal with managerial overreach. The traditional hierarchy partly protects against overreach by introducing distance—both informational and psychological—between employees at different levels. In a flat organization, because management is so close to operations, managers may be tempted to micro-manage and overreach. Managers may *say* that they are willing to relinquish control, without really meaning it. Or the employees may not believe them.

Ostensibly, Holacracy solves this problem by having the CEO publicly embrace the Holacracy constitution. The problem, however, is that it is not clear what course of action Holacracy suggests when a CEO breaches the constitution.

HOLACRACY IN ZAPPOS

In 2013, Zappos became the most prominent adopter of the Holacracy model. It is easy to see why Holacracy would appeal to Tony Hsieh: it promised a way of scaling up Zappos while keeping the company innovative and entrepreneurial. It would simultaneously offer coherence and decentralization—one being a condition for a balanced growth process, the other for innovation and entrepreneurship. In March 2013, Hsieh wrote in an internal memo: "We haven't made fast enough progress towards self-management, self-organization, and more efficient structures to run our business. . . . We are going to take a 'rip the Bandaid' approach to accelerate progress."[37]

However, Zappos encountered a few surprises on its Holacracy journey. First, many employees got frustrated with the implementation. Hsieh seemingly thought that some employees simply didn't fit with the new approach. In 2015 he offered Zappos employees a special version of the Zappos "offer" (the quit bonus mentioned earlier):

> Self-management and self-organization is not for everyone. . . . Therefore, there will be a special version of "the offer" on a company-wide scale, in which each employee will be offered at least 3 months' severance (and up to 3 months of COBRA reimbursement for benefits) if he/she feels that self-management, self-organization, and our Best Customers Strategy and strategy statements as published in Glass Frog are not the right fit.[38]

Over the coming months, 18 percent of Zappos employees took the offer, including, problematically, 38 percent of Zappos's tech department. In early 2020, Zappos watcher Aimee Groth noted that Zappos had decisively, if quietly, backed away from Holacracy.[39] It hasn't abandoned

Holacracy entirely. For example, the idea of the "circle" remains. But traditional managers are back.

What went wrong? At least three things, none of which a Holacracy believer would expect. They were less surprising, however, to those who appreciate the benefits of traditional hierarchy.

First, Holacracy made Zappos overly bureaucratic. Not because of too much red tape, or intractable lines of command and reporting, but because of excessive meetings. Doing away with formal job descriptions and organizing all activities around roles and circles required that a lot of the ongoing coordination normally handled by managers in a "vertical," hierarchical way now be handled by employees in a more lateral way. This increased the sharing of information and joint decision-making, but it also led to longer and more frequent meetings. While traditional hierarchy is often blasted for its alleged slowness in passing information up and down hierarchical layers, it is sometimes forgotten that the alternative can be worse.

Second, as many other adopters of Holacracy have come to realize, the model is hard to scale, partly because coordination involves so much lateral communication. This problem is related to another point, namely, that growth usually involves taking care of *interdependencies*, that is, "spillovers" between the various units. Companies are not loose collections of self-contained organizational atoms. Even at the most "modular" companies, many interdependencies exist between organizational units. No unit is entirely an island. Not all activities can be "decomposed" into smaller units.

Companies realize this when they grow. A sudden, unexpected increase in sales puts pressure on production, support functions, and much else, potentially straining the company. This is a well-known challenge for start-ups: once they start growing, they find it difficult to control costs, partly because of how managers and employees struggle to handle interdependencies in the growth process. Managing that process can be difficult even for a streamlined hierarchical company; it is likely far more challenging for a company based on significant delegation and coordination between circles run by dedicated coordination "roles" with little authority or ability to make their cases except by argument and persuasion.

Third, the adoption of Holacracy led to less customer focus, perhaps because of all the attention devoted to making the model work. Clearly, for a company that made customer-centricity its lodestar, this was a deal-breaker.

READ THE FINE PRINT!

Spotify and Zappos are great companies, both of them innovative and successful. Spotify's lingo of "squads" and "tribes" has gotten a lot of press and helps attract knowledge workers looking for an innovative, challenging environment. Zappos's embrace of Holacracy has likewise drawn attention to the company. Good for them!

There is a lot to like in Spotify's matrix structure and the decentralized, holacratic system. But they aren't substantially new, and they certainly aren't bossless. Managers have implemented cross-functional teams, multiple reporting lines, overlapping circles of interaction, and similar structures for decades, if not centuries. Not only does the bossless company narrative oversell the benefits of highly flat structures and downplay the role of good management, but it also exaggerates the novelty of the former. Both structures lead to dangers, of different types. Highlighting the benefits of flat structures while downplaying their drawbacks, and falsely implying that these structures always work well for all firms, can lead managers to embrace a model that's not right for them. Claiming that a well-known structure is something new and different encourages managers to embrace that structure as a quick fix for various company problems, not realizing that their changes are merely window dressing.

In the next chapter, we take one more step toward clarifying when a bossless organization structure may work—and when it is not going to work.

6

WHAT THE BOSSLESS COMPANY NARRATIVE GETS RIGHT—AND WHAT IT GETS WRONG

THE BOSSLESS COMPANY NARRATIVE IS RIGHT THAT DELEGATION, decentralization, and empowerment can be beneficial. But it gets many other things wrong. It misses that flattening the hierarchy brings costs as well as benefits. It fails to recognize that the design of a company is *contingent* on the key elements of the business environment—products, markets, technologies, and worker preferences. The theory of organizational complementarities discussed in Chapter 4 fleshes out these contingencies in the context of job design. The notions of contingencies and complementarities (or "positive interdependencies," or even "synergies," if you prefer) are important for understanding the limitations and perils of the bossless company, as we will see with the rise and fall in the 1990s of a near-bossless experiment at Oticon, a Danish hearing-aid producer. The Oticon story illustrates the importance of contingencies and complementarities and shows more clearly what the bossless company narrative gets (partly) right and what it gets wrong.

What the Oticon story most of all shows is the fundamental misconception at the root of the bossless company narrative: that companies are essentially the same as markets. By overemphasizing flat structures, decentralization, and autonomy, the narrative suggests that all the great features of the market—exchange, competition, survival of the fitter, and so on—can be re-created inside the firm. But the forces at work inside organizations are different from those at work in markets. Pretending they are the same leads to trouble.

Oticon's "spaghetti" organization—its experiment with "bossless" organization—was explicitly seen as introducing markets into a company. The catchy metaphor, invented by CEO Lars Kolind, was meant to illustrate the idea that while the new flat organization would be flexible and adaptable, it would still have form and shape, like a pile of spaghetti in a good *sugo* on a plate tossed by a fork. He probably didn't have in mind another spaghetti idiom, namely, throwing it against the wall to see what sticks (though it does describe how organizations often change by trying many things, seemingly at random, to see what works). In any case, Kolind's metaphor stuck, and the spaghetti model has entered the lexicon of business jargon.

Oticon was among the first important firms to flatten its hierarchies to increase employee satisfaction, create an organization that was better at sharing knowledge between employees, produce new ideas, and improve overall performance. Its experience received enormous attention and widespread acclaim in the business press and has been studied and taught in business schools around the world. Oticon supposedly showed that flattening the hierarchy could drive organizational learning and renewal, even at an established firm in a low-growth environment. But some of the most important lessons from the Danish company's spaghetti experiment are less well known.

OTICON: FROM SPAGHETTI TO LASAGNA

At 8:00 a.m. on August 8, 1991, in the Copenhagen suburb of Hellerup, reporters from CNN were standing by for the kind of occasion that normally would not interest the world's largest cable news organization: the

opening of the new headquarters of a Danish company, Oticon, a leading supplier of hearing aids. Just a few months earlier, CNN had been
reporting on Operation Desert Storm, the US-led military operation
against the Iraqi occupation of Kuwait, a story that had vastly influenced
CNN's global reach. The BBC would run a feature on Oticon, as did international newspapers such as the *New York Times*, *Der Spiegel*, and the
Guardian.

These media outlets weren't reporting on a cure for hearing loss or a
breakthrough technological innovation. Oticon would be highly innovative in the years to come, but it had no new technology to announce
that day. This was a medium-sized company in an industry that was not
particularly exciting, operating in a smallish city in a small European
country. What brought CNN, as well as other international broadcasters
and newspapers, to Copenhagen that August morning?

These people were there to see Lars Kolind, Oticon's intellectual,
media-savvy CEO. Kolind was well known to the international business
press, and that day he had something to pitch—nothing less, as he saw it,
than a revolution in management and organization. Kolind was there to
introduce the spaghetti organization—the new, radically decentralized,
empowering, and IT-supported Oticon organization.

Kolind's pitch convinced the leading management guru Tom Peters,
the coauthor of the international best-seller *In Search of Excellence*, who
was already thinking along similar lines about the relations between strategy, organization, and performance. In his subsequent book, *Thriving on
Chaos*, published in 1988, Peters had told managers to do as his title suggested. The book opens with a description of a business world made unpredictable because of constant change, much of it driven by technology.
Since the publication of Peters's book, the story of rapid technological
change and its disruptive effect on business has become almost a boiler-
plate opening for leadership books. In 1988, however, Peters described
other major challenges to the US economy, such as lagging productivity, a large trade imbalance, and political and competitive threats from
new parts of the globe (yes, not much new under the sun). Dealing with
this "chaos" requires "world class superior service" and "extraordinary

responsiveness"; fast-paced and constant innovation based on a "piloting culture" that supports constant, incremental change as well as major innovation projects; "partnering" with relevant stakeholders; leading based on an encompassing and motivating vision; and measuring the truly important things in the organization. Oh, and of course all of these efforts must be entirely people-driven. Employees need to be flexible, empowered, and involved in everything.

If Peters's list of chores for the modern company sounds a little clichéd, that's because it is. These words and phrases sound good and are often incorporated into consulting reports, TED tasks, and keynote speeches by famous professors and authors. But achieving consensus, articulating a vision, and getting buy-in are mundane management tasks. What was fresh was Peters's framing and language; he made these ordinary ideas sound radical, exciting, and new. He needed examples of firms living out his ideas, and he latched onto Oticon, giving the company an entire chapter in his 1992 book, *Liberation Management: Necessary Disorganization for the Nanosecond Nineties*. (Sadly, unlike his earlier best-sellers, the book did not seem to grab readers' attention for more than a nanosecond, and it quickly faded into obscurity.)

What was going on at Oticon to generate such *Sturm und Drang*?

Looking back, we can see that some features that looked so revolutionary back in 1992 have become nothing special. The media swooned over the open office spaces (still unusual in those days outside of newspaper offices) with their temporary workstations where members of project groups, moving their paperwork around on carts, would gather. They noticed the ostensibly paperless organization (the headquarters featured a big glass tube that showed paper falling down to a lower floor, apparently toward the brutal fate of shredding), a precursor of today's fully digitalized office, and the overall design intended to foster spontaneous interaction and knowledge-sharing.

Again, if none of this seems very novel, it's because so much has changed in how we think about management and the nature of organizations. But at the time, these changes at Oticon were mainly symbolic. Underneath, something real was happening at Oticon, what we might now call a change in the organization's DNA. Kolind really was completely redoing Oticon's management model as he tried to turn company culture dramatically around.

ENTER LARS KOLIND

Oticon's lackluster financial performance, declining innovativeness, and loss of market share toward the end of the 1980s had brought changes to its C-suite. The old team had been at the Oticon helm for almost three decades. In came new CEO Lars Kolind, who launched a program of extensive cost-cutting. Initially, he strongly centralized the firm's decision-making structure to give himself the power to break resistance to his cost-cutting measures. Although this program was successful, restoring revenues and profits to their former levels, it was also clear to Kolind that Oticon was on a long-term decline. Oticon's increased financial distress convinced Kolind to change his fundamental thinking about the company he was managing. Something more radical than a standard cost-cutting exercise was needed. To see how this more radical thing emerged, let's take a closer look at Kolind.

It would be hard to characterize Lars Kolind as "charismatic" in the usual sense—at least compared to someone like Steve Jobs. Kolind is thin and bespectacled, speaks English with a characteristic Danish accent, and comes across as an introvert. But he is also highly intelligent, driven, and committed to a set of fundamental values that may have sounded slightly eccentric in the 1990s but have become nearly mainstream.

For Kolind, the purpose of the firm is not to maximize returns to shareholders, but to change the world for the common good. Employees are partners in this endeavor who should be trusted and given the freedom and flexibility to explore their own ideas for improvement. These are the basic values that formed the basis for Kolind's turnaround at Oticon. They are also values he has continued to endorse, notably in his 2012 manifesto *Unboss*.[1]

Kolind was trained as a mathematician and served as a deputy at Denmark's (so far) only nuclear test facility (Risø). His active participation in the international Boy Scout movement also influenced him, especially its strong values-driven orientation (remember those Twelve Scout Laws!), focus on local control, and little central direction. Scouting is about commitment to a movement and its values and about doing good. Thus, being a scout means participating in building "a better world where people are self-fulfilled as individuals and play a constructive role in society."[2] There is hierarchy, to be sure, but it is a hierarchy of supporting adults. Leadership is mainly peer-to-peer leadership.

It is tempting to interpret Kolind's new experiment in radically flattening the Oticon hierarchy, empowering employees, strengthening customer orientation, and establishing strong cultural values of initiative and trust as bringing Boy Scout principles into Oticon. Kolind himself said as much: "I see most companies as a waste of resources. In contrast, when I take a look at the scouting movement I see a strong volunteer aspect. When scouts come together they cooperate effectively without hierarchy, like a family brought together through common goals. That's why the scouting movement is accomplishing loads of remarkable things with limited resources."[3]

This mathematician–Boy Scout–CEO spent New Year's Eve 1989 making the first sketch of a new radical organizational structure for the company he had been managing for over a year and was desperately trying to save from an impending bankruptcy. The magic bullet in that sketch was killing the hierarchy, quite literally. Kolind wanted Oticon to operate based on "internal market forces." What he had in mind was a real market, but one that would be delicately steered by a management board. Because what he proposed was so radical—Kolind knew that, traditionally, markets and hierarchies are seen as very different things—he titled his memo "Think the Unthinkable."

THINK THE UNTHINKABLE

"Think the Unthinkable" was presented to the organization on April 18, 1991. It offered a radical proposal for a new kind of organization without bosses or hierarchy. Kolind used the metaphor of the market: like that system of decentralized, voluntary exchange, Oticon would be run on the self-organizing efforts of highly motivated people, acting in an entrepreneurial manner to bring about innovations in technology and marketing. Accordingly, the memo laid out a design for a very flat, creative, informal, self-organizing, and knowledge-based company driven by a culture of trust, empowerment, and enthusiasm. The concrete financial goal was to increase profitability 30 percent in three years. (The change project was sometimes referred to as "project 330.")

Kolind constantly contrasted the Oticon of yesteryear, "Old Oticon," to the Oticon with the new structure, "New Oticon," the so-called "spaghetti organization." Kolind wanted Oticon's plate of spaghetti to accomplish the following:

Abolish the hierarchy. All managerial positions and formal job titles were eliminated. There would be no departments, only self-organizing, temporary projects. All employees were treated as associates or partners (though legally they remained employees). While hierarchical layers were drastically reduced, hierarchy wasn't eliminated: the so-called Products and Projects Committee (PPC) remained at the apex of the organization. This committee was given the task of evaluating and approving projects and had discretionary powers to intervene in them. That is, if the committee thought that a project was not developing in the right way, it could close it or merge it with another project.

Empower employees and decentralize. Employees were no longer assigned to certain projects but could join as many different projects as they wanted. An early version of a company intranet established an internal job market where any employee could join any project she wanted to join (subject to approval by a project leader). Kolind's new structure also allowed employees to start any project relating to Oticon's core business areas, provided that they obtained permission from a designated committee to implement and manage the project. The criteria for approval were relevance and a simple rule of a fixed rate of return over three years. Finally, project leaders were empowered to exercise real leadership. Running a project was to feel like running an entrepreneurial start-up, with the project leader, the entrepreneur in charge, exercising leadership not as a traditional boss but as a supporter, based on experience and the respect enjoyed in the project team and the organization at large. Project leaders were given substantial discretion over the remuneration of project members.

Encourage multitasking and skill upgrading. Employees were encouraged to learn new skills and to multitask. The relationship between job and employee was rethought: instead of employees having to fit certain jobs, jobs were redesigned into unique combinations of functions that would suit employees' needs and skills.

Make rewards high-powered. In "Old Oticon," employees received their monthly paycheck and that was it. In the new organization, salaries were heavily (for that time) based on performance, specifically the financial performance of projects. To emphasize the "partner" status of employees, Kolind also introduced an employee stock ownership program.

Stress the artifactual dimension of the organization. This was what made the media swoon: those open office spaces with mobile desks and carts; the huge glass cylinder in the middle of the office space with redundant paperwork silently flowing down toward its destiny in the shredder; the carefully designed staircases where employees (sorry, partners) met and shared knowledge. Of course, all these features were in tune with the times: "culture" was *the* big thing in management consulting around 1990, when more "humanistic" management practices were displacing the "management by the numbers" culture of the 1960s and 1970s and the cost-cutting, financial-results-driven emphasis of the 1980s. (Remember the notorious CEO "Chainsaw Al" Dunlap?) A best-selling 1992 book by Harvard Business School professors John Kotter and James Heskett, *Corporate Culture and Performance*, argued that "soft" characteristics like shared values and unwritten rules mattered more for company performance than technical efficiency or productivity.[4] Physical spaces designed to encourage spontaneous interaction and stimulate creativity were seen as enablers of a strong corporate culture.

Embrace knowledge and communication. In "Think the Unthinkable," Kolind urged Oticon to embrace being a "fully knowledge-based company," anticipating the "knowledge management" language that exploded in the 1990s along with the rapid growth of the internet and the idea that knowledge was the key competitive resource. Here, employee knowledge-sharing was seen as crucial to company performance. The argument was that knowledge didn't just flow up and down the hierarchy; it also had to move laterally because ideas for new products, new marketing initiatives, and so on, would emerge from combining knowledge in novel ways. Thus, Kolind stressed the importance of cross-functional projects— putting marketing people and R&D people on the same project—as a key driver of innovativeness. He also emphasized clear and transparent communication that outlined key organizational priorities as pivotal.

It seemed radical at the time—and still does today. In retrospect, Kolind was betting the organization's future. But it worked, at least for a while. Profitability soared as the organization cranked out one innovative hearing aid device after another. The Oticon spaghetti organization was quickly picked up by management consultants, writers, and professors. It has been one of the most used cases in business school teaching on organizational change management. And the Oticon spaghetti organization has become a key poster child for the death-of-hierarchy narrative. It is rightly seen as one of the very first successful experiments in a radically decentralized organization with almost complete employee empowerment and a very flat structure.

PARADISE LOST

However, there is a snag. Media accounts and business cases mention only the rosy aspect of the spaghetti organization and leave out the problems. Even recent accounts fail to mention that it was abandoned in 1996. One of us conducted a series of interviews in Oticon in 2016, and there was little memory of the spaghetti organization within the company.[5] If it was such a fabulous success, why was the spaghetti organization abandoned?

In one sense, the radical spaghetti organization was killed by its own success: it generated too many ideas and also brought confusion, turmoil, and general chaos. Management began to wonder if the idea pipeline was filling up too quickly. At the same time, employees were fed up with colleagues who promised time to so many different projects that their total work time amounted to 300 percent of the required time on the job. Employees were frustrated by the lack of planning regarding resources and deliverables across projects and the absence of clear routines and rules. They were missing what hierarchy supplies: predictability and order.

Employees were also frustrated with erratic and arbitrary intervention by the only remaining management layer in the company: the Products and Projects Committee, which, remember, was tasked with approving or rejecting projects and checking on project execution. The PPC would often close or merge projects without sufficiently explaining why. To employees, such intervention clashed with the ethos of freedom and trust and being treated like adults that Kolind had worked so hard to establish. It might seem as if employees were rebelling against hierarchy, but they weren't.

This seemingly arbitrary interference in projects illustrates what Oliver Williamson called the impossibility of "selective intervention."[6] In principle, management rarely intervenes in a firm with an extremely flat organizational structure, doing so only when it would create value through coordination, improved communication, or conflict resolution. Yet there's a problem. Employees know that such intervention could be coming, but not exactly when, and not exactly to what purpose. The idea that someone is looking over your shoulder, second-guessing your decisions and overriding your actions, can make you reluctant to do as much or as well as you otherwise would. The knowledge that management could always come along and interfere—even if management does so only rarely—is a disincentive to show initiative, assume responsibility, and invest in outcomes. That is a key limit to the size of the firm: while managerial coordination provides great benefits, it is costly if used to excess.

In a well-functioning hierarchy, higher-level managers do intervene. Projects that have been given a "go" are sometimes shut down, merged with other projects, or postponed. Promises are not always kept. Yet intervening, overruling, and reneging are *minimized* in a well-functioning hierarchy. Managers take the time and make the effort to explain why they are intervening so that employees, even if they disagree with a particular managerial decision, view the process as transparent and fair.

A classic example concerns performance reviews. Researchers have consistently found that employees care not only about the pay increases that they and coworkers receive based on performance ratings, but also about the process by which pay raises are determined. For instance, they appreciate knowing the ratings criteria ahead of time, being allowed to express their opinions and feelings about their jobs, and receiving their assessments in a timely fashion.[7] As scholars, we frequently submit our written work for formal peer review, part of the process of getting published in academic journals. We have each had our fair share of rejections! These sting, but what really irks us is a poorly done review, a long wait for the decision, or some other breakdown in the process. We are more likely to accept the outcome if we think the procedure was transparent and fair.

What happened at Oticon in 1996, five years after the introduction of the spaghetti organization, was that employees had come to want the good kind of hierarchy back. They wanted stability, predictability, and fair processes, even if these came at the expense of autonomy and spontaneity. So a more conventional organizational structure—something more like lasagna—was restored. The company was divided into three large units according to the markets they primarily targeted—in other words, something like the product-based divisions characteristic of the traditional multidivisional form—with strong lateral connections between these units. So in essence Oticon went from a radical, project-based, almost entirely flat organization to something resembling a "matrix" organization.

LESSONS FROM THE SPAGHETTI ORGANIZATION

What do we learn about the bossless company narrative from Oticon's experience with creating the spaghetti organization?

First, radical decentralization is possible and can bring benefits. Oticon's radically decentralized organization based on employee empowerment did generate lots of excitement, creativity, and energy (and media attention)—for a while.

Second, excitement disappeared as self-organizing processes ran into all sorts of trivial but nevertheless deeply frustrating daily problems with coordinating work and motivating employees. Perhaps these frustrations could have been remedied by more clearly codified procedures, such as a simple system for registering the time employees spent on tasks in different projects. Perhaps rewards could have been changed to improve motivation. But these would only have been minor tweaks and could easily have violated the spirit of self-organization on which the new organizational form was based.

Third, even in a radically decentralized form, management doesn't really go away. Perhaps the exercise of management in a radically decentralized form is more informal, as it was at Valve. But that is part of the problem. The lack of formality creates unpredictability and hampers performance. With fewer layers of middle management, senior managers are closer to employees, and that can make employees uncomfortable. While employees may initially appreciate that bosses are now less distant, they also come to realize that greater proximity could make bosses more prone to meddling. Micro-management and other management behaviors that are, from the point of view of the employees, simply annoying begin to proliferate. This is what happened in the spaghetti organization. Employees of other companies with radically flattened hierarchies have had similar experiences.

THE BASIC MISTAKE: FIRMS AREN'T MARKETS

The story of Oticon helps us see the problem that arises when proponents of the bossless company make the mistake of describing firms using the language of markets. Emphasizing freedom, autonomy, and empowerment and touting the advantages of self-organization, voluntary interaction, and spontaneous creativity push the need to bring the market inside the firm, substituting negotiation, persuasion, and community for command and control. The resulting company is flat, bossless, entrepreneurial, and agile—like the market.

The key point is that while firms operate within the market, what goes on inside the firm is categorically different from what goes on in market transactions. Of course, workers inside a firm typically have some autonomy—line workers a little, knowledge workers a lot—and managers often design incentive systems, internal competitions, bargaining procedures, and other mechanisms to motivate employees and take advantage of their unique knowledge, and so on. Both the managers who design such systems and the employees who participate in them must experiment, learn, adapt, and adjust to changing circumstances. But these aspects of firm organization are designed—they do not emerge spontaneously in the absence of purpose and plan.

In other words, companies simply are not markets, and it is wrong to ascribe the property of being a market to a company. This is a key theme in this book. What do we mean by it?

In markets, people are free to transact with each other; prices regulate who buys and uses the goods, services, and inputs in the economy; resources tend to flow toward the places where they are valued the highest; and entrepreneurs test new ideas and projects against the profit-and-loss test of market competition. The market isn't a thing, or a place, or an organism, but a process, one shaped by the rules of the game embodied in institutions, norms, and contracts. The market system itself doesn't have a specific purpose; as F. A. Hayek put it, markets are "orders" rather than "organizations."[8] They aren't designed by anyone, though they serve the purposes of those who participate. They lack what the Greeks called *telos*—a single, ultimate objective or aim.

Companies, by contrast, are established by specific people at specific times and places for specific purposes: producing particular products or services, making the founder wealthy, preserving a family name, allowing an entrepreneur to find her passion, possibly even contributing to broader social causes such as protecting the environment or helping certain workers. This is why managers matter: to achieve these purposes, the leaders of the business adopt operating procedures, establish business processes, purchase and deploy resources, and hire and manage employees. For example, Tesla's mission, according to Elon Musk, is "to accelerate the advent of sustainable transport by bringing compelling mass-market electric cars to market as soon as possible."[9] To accomplish its mission, Tesla eschews the auto industry's conventional business model of selling through franchised dealerships in favor of a direct-to-consumer model that includes home delivery and service. It invests not only in vehicle manufacturing, sales, and service but also in rolling out the charging stations that are often vital for Tesla owners who have limited battery-charging capacity. Lobbying for tax benefits for electric vehicles and trying to change public perceptions of renewable energy are also part of the business plan. All these aspects of the mission are designed, part of a carefully crafted, though sometimes clumsily executed, strategy to make Tesla the world's leading auto producer. (As of this writing, Tesla is small by sales volume, but the world's largest auto manufacturer by market capitalization.)

Of course, plans change, companies pivot, and things don't always work out as expected. A designed object or institution, such as a firm, isn't static and fixed—it can be adjusted and even totally redesigned if needed. The design can include options and contingencies. But this basic distinction between markets and firms holds for all companies, even those that are highly decentralized.

The bossless company narrative seeks to make companies into markets—something they are not and never can be.

BIG COMPANIES ARE ALSO PART OF THE MARKET

Yet markets and companies coexist and very much need each other. Markets can do some things well, but certainly not all. Most valuable business activities take place in the organized, structured groups that we call companies. Think of Walmart. Most Walmart customers probably don't notice, but shopping at Walmart is the result of a logistics and operations management miracle. In 2020 Walmart managed $44 billion in inventory over its nearly twelve thousand stores across twenty-eight countries around the world. In fact, Walmart is synonymous with successful supply-chain management. This business activity surely adds value for basically everyone—the other companies that are part of the supply chain, Walmart's customers, and its 2.3 million employees. The basic management of the supply chain is done by Walmart itself. So is the actual selling of all the stuff that the supply chain provides. But the products that are offered for sale by Walmart aren't produced by Walmart; the production of vegetables, meat, electronics, and so on, is handled by other organized, structured groups—that is, other companies.

Of course, Walmart trades with these other companies. So some activities or "transactions" are handled inside Walmart, as it were (notably, logistics and sales), while other activities are handled by other companies. Walmart accesses the results of those activities (that is, the actual products) by engaging in *market* transactions with them. So, although productive activities are undertaken by companies, transactions can take place in markets. But again, companies and markets are different beasts, with different natures and purposes. Markets are (partly) self-organizing systems, while companies are based on (some measure of) direction and planning. The one should not be mistaken for the other.

CONTINGENCIES IN TECHNOLOGY AND ORGANIZATION

We've seen from Oticon that ideas about flatter hierarchies, companies without bosses, worker-owned firms, and radical decentralization may work in some contexts, at least for a while. In Oticon they helped to reboot a company that seemed destined for bankruptcy, but Oticon's success doesn't mean these ideas will work elsewhere. There are plenty of drawbacks to this way of organizing companies, and those drawbacks explain why the radically flattened hierarchy never became the dominant form for organizing a company.

Why did it work for Oticon in the 1990s? And why do we hear so much about flatness today? Is it just a fad, or is something going on in the economy and society at large? There are in fact some contingencies that give an edge to flatter structures and management, because of the way they set and enforce rules, over command and control—technological change, the rise in outsourcing, and modularity and simplicity.

TECHNOLOGICAL CHANGE

An obvious shock to the business environment over the last three decades has been rapid technological advance. Since the late 1980s, management writers and gurus have emphasized technological change—and for good reason! Over those three decades, we have seen the advent of cheap and almost-universal high-speed internet, mobile telephony, and smart devices, as well as the production and distribution models they enable, such as social networks, platforms, cloud storage, streaming services, and the gig economy. More people now get their news from Facebook and Twitter than from the *New York Times* or the BBC. TikTok went from zero to a billion users in two years of operation, with young stars like sixteen-year-old dancer Charli D'Amelio grabbing 100 million followers in just a few months—without any direction from management. Algorithms, not editors or managers, increasingly decide what information we receive. We share rides with strangers via Uber and Lyft and share their homes via Airbnb and VRBO. Companies like Spotify and Zappos capture our imagination not only because of their heavy digital presence but also because they embrace the loosely structured, "democratic" nature of the internet itself.

There is more to the story, however. Interest in the bossless company accompanies a broader shift in how people are thinking about large organizations, about capitalism, and about the nature of business in society. The increasing interest in "stakeholder" capitalism—the proposition that firms should look out for the broader interests of society rather than simply earn money for their owners—reflects this broader shift. Increasing global competition, rapid innovation, an emphasis on entrepreneurship, and the importance of knowledge assets, rather than physical assets, have heralded what many see as a new type of capitalism.

THE RISE IN OUTSOURCING

The famous eighteenth-century economist Adam Smith used the metaphor of the "invisible hand" to illustrate how resources are allocated in a decentralized market system. Production and consumption are coordinated, not by the wise actions of state planners, but by prices and markets—or as we would say today, by the forces of supply and demand. Even large factories (such as the pin factory memorably described in Smith's 1776 book *The Wealth of Nations*), which rely on managers to arrange workers and tasks to take advantage of the division of labor, are competing against other firms and are forced to adjust their behavior in response to market conditions.

The rise of large, vertically integrated manufacturers in the late nineteenth century, followed by diversified multidivisional firms such as General Motors and DuPont in the twentieth, led Harvard professor Alfred Chandler to suggest that the "invisible hand" was being supplanted by the visible hand of management. In *The Visible Hand*, Chandler claimed that the centralized managerial hierarchy, not market competition, was the main engine of production and economic progress. The Nobel laureate Herbert Simon, writing in 1991, asked us to imagine an alien viewing the Earth from space, equipped with a telescope that reveals social structures:

> The firms reveal themselves, say, as solid green areas with faint interior contours marking out divisions and departments. Market transactions show as red lines connecting firms, forming a network in the spaces between them. Within firms (and perhaps even between them) the approaching visitor also sees pale blue lines, the lines of authority connecting bosses with various levels of workers. . . . No matter whether our visitor approached the United States or the Soviet Union, urban China or the European Community, the greater part of the space below it would be within the green areas, for almost all of the inhabitants would be employees, hence inside the firm boundaries. Organizations would be the dominant feature of the landscape. A message sent back home, describing the scene, would speak of "large green areas interconnected by red lines." It would not likely speak of "a network of red lines connecting green spots."[10]

In other words, even a modern, networked economy is dominated by organizations, many of them quite large. This is the world of *Mad Men* and *The Man in the Gray Flannel Suit*, as described earlier.

As many have argued, however, the large twentieth-century organization seems to be giving way to the flexible, networked, decentralized firm. The flattening and decentralization of the internal organization of companies (how companies do what they do) has been accompanied by changes in what they actually do. Many companies have divested unrelated business areas, concentrated on doing what they are good at (their "core competences"), and outsourced non-core activities to other firms. (Such outsourcing not only occurs within national borders but often involves offshoring—moving activities to companies in other countries.)

The University of Connecticut economist Richard Langlois calls this phenomenon the "vanishing hand" of the twenty-first century.[11] He argues that large Chandlerian firms that assume ownership of both suppliers and buyers and produce a broad range of different products and services are increasingly being supplanted by smaller and more specialized firms. In this view, the balance is changing from organizations to markets: Chandler's "visible hand" is "vanishing" as firms outsource and spin off business units. However, even in industries where firms are getting smaller and the external market is playing a bigger role, hierarchy is still important. Nor are the hierarchies in those firms becoming more like markets. The vanishing hand at work in these industries simply means that, compared to the heyday of the vertically integrated industrial company, fewer resources are being directed by planning and direction inside firms and more are being coordinated by market signals that facilitate cooperation between independent companies.

Why did the visible hand start to vanish? Langlois emphasizes changes in technology, such as the shift from proprietary, vertically integrated systems like the mainframe computers of the 1960s and 1970s to the open-architecture, modular, vertically disintegrated personal computers of the 1980s and 1990s. Think of the classic IBM System/360 family of mainframe computers that dominated IBM's industry for more than a decade. Virtually all the hardware components, the operating system and application software, and the installation, service, and support were provided by IBM, whose products were not compatible with the products of other manufacturers. In stark contrast lies Dell, the leading PC maker of the 2000s, which specialized in assembling made-to-order PCs using off-the-shelf components manufactured by other firms, using an open, modular architecture.

In other words, because many firms are getting smaller in the new economy, a larger share of the coordination of resources, people, and tasks is taking place between firms, via the market, instead of inside large firms, via the managerial hierarchy. For example, as solid-state disk drives (chips printed on a circuit board with no moving parts) became easier to manufacture, they fell rapidly in price, making them more attractive than conventional disk drives (spinning magnetic or optical disks with motorized "heads" that move around the surface as they read the data). If the same company made both the computers and the drives—say, a 1960s-style IBM—managers would have to decide which technology was best in terms of size, weight, cost, reliability, and so on, then shift production and installation from one technology to the other. But in the vertically disintegrated world, where computer makers buy disk drives on the market, all they have to do is shop on price. The market tells them to switch from the old (more expensive) to the new (less expensive) technology—an example of what Hayek called the "marvel of the market."

Of course, a substantial amount of coordination still takes place within these firms, even if they are smaller than their ancestors. As pointed out earlier, firms are not markets! But the boundary between firm and market has been shifting, with a move toward more coordination via the market and less via the managerial hierarchy, at least in some industries.

Another example of the vanishing hand is the movie industry, where large firms have relinquished their ownership and control of the value chain in favor of more flexible outsourced production. For example, under the Hollywood studio system of the 1930s and 1940s dominated by the Big Five studios, Paramount, RKO, MGM, Warner Brothers, and Fox (along with the "Little Three" of Universal, United Artists, and Columbia), film production and distribution were heavily vertically integrated. Actors, directors, and crew were long-term employees of a studio and worked in the films they were assigned; the studios even owned the movie theater chains.

After World War II, the industry became much more disintegrated. A 1948 antitrust settlement forced the studios to divest their theater holdings. Eventually the "talent" became freelancers who could negotiate movie deals or sign on with TV series one at a time. Finance and production became syndicated and shared (as parodied in a funny scene from the animated comedy series *Family Guy* about the long string of logos that precede today's movies). Remember the opening seventeen-minute sequence of the 2013 science fiction thriller *Gravity* in which the Space Shuttle is being destroyed by a hailstorm of space debris, sending astronaut Ryan Stone (played by Sandra Bullock) into space? That was the work of the London-based specialized visual effects company Framestore. There are now companies that specialize in trailers. Or in editing. In other words, the filmmaking value chain has been "broken up" in the sense that many of its stages are occupied by small specialist companies. As with the computer industry, the boundary between coordination inside the firm and coordination among firms has shifted.

Does that mean that smaller, more specialized companies are bossless? Not at all. Even a broken-up value chain requires a managerial hierarchy to organize, supervise, adjust, and sometimes renegotiate the operations at each stage of production. A truly bossless value chain wouldn't have companies at all—each worker would be a tiny element in a giant vertical structure of production! Moreover, the specialized companies in a vertically disaggregated production system can actually be quite large; they specialize in only one stage of production, but they may do so at a very large scale. For example, in 2021 the most heavily concentrated US industries—that is, the ones dominated by just a few large firms—included beef packing, domestic air travel, and broadband internet; all provide specialized services that create value only as part of a larger vertical chain.[12] The industries that experienced the greatest rise in concentration from 2002 to 2017 included newsprint production (not newspapers but the mills producing the paper), ammunition manufacturing (bullets only, not weapons), and geothermal electricity generation.[13]

The same is true for larger, more diversified firms spinning out activities that are not in their core competence: they often build up their other activities, leading to a firm that is just as large as ever (or even larger).[14] So even if the visible hand of management is directly controlling fewer stages in the value chain, it is still setting up that chain, coordinating the upstream and downstream links, and often managing more activity within its preferred stage. Even if the technology is highly modular (meaning that customers can mix and match pieces from different manufacturers), the technological specifications are open instead of proprietary, and the industry is vertically disintegrated, we still have firms—often large and important firms—and these firms are still managed by managers.

MODULARITY AND SIMPLICITY

Although the bossless company narrative is wrong about the fundamental difference between firms and markets, it is right that very flat hierarchies with a high degree of employee empowerment can work—but only under special circumstances. These circumstances are similar to those underlying the "vanishing hand." One reason we're seeing more outsourcing and more decentralized supply chains is that industries ranging from construction and automobiles to business services and smartphones are moving toward standardized, transparent interfaces and specifications. In other words, buyers announce their technical requirements and how they want components to fit together, and lots of suppliers can bid on providing those components. If the suppliers know what is expected, they don't need instruction in how to meet the standard but can rely on their own skills, knowledge, and efforts to do so.

If it's obvious how components fit together to form a value proposition, then there is not much for managers to coordinate, as well as less need for Chandler's vertically integrated corporation. The same is true of workers inside companies: if the production process is simple or tasks can be broken down into self-contained "modules," then the need for management is diminished.

Valve and Oticon, two companies we have examined, are in conventional industries: video games and hearing aids. Both are important companies in their respective industries. Valve is a big player, though not the biggest in its industry. While neither has the consumer brand recognition of an Apple or Amazon, they are still viewed as exemplars of the trend toward bosslessness, partly owing to their savvy branding. Lars Kolind enjoyed sharing his dramatic narratives of radically different workplaces that empower employees, foster innovation, and put the customer first.

Cool words and phrases like "team members" and "colleagues," "spaghetti" and "circles," make good copy.

A more detailed look at both companies reveals some common themes. First, their production processes have relatively few interdependencies, allowing workers and teams to operate with a lot of autonomy. A central role of managerial authority is coordination—making sure all the pieces fit together and resolving problems when they don't. Oticon during its spaghetti organization period was essentially a portfolio of autonomous development projects that shared overhead, marketing and branding, and some R&D. Individuals and teams could do what they needed to do without a lot of coordination with other individuals and teams. This is even truer for Valve, where small teams can design bits of code and even entire games with relatively little input from other teams.

In other words, flatter structures can work for companies where no significant amount of coordination is required of managers. But they don't work for most companies. Extreme decentralization fails in most cases for the same reason it failed at Oticon: the pieces don't fit together. Most businesses involve a lot of interdependencies that have to be managed— both in advance, by creating systems and structures that enable coordination (as with Wikipedia), and after the fact, through careful, but not too frequent, intervention to align individual and group decisions with each other and with overall company objectives.

So the "bossless" companies still have bosses. They may be highly visible, like Lars Kolind, or they may operate informally and behind the scenes, like the "cool kids at Valve." The Iron Law of Oligarchy again.

We are not arguing, however, that bossless companies are always just conventional companies dressed up in fancy terminology. These companies often do give their employees considerably more autonomy than more conventional companies. They are allowed to do much more with company resources than is usually possible for employees in conventional companies. However, the designers of the "bossless" companies— CEOs like Kolind—realize that, despite the official rhetoric, it usually will not work to just give your employees well-nigh unlimited freedom. The result will not be a thousand flowers blooming, but rather no flowers blooming at all. So they discreetly keep some management function in the design.

Moreover, designers of bossless companies also replace the management layers and functions they choose to forgo with new management technology. This was anticipated by the Austrian Peter Drucker, perhaps the first real management guru. Decades ago, Drucker not only anticipated the idea of "self-management," an important part of the bossless company narrative, but also pointed out that "to make management by self-control a reality requires more than acceptance of the concept as right and desirable. It requires new tools and far-reaching changes in traditional thinking and practices."[15] So Oticon had its detailed performance reviews, employee ownership schemes, and performance incentives—all quite revolutionary for an early 1990s company, but quite standard nowadays. Valve has its stack ranking system—and its high school gossip.

The bottom line: it is possible to delayer, cut management roles, and give workers more discretion, though doing so does not result, of course, in a bossless company. As we have seen, such organizations normally have very powerful bosses, cliques, and other sources of authority—and even the most bossless companies have bosses who set them up and make sure the model is working. Most important, this style of running a company can work only under special circumstances. For most companies—and with any kind of cooperation involving strong interdependencies—it won't work. Moreover, it's not obvious that going "bossless" makes a company more efficient and less bureaucratic; as we saw in Chapter 1 with Blinkist, going bossless can lead to more meetings, more arguing, and less time spent working!

In short, even if near-bosslessness brings benefits in certain cases, it also brings costs. Is it the right structure for you? If you use a straightforward technology, operate in a stable environment, and supervise tasks that can be performed independently of each other, you might give it a try. Even so, proceed with caution.

SHOW US THE EVIDENCE!

WE ALL LOVE A GREAT STORY. ALL THOSE COOL WORKPLACES! THE futuristic factory churning out those SpaceX rockets! But while colorful examples and detailed Harvard-style cases can be informative, they don't paint a complete picture. Anecdotes are just that—anecdotes. What do we learn from a more comprehensive look at the evidence about how managers should organize a company?

The bossless company narrative doesn't give us very good answers. Often the claims are loose and squishy, such as Frederic Laloux's call for business to adapt to the "Next Stage of Human Consciousness" and Gary Hamel and Michele Zanini's focus on "freeing the human spirit at work" and making "organizations as amazing as the people inside them."[1] Other writers stress more mundane aims, such as boosting employee motivation by giving them "ownership" of their work, allowing those lower in the hierarchy to act on their specialist knowledge, or truly harnessing the forces of digitalization. The bossless company narrative also makes sweeping claims ("with the advance of the digital tools, there will be little for future managers to do") and asks rhetorical questions that poke fun at traditional management structures ("if employees know better than managers what should be done, why do we need managers bossing them around?"). Then out comes the colorful example: "Look, Valve can do it! It works in lots of industries. It's just better. So why don't you go and do the same?"

These writers are not providing very good guides to action. What should the manager reading a book like *Unboss* or *Humanocracy* do to craft job descriptions and reward systems? Or to redesign the office layout or business processes? Should she herself resign her job title and embrace the bossless company model? In fact, what does "bossless" mean exactly? Can we have, say, charismatic founders of the "bossless" company who, although they may not intervene in day-to-day operations, still pull the strings by exercising the influence that comes with their founder status and, perhaps, their wisdom (like Valve's Gabe Newell)?

Too often, we get no answers from the literature. In *The Future of Management*, for example, Gary Hamel and Bill Breen conclude their diagnosis of what is wrong with modern management by calling for "a top to bottom remodeling of modern management's creaking edifice of principles, processes and practices." That conclusion arrives on page 241 of a 288-page book—one that is ostensibly about the future of management. A few pages later, we are told: "So far, I've resisted the urge to share my own vision of the future of management. Mostly this is out of modesty. The future of management has yet to be invented, and when it arrives, I expect to be surprised." Clearly, we the readers are supposed to invent the future of management and surprise Gary.

Meanwhile, the case that the traditional hierarchical company organization is outmoded, nonfunctional, not hip at all, a broken paradigm . . . hasn't been made. Moreover, the bossless company narrative fails to offer a clear, convincing, and well-described *alternative*. The only real answers we get are indirect—that is, they come through isolated company examples.

KARL POPPER WARNS US

Managers have much to learn from Sir Karl Popper, the Austrian-British philosopher known for "falsificationism," the notion that theories in the empirical sciences can never be completely proven. When we say we have proven a theory in biology or physics, we really mean something like,

"This is the best we can say for the moment given the data we have, and we may have to revise our theories in the future." The most we can say is that a particular theory has not yet been disproven or "falsified" by the data. Our knowledge of empirical reality is always tentative and conjectural, never definitive.

Although such theories cannot be decisively proven, they can be more or less consistent with the data at hand. Empirical science progresses by scientists formulating theories and continually testing those theories through experiments. Popper thought that everyone, not just scientists, should embrace the idea of falsification: we should be exposing our ideas, beliefs, and expectations to critique and therefore to potential "falsification." This is how we learn.

In this spirit, one of Popper's last articles was a warning to managers and management thinkers about the dangers of authoritarianism in companies as well as in society. Authoritarian leadership is bad, he said, not just because it oppresses people and violates rights and standards of humanity, but also because it stymies learning. If free discussion and the exchange of ideas is harmed, this is bad for everyone. In contrast, as managers we should "learn to make the best of our mistakes" by "welcom[ing] having a mistake pointed out to us" and, "in pointing out another's mistake," "doing so in the full consciousness of our own fallibility." "Only in this way can we learn to discuss our hypotheses, our proposals, plans, decisions, impersonally and rationally, without degenerating into mutual accusation, into personal attacks."[2]

PICKING CHERRIES

People who push the bossless company narrative have an unfortunate tendency to cherry-pick: they point to data, examples, or cases that seem to confirm their position while ignoring similar or related data, examples, or cases that may contradict it. This is as anti-Popper as it gets. Given that there are close to 50,000 publicly traded companies out there—estimates of the total number of registered businesses range between 100 and 200 million, with China alone having 80 million!—we can pick almost any business model, company strategy, or organizational structure and find examples that "prove" it's the next big thing. And we can also find some "bossless" companies and "prove" that what they are doing is the next big thing. This kind of cherry-picking is an example of what psychologists call "confirmation bias"—searching for evidence that supports a cherished idea, belief, ideology, or finding and disregarding anything that contradicts it. That's why there are so many articles and books about Valve, Zappos, Morning Star, Gore, and Oticon, and why it is so difficult for those authors to recognize the special circumstances that made the near-bossless model work in those cases.

THE PLURAL OF "ANECDOTE" ISN'T "DATA"

In science, we are regularly warned not to draw general lessons from extreme cases. "Hard cases make bad law," as the legal theorists tell us. In telling the stories of extremely successful individuals and groups in sports, education, and business in his 2008 book *Outliers*, Malcolm Gladwell argues that hard work (such as the ten-thousand-hour rule, which Gladwell invented), rather than gifts of nature, is largely responsible for success. But clearly not everyone can be an outlier, or they wouldn't be outliers. How much can be learned from these examples, really? Without a more comprehensive look at the evidence, it is hard to know if Gladwell's theories are true. As one reviewer noted: "Gladwell chooses his anecdotes well, but they are ultimately just stories." Indeed, the ten-thousand-hour rule has largely been debunked by more careful studies.[3]

In *The Halo Effect: . . . and the Eight Other Business Delusions That Deceive Managers*, business professor Phil Rosenzweig calls the attempt to draw general conclusions from extreme cases the "Delusion of Connecting the Winning Dots." He points out that classic management texts like *Good to Great* or *Built to Last* look at a set of very successful companies, then try to draw lessons for all of us from those companies' experiences. We've all seen the "Ten Habits of Extremely Successful X" genre, and we know it's bogus. Imagine a study claiming, "These 100 people never got cancer, and they also brushed their teeth every night. Therefore, brush your teeth to remain cancer-free!" To see if good dental hygiene prevents cancer, we would need a sample of people who brush daily, and a sample of otherwise similar people who don't; we could then see if members of one group or another are more likely to develop cancer. We need to look at successful *and* unsuccessful cases, not just at one or the other.

WHAT DOES THE EVIDENCE TELL US?

So what do we know about how company organization has changed over the last few decades, based on more systematic evidence? As it turns out, this question is difficult to answer, because there are few economy-wide studies that attempt to measure delayering, worker empowerment, and "unbossing" over time and for a large sample of firms.

In most countries, economy-wide data on companies comes from public disclosures (quarterly or annual reports from publicly traded corporations), tax and census records, industry surveys, or other information of interest to investors or regulators. These databases contain information on firm age, firm size (measured by sales, assets, or employees), financial and accounting data such as share prices, costs and revenues, assets and liabilities, and other information found on balance sheets and income statements. Larger firms provide the names and salaries of top executives, board members, and other key personnel. Firms with multiple subsidiaries typically provide some of this information for the individual subsidiaries or operating units as well as consolidated, corporation-level data. Contracts for procurement, distribution, or other collaborations that are deemed "material" to investors or regulators must also be disclosed. Firms that are about to be listed on a stock exchange through an initial public offering (IPO) typically reveal other details through the offer prospectus. Mergers, acquisitions, and other changes in the firm's asset base are tracked by regulators, stock exchanges, and credit ratings agencies.

While these data sources can be used to construct some crude measures of flatness (for example, the ratio of employees to sales or assets, the presence or absence of a multidivisional structure, or the extent of vertical integration), we have little systematic information in most countries on what we are interested in here: How many hierarchical layers does the firm have? Has this number changed over time? How decentralized is the firm? How much delegation does it have? It is only very recently that statistical authorities in the United States, such as the Census Bureau's Center for Economic Studies, have begun collecting data on the internal organization of companies. Still, we do know something, and the rest of this chapter will walk you through what we know.

CHANGES IN SKILLS AND JOBS

We noted before that today's employees, compared to workers of the past, are more educated, are more aware of their options, care more about work-life balance, and have a stronger desire to be involved in decision-making. Although these attributes may make them a challenge to manage, they also have much more to contribute. So empowering employees by giving them more rights to make their own decisions seems like a win-win situation.

Employee education and skill levels have indeed been rising for decades, and investments in education lead to higher wages.[4] The story is a bit more complex, however, because we have seen increases in both high-education, high-wage jobs *and* low-education, low-wage jobs.[5] This data suggests that there really is something to the notion of a "knowledge economy," one that is not just more digital, virtual, or science-based, but also—perhaps mainly—one in which people get more education and do more cognitively demanding work. This has implications for turnover, hiring, retention, and wages. Companies that hire workers with degrees in, say, biotechnology, molecular chemistry, or statistics from top US universities face a retention problem: employees who are knowledgeable about the scientific frontier in fields that are open to commercialization may create their own spin-off companies or be lured away by competitors. Obviously, HR practices and compensation policies will take into account not only employee education and skill levels but also this possibility. Other aspects of company organization, such as job descriptions and how much discretion is left to employees, will also reflect employees' education and skill levels.

To see how this works, let's start with a well-known stereotype (or caricature) of the traditional hierarchical firm, the "Taylorite" factory. The term "Taylorism" is seldom meant as a compliment, representing as it does single-minded pursuit of efficiency at the expense of all other aims. Here is the background.

FREDERICK WINSLOW TAYLOR AND SCIENTIFIC MANAGEMENT

In 1911, Frederick Winslow Taylor published his slim volume *Principles of Scientific Management*. Taylor had conducted thousands of experiments with metal cutting at the Midvale Steel Company in Nicetown, Pennsylvania. He was trying to figure out the optimal way of cutting steel given that faster cutting speeds wore out tools more quickly. He came up with a series of equations for optimal cutting speed, cutting depth, and metal feeding rate. Taylor's scientific and experimental approach generated the key insight that applying a standard method not only to individual manufacturing processes but also to factory organization itself would increase productivity. This approach became known by the term "scientific management" and would be underpinning "American efficiency."[6] Peter Drucker put Taylor rather than Karl Marx in his "trinity of makers of the modern world, along with Darwin and Freud."[7]

The term "scientific management" was actually coined in 1910 by the future Supreme Court justice Louis Brandeis when he argued that increases in railroad rates were unnecessary even if labor costs were increasing. Application of scientific management principles would keep overall costs from increasing; though hourly wages might rise, reorganizing work processes and managing them better, he contended, would save more than enough to make up for the increase in direct labor costs.

Scientific management sees the key to increasing productivity as breaking work processes into elementary tasks, and tasks into individual motions of workers. With this information at hand, the production planner, with the help of a stopwatch, can eliminate unnecessary tasks and motions, optimize movements and sequences of tasks, and get workers to concentrate on simple, routine tasks. Such "time-and-motion studies" were popular in twentieth-century manufacturing processes.

This thinking was highly complementary to a new process innovation in manufacturing, namely, the moving assembly line. In 1908, Henry

Ford had launched the Model T and sold ten thousand units. That same year he hired Taylor as a consultant. Building on Taylor's observations, Ford implemented numerous efficiency-enhancing improvements of the assembly-line approach. For example, the large parts of the car were to be more stationary than the smaller parts, so the chassis and the body would stay put at one station while smaller parts were brought there and mounted on the larger parts. With each set of work processes completed, the semiprocessed car was then moved (by workers pulling ropes) to the next station, where the next set of workers would, for example, paint the car. Most workers remained stationary, performing one or a few routine tasks.

ADAM SMITH ON STEROIDS

Adam Smith had told the story of the pin factory in *The Wealth of Nations* to show that production of a simple commodity could be dramatically increased if it was rearranged to have workers engaged in specialized tasks rather than carrying out multiple operations. Taylor told the story of "Schmidt," a pig-iron loader at Bethlehem Steel. Before his workplace was redesigned by Taylorist principles, Schmidt could load twelve tons of the ninety-two-pound iron pigs each day. After the workplace was redesigned using Taylor's principles, Schmidt's output jumped to forty-eight tons per day—a huge gain. That increase in his individual work productivity resulted in Schmidt's daily wages going from $1.15 to $1.85.

Higher productivity and wages seemed like a good deal to both industry and workers. But it is also easy to see how Taylorism came to be seen as the quintessence of dehumanizing hierarchical industry—with hierarchical layers of worker drones mechanically carrying out their simple, repetitive work processes—even though Taylor himself endorsed worker training and put much emphasis on properly rewarding employees. Marxist writers viewed the "factory system" as a deliberate conspiracy to "deskill" workers. When people have few or no distinctive skills, they have zero bargaining power and are particularly easy to exploit. At first glance, Taylorism might seem to have the same effect. But Marx was wrong: there is no evidence that managers pursued deskilling as a deliberate strategy. (On the contrary, industrialization was accompanied by a massive increase in education.) Moreover, while Taylorism, like any extreme division of labor, might have been boring, it was also highly productive and was one of the key drivers of the twentieth-century explosion in incomes and wealth.

The bossless company narrative often points to Taylorism as a foil. As Hollywood's "Charlie" did for his fictional "Angels" detectives, "I took them away from all that!" Indeed, who today wants a job like Schmidt's? Taylorism tends to be applied to production systems that are linear (tasks are sequential), predictable, and based on a manufacturing model epitomized by the moving assembly line. This is the soulless mass production lambasted in Chaplin's *Modern Times*—the last movie in which Chaplin played his tramp character (and one of the last major silent movies). As he works the assembly line, the tramp suffers because of the monotonous, dull work and eventually melts down, causing chaos in the factory.

Chaplin's biographer Jeffrey Vance claims that *Modern Times* is perhaps more meaningful now than at any time since its first release. "The twentieth-century theme of the film, farsighted for its time—the struggle to eschew alienation and preserve humanity in a modern, mechanized world—profoundly reflects issues facing the twenty-first century. The Tramp's travails in *Modern Times* and the comedic mayhem that ensues should provide strength and comfort to all who feel like helpless cogs in a world beyond control."[8] This is the world from which bossless company proponents promise to rescue us.

The problem with that promise is that most modern, hierarchical firms aren't Taylorist. Indeed, while *Modern Times* may indeed carry a universal message, it is most directly a critique of a system that was being superseded in large parts of the world when Vance wrote his biography in 2003. One reason is that productive activity shifted in relative terms from manufacturing to services. Personal trainers, lawyers, hairdressers, consultants, nurses, and teachers have become much more important in the economy, in absolute as well as relative terms.

In services, the producer of the service is in direct contact with the customer. Your personal trainer directly interacts with you, instructing you by showing you the various exercises that will increase your muscle mass, reduce your BMI, improve your overall well-being, or otherwise achieve the specific purpose of your training sessions. It normally makes sense to have a single trainer supervising your entire workout, rather than having you be shuttled from trainer to trainer for each exercise or routine. This is true for the services sector more generally: managers tend to be generalists, not specialists. Managers do a lot of different things, as Henry Mintzberg famously documented, but because those things are closely related and feed on each other, it makes sense for each manager to be providing some direction, some task monitoring, some dispute resolution, and some document review.[9] Management is a generalist skill because the interdependencies among tasks are high.

More than two decades ago, the US National Research Council documented the changes over time in the managerial job role.[10] Although old-fashioned Taylorite monitoring didn't disappear entirely, managers became less focused on it. They still did lots of other things, engaging in much more customer interaction, team building, and coaching than had previous generations of managers. This trend has only accelerated in the twenty-first century.

HOW JOBS HAVE EVOLVED

If our modern service-oriented and knowledge-based economy needs fewer jobs involving routine, repetitive tasks and more jobs featuring multitasking, decision-making, and the use of formal education, then what happens to all those boring jobs? We still need assembly-line workers, even if some routine tasks are now performed by robots (such as the large industrial robots that work in automobile assembly or the self-powered, autonomous trams and loaders in an Amazon warehouse). Construction requires many tedious person-hours of on-site labor, even if subcomponents can be manufactured off-site. Workers in a fast-food restaurant kitchen, a textile plant, or a steel mill may imagine Frederick Taylor peering over their shoulders.

But many of these jobs and tasks have been made obsolete by technology; new smart machines have now been substituted for workers doing

people replaced by technology

simple, repetitive operations.[11] Although occupations such as line workers and assemblers are still around (despite a few exceptions such as elevator operators), automation has replaced many jobs and reshaped those that remain. It's not just factory work; routine office tasks and intermediary services such as making reservations, booking tickets, arranging meetings, transcribing, and the like are performed by software or directly by customers, without the need for human assistance. This kind of automation, in both hardware and software, is the main reason why occupations that revolve around routine tasks have fallen as a share of total employment. However, occupations that involve nonroutine tasks and require social and cognitive skills, such as management, have grown. But interestingly, the same is true *within* occupations. It's not just management that has become more relational and more dependent on multitasking.

Fascinating recent research shows the evolution of job tasks in the United States from 1950 to 2000.[12] This evolution is hard to document because we lack comprehensive data on how, for example, the tasks that a bank clerk carries out have changed over the decades. However, the researchers got a bright idea: Why not use job ads? After all, ads specify job content, at least to some degree. So they built a data set from the text of all 7.8 million job ads that appeared during this period in the *Boston Globe*, the *New York Times*, and the *Wall Street Journal*. They sorted the description of tasks into "routine" and "nonroutine" categories and linked the job titles in the ads to the Standard Occupational Classification codes (all with the help of artificial intelligence or "machine-learning" algorithms).

The results show that, since 1950, words relating to nonroutine tasks have become more frequent, while the opposite is true for words relating to routine tasks, particularly routine manual tasks. In other words, routine occupations have become even more routine, while nonroutine occupations have become even less routine!

HYPERCOMPETITION

"Life comes at you fast," as the saying goes, particularly in the modern global, networked, high-tech economy. The strategy guru Richard

D'Aveni coined the term "hypercompetition" to describe those markets and industries where innovation in products, processes, and business models, changes in what customers want, and the emergence of new competitors are not only frequent but also hard to predict.[13] D'Aveni argued that hypercompetition would come to any industry, and that no firm could expect an advantage to be anything more than temporary.[14] Under such circumstances, it often makes sense to delegate decisions to the person on the spot. In fact, some research suggests that there is more decentralization and delegation in companies that are placed in more dynamic environments.[15] Where things move fast, decisions must be made.

An email from Tesla CEO Elon Musk to the company's employees nicely summarizes the two basic ways to handle these situations:

> There are two schools of thought about how information should flow. By far the most common way is chain of command, which means that you always flow communication through your manager. The problem with this approach is that, while it enhances the power of the manager, it fails to serve the company.
>
> To solve a problem quickly, two people in different depts should simply talk and make the right thing happen. Instead, people are forced to talk to their manager, who talks to their manager, who talks to the manager in the other dept, who talks to someone on his team. Then the info has to flow back the other way again. This is incredibly dumb. Any manager who allows this to happen, let alone encourages it, will soon find themselves working at another company. No kidding.
>
> Anyone at Tesla can and should email/talk to anyone else according to what they think is the fastest way to solve a problem for the benefit of the whole company.
>
> You can talk to your manager's manager without his permission, you can talk directly to a VP in another dept, you can talk to me, you can talk to anyone without anyone else's permission. Moreover, you should consider

yourself obligated to do so until the right thing happens. The point here is to ensure that we execute ultra-fast and well.[16]

Passing information up and down the hierarchy slows down decision-making and is costly in other ways, such as what it takes to set up and maintain communication channels with specialized middle managers. When things move fast, companies may make fast decisions by delegating decision authority to the person on the spot.

That people on the spot know what to do is supported by two arguments. The first is Hayek's point that the knowledge necessary to make good decisions is typically dispersed throughout an economy or an organization. Things are too complex for the CEO (or, in an economy, government central planners) to have all the relevant information—especially what Hayek called "the knowledge of the particular circumstances of time and place"—so decision-making should be spread out as much as possible.[17]

The second argument is that employees today have, on average, much more formal education than those in the Taylorite factory.[18] Of course, there are plenty of complaints about the modern education system and questions about whether it provides the skills necessary for workplace success. Still, educated employees have a sense of worth and even entitlement lacked by the factory workers of the early industrial period. Many are also specialists, by virtue of their education or on-the-job experience or both, making them less eager to take direction from supervisors without specialized expertise.

Moreover, many modern employees are specialists who are in high demand. This gives them power vis-á-vis the company and workplace, power that they can leverage to gain more influence and freedom in the workplace. Needless to say, managing such employees can be a challenge.

Consider the banking industry and the role of the loan officers. In the 1950s and 1960s, commercial loans were simple and fairly standardized. Increasingly, however, loans have become much less straightforward and much more customized. Setting up customized loans requires knowledge of the client. What becomes important is "controlling the client list," and so the valuable employees are those who have the important knowledge of the clients. Today's loan officers are more knowledgeable and effectively control an important asset that gives them considerable bargaining power. No wonder banks try to set up knowledge-sharing schemes that basically amount to sharing the client lists. Understandably, loan officers are known to be less willing to engage with such schemes.[19] The bottom line is that these employees effectively have much real power. More generally, when employees know the best decision to make, why not delegate the right to make the decision to them?

In short, there are real reasons why we expect to see more delegation in a modern knowledge economy. We will return to this theme time and again throughout the rest of this book. But notice something important here: the fact that there is more delegation doesn't necessarily mean that there is less hierarchy; decision-making power may just be shifting down that hierarchy. Although we often speak as if more delegation means less hierarchy, it often does not. There is still a hierarchical superior who can check decisions and, if necessary, take back the decision authority delegated to subordinates.

Of course, when decision-making power shifts downward, more delegation leads to flattening hierarchies and fewer managers are needed. There is in fact some solid evidence based on large data sets and rigorous statistical analysis that hierarchies are flattening. For example, an important study of managers' job descriptions, reporting relationships, and compensation structures at three hundred large US companies found that the number of positions reporting directly to the CEO has gone up over time—that is, a given manager's "span of control" has increased. At the same time, however, the number of levels between the division heads and the CEO has decreased. Hierarches are delayering and firms are flattening. Moreover, more managers are reporting directly to the CEO. Those managers closer to the CEO receive higher pay, indicating that these organizational changes are not window dressing; they are happening for a reason.

These findings are consistent with an increase in delegation at US firms. But more delegation does not necessarily imply more decentralization; in some ways, as CEOs have gained more direct reports and, because of delayering, come closer to the real action, they are becoming even more powerful!

A follow-up study found that large firms flatten their hierarchies in response to increased competition.[20] The likely explanation is the one we offered earlier: more competition leads to more frequent changes as firms adjust prices, try new sales initiatives, launch new products, and acquire new production technology to drive down costs, and all of these actions require quick decision-making. Delegation can make things move faster.

But top managers may still want to keep tabs on what goes on at lower levels. One way to do so is to delayer the company. This is partly what happened at Valve and the other poster children for the bossless company narrative: with fewer middle managers to serve as buffers between bosses and employees, bosses become more powerful.[21] And employees don't like it, particularly when they have been fed a steady diet of empowerment language and culture![22] We can see now that *increasing the power of bosses is not some weird quirk that contradicts the bossless company narrative, but exactly what we would expect as a result of delayering.*

In a sense, therefore, the middle managers and procedures of the typical hierarchy often serve not as an enforcer but as an intermediary between the desires of a strong-willed boss and the day-to-day activities of employees. Middle managers shape the flow of information, interpret actions and behaviors, and help establish organizational culture. They are far from useless! Without that buffer, those at the top of the hierarchy can exercise their will directly, given the short distance to individual employees. Is that a good idea? On the one hand, a flatter structure can make the company more agile, as the wishes of senior management can be implemented more quickly. At the same time, employees often prefer to have a middle manager "on their side," representing their interests and communicating knowledge "on the ground" to the executives at headquarters who may be too isolated from day-to-day activities. As business professor commentator André Spicer puts it, "Fantasies of no rules, no bosses and no hierarchies are seductive. Hierarchies can be repressive, rules can be absurd, and bosses can be toxic. But not having these things can be worse."[23]

Part II

WHY HIERARCHY WORKS

Even in the new economy characterized by knowledge workers, empowerment, and rapid technological change, managerial hierarchies are useful. Managers perform the essential tasks of coordination and cooperation inside organizations. Hierarchies can even promote innovation and entrepreneurship. Much criticism of hierarchies, historical and contemporary, is misplaced.

8

MANAGEMENT ISN'T GOING AWAY

THERE ARE MANY COUNTEREXAMPLES TO THE BOSSLESS COMPANY narrative. The most successful companies are often run by powerful, opinionated figures. For many years at Apple, CEO Steve Jobs made key decisions in a way that can only be described as dictatorial. Under Jobs, according to author Adam Lashinsky, "only one executive 'owned' a [profit-and-loss-statement], and that was the chief financial officer."[1] Everything else belonged to Jobs. Charismatic figures such as Elon Musk fill the headlines in the business press, though they may often be better known for their visionary leadership than for their managerial effectiveness. Amazon founder and former CEO Jeff Bezos was said to be relentlessly obsessed with data and measurement, touting what he calls Amazon's "culture of metrics"—which features at least five hundred measurable performance outcomes, all easily accessible to the CEO—as the key to its rapid growth.[2] If anything, these examples demonstrate a heavy concentration of power and authority in many of our leading firms.

Companies such as Oticon and Zappos, as we have seen, often have dominant, even overpowering, central leaders. Highly visible celebrity

CEOs are unlikely to practice a hands-off management style, no matter what they tell journalists.

Not only is concentrated managerial power here to stay, but managerial authority has become even more essential than it was in earlier eras. Knowledge-based, networked economies are characterized by rapid technological change and high levels of uncertainty and complexity. Companies increasingly need to deal with potentially massive "tail risks"—the "unknown unknowns," in former defense secretary Donald Rumsfeld's pithy phrasing. Small changes can be dealt with locally, even if unanticipated. This is rarely the case when unforeseen events happen that can disrupt entire industries or economies. As we show in this part of the book, centralized, even authoritarian, decision-making may then be required.

Many companies that have survived major technology shocks, regulation, and global competition have had strong, charismatic leaders with highly authoritative styles. In what is arguably the greatest corporate comeback of all time, Steve Jobs, faced with a major restructuring, rescued Apple by making tough decisions against considerable resistance (cutting the Newton project, setting up a partnership with Microsoft). It is no coincidence that many of the best-known successful corporate turnarounds were pinned to single individuals, such as Jobs at Apple, Louis Gerstner and later Samuel Palmisano at IBM, Carly Fiorina at Hewlett-Packard, Howard Schultz at Starbucks, Carlos Ghosn at Nissan, and Peter Cuneo at Marvel. The lesson is that centralizing decision authority can often reduce the delays resulting from more collaborative and consensus-driven approaches.

Also, evidence points to the interesting fact that while corporations do indeed delayer their hierarchies, the purpose is often not to decentralize—quite the contrary. For example, Lego, the Danish toy company, has spent the better of the last fifteen years reorganizing to reduce internal complexity. This effort has reduced the number of middle manager layers. But it has been accompanied by an expansion of the size of the top management team as the company brings in functional specialists and moves senior managers much closer to operations. Lego's moves may be part of a broader trend. In a study about management hierarchies and compensation at three hundred Fortune 500 companies over a fourteen-year period (which we will have more to say about later), researchers found that while companies were delayering, the size of the executive team (defined as the number of positions reporting directly to the CEO) doubled from an average of five to ten. What's more, executives were intervening more frequently in operating decisions.[3] The result is counterintuitive: *flat management structures can induce more micro-management than vertical hierarchies.*

This is the case even in creative organizations. Listen to "The Boss" (Bruce Springsteen) himself: "Democracy in a band . . . is often a ticking time bomb. If I was going to carry the workload and responsibility, I might as well assume the power. I've always believed that the E Street Band's continued existence is partially because there was little to no role confusion among its members." That is, everyone understood that The Boss was running the show.

Clear leadership is not, of course, autocracy! Charismatic leaders in creative industries not only control membership and resources but also inspire, shape, goad, and cajole. A strong boss knows how to bring out the best in each team member and can persuade strong-willed individuals to subordinate their egos and play as a team. This is true of great symphony conductors, film directors, and sports coaches. Or to take an example from the culinary world, consider these words from the late Anthony Bourdain:

> You have a tremendous amount of personal freedom in the kitchen. But there's a trade-off. You give up other freedoms when you go into a kitchen because you're becoming part of a very old, rigid, traditional society. . . . Absolute rules govern some aspects of your working life: obedience, focus, the way you maintain your work area, the pecking order, the consistency of the end product, arrival time.[4]

Many leaders in the creative industries have been autocrats. Herbert von Karajan, conductor of the Berlin Philharmonic from 1955 to 1989, became heavily dictatorial in his later years. The great Austrian conductor Karl Böhm, famous for his performances of Mozart, Wagner, and Strauss, was an even harsher autocrat. In jazz, the "greatest drummer who ever lived," Buddy Rich, was a terrible tyrant. His "bus tapes," recorded by members of his band as he lambasted them, have racked up hundreds of thousands of views on YouTube.[5]

Restaurant Noma in Copenhagen is known for reinventing and reinterpreting Nordic cuisine. It has repeatedly been ranked as the best restaurant in the world by *Restaurant* magazine (and is currently number two). Noma is run and co-owned by the charismatic chef René Redzepi. A program that aired on Danish television showed Redzepi screaming and yelling at young chefs in his kitchen. When a chef carves a lamb leg incorrectly, Redzepi shouts, "I will write this day down. What day is it? This is the worst day in Noma's history." The previous year the actor Christian Bale famously had a meltdown while filming a scene from *Terminator Salvation*, screaming profanities at the director of photography, Shane Hurlbut, who had accidentally walked into Bale's line of sight. "I'm trying to [expletive] do a scene here, and I'm going, 'Why the [expletive] is Shane walking in there? What is he doing there?' Do you understand my mind is not in the scene if you're doing that?"[6]

For creative geniuses like Rich, Redzepi, and Bale, nothing short of perfection will do. Every member of the team must perform at the same high level as the leader. This was, of course, Steve Jobs's model as well.

Many of the great autocratic leaders like these did not take pleasure in the drama they created. Their reactions reflected their passion and their desire to achieve the very best. This is obvious if you listen to Rich in the bus tapes: he yells that he has been playing with the very best, that the audience deserves only the very best, but that "you [expletive] aren't capable of delivering!" And to some extent, all the screaming and even humiliation worked. Success in this instance doesn't prove, of course, that a softer approach wouldn't also have yielded results. Gandhi and Lincoln, for example, were known for taking action with quiet resolve rather than histrionics.

In any case, the days of the leadership styles of a Böhm, Rich, or Redzepi are increasingly over. Employees don't accept it anymore, and neither does the public. But we still have conductors, orchestra leaders, and master chefs. Their role and their function may be changing—but they are still here.

SAME AS IT EVER WAS

The insight that leadership, authority, and hierarchy perform useful functions is as true today as it was in the days of important organization and management thinkers such as Max Weber, Chester Barnard, Ronald Coase, Alfred Chandler, Herbert Simon, and Oliver Williamson. These thinkers, three of whom won Nobel Prizes for their work on management and organization, are among the most famous social scientists of the twentieth century (and we will discuss their work in more detail later in this book). They all saw the managerial hierarchy as an indispensable part of the company—indeed, as its defining feature. To them, the company represented a way of getting things done—by means of hierarchy and authority.

Although we agree with these great thinkers, a fresh statement of their basic theme is needed, and not just because it has been badly misunderstood and misrepresented, particularly by proponents of the bossless company narrative. Surprisingly, and perhaps counterintuitively, managerial authority is more important than ever in our knowledge-based, networked economy, even if it works in different ways. These thinkers' ideas, as well as our own research, show that management (and hence executive authority) is essential in two conditions that are hallmarks of our modern economy: an emphasis on knowledge as the key competitive resource, and competition based on innovation. Under these conditions, firms seek to beat their rivals by offering something more technologically advanced to the customer.

Innovations are hard to predict. In hindsight, it seems obvious that a handheld device with Wi-Fi, a large color touch screen, a powerful processor, and access to an ecosystem of third-party apps is more attractive than a traditional cell phone or pager; there's a reason we call the latter a "dumb phone." But it was not obvious to the executives at Research in Motion (BlackBerry) or Nokia, the two companies that dominated the mobile telephony market at the launch of Apple's ambitious iPhone, which was considered a risky and very expensive bet. To bring such a device to market—ultimately upending an entire industry and creating a new one—required foresight and careful planning. Of course, managers often get it wrong; just ask BlackBerry creators and former RIM co-CEOs Mike Lazaridis and Jim Balsillie. But such breakthroughs don't happen spontaneously; while a lot of coordination takes place through the market and across participants in an industry, platform, or ecosystem, managers leading teams of people within companies are the driving force.

Management is also crucial in a networked economy where small changes in one part of the economy may have major unanticipated consequences in another part. The introduction and eventual domination of the smartphone had ripple effects not only in software and hardware development and production but also in music (where downloading and streaming replaced the sale of physical media), financial services (where mobile apps have largely displaced bank tellers and loan officers and mobile payments are displacing cash, checks, and even credit cards), taxis, TV and movies, travel, and more. In each of these affected industries, management was needed to react, adopt, shape, restructure, and produce complementary innovations.

In other words, ours is an economy with a strong element of surprise, and firms must be quick to react in the face of major, potentially disruptive changes. Decisions made at various management levels are thus time-sensitive—managers must react now, not tomorrow. Often the necessary changes involve not just one task, routine, or behavior, but many, in a tightly coordinated fashion. And often the knowledge about what should be done and when is concentrated in the management team.

It is exactly because of these conditions and the resulting time-sensitivity, need for expert decision-making, and focus on internal alignment that we have seen top management teams expanding even as companies have been delayering. Top management teams have grown to include a greater number of functional specialists as well as generalists as these teams get closer to the action. At the same time, they are investing heavily in new digital tools (including big data, AI, and machine learning) to collect and analyze data on customers, employees, and rivals. These changes may have made top managers more effective and powerful than ever. That doesn't look like bosslessness to us!

The bottom line is that, while management has been changing in form and appearance over the last decade, it is not going away. It performs essential functions. It is an inherent part of companies and central to their nature and functioning. In the rest of this book, we show you why.

9

WHAT IS A COMPANY ANYWAY?

Everyone knows what a company is, right? Companies are business ventures that are established as legal entities to create value for stakeholders and make a profit. Nonprofits, educational associations, and investment groups can be companies as well. Companies can grow and contract like other organizations, they interact with other companies, and they have legal standing to write contracts and to sue or be sued. This is how the business press, college textbooks, the media, and businesspeople themselves talk about companies.

This understanding, however, is recent. According to the Online Etymology Dictionary, the modern definition of "company" in the sense just described originated in 1553, and the abbreviation "co." dates from 1769. And company law is evolving, especially regarding the idea that companies do not belong exclusively to their owners but must take into account the interests of a broad set of stakeholders. The boundaries of the company can also be a bit fuzzy; Uber says that it's just a software platform that matches drivers and riders, while several countries and US states claim that the company is the entire Uber network and the drivers are its employees—a claim Uber vigorously contests.

In many ways, as we show in this chapter, companies and their hierarchical structures have evolved as society and norms and culture have changed. Not only does the bossless company narrative cherry-pick its examples, but it also mischaracterizes the more conventional, hierarchical firm, which in fact has changed, in some ways radically, since the 1950s. It is time to move beyond caricature.

HOW THE MODERN COMPANY EMERGED

The modern company, with its owners, executives, middle managers, and employees, is the most salient of what Oliver Williamson called the "economic institutions of capitalism."[1] Williamson won a Nobel Prize for his lifelong attempt to understand the nature of the business firm. When economists seek to understand an enduring institution like the business firm, they typically ask: What role does it play in a market economy? And why is it beneficial to someone that it exists? So why do companies exist if, as Williamson liked to say, "in the beginning there were markets"? The obvious answer is—to make a buck! But bucks can be made in different ways.

For example, here's how a gun-making entrepreneur made a buck in nineteenth-century Britain:

> The master gun-maker—the entrepreneur—seldom possessed a factory or workshop. . . . Usually he owned merely a warehouse in the gun quarter, and his function was to acquire semifinished parts and to give those out to specialized craftsmen, who undertook the assembly and finishing of the gun. He purchased material from the barrel-makers, lock-makers, sight-stampers, trigger-makers, ramrod-forgers, gun-furniture makers, and, if he were engaged in the military branch, from bayonet-forgers. All of these were independent manufacturers executing the orders of several master gun-makers. . . . Once the parts had been purchased from the "material-makers," as they were called, the next task was to hand them out to a long succession of "setters-up," each of whom performed a specific operation in connection with the assembly and finishing of the gun. To name only a few, there were those who prepared the front sight and lump end of

the barrels; the jiggers, who attended to the breech end; the stockers, who let in the barrel and lock and shaped the stock; the barrel-strippers, who prepared the gun for rifling and proof; the hardeners, polishers, borers and riflers, engravers, browners, and finally the lock-freers, who adjusted the working parts.[2]

If this process sounds familiar, that is because it is what today we label "outsourcing"—gun production à la Michael Dell's computer company. This is not the current norm, however, for gun production. Consider Smith & Wesson, which acquired Battenfeld Technologies in 2014 for $130.5 million and acquired Tri Town Precision Plastics for $22.8 million. The modern-day US equivalent of the nineteenth-century "master gun maker" works with a "vertically integrated" business model in which the firm either acquires its key suppliers or develops their capabilities internally, keeping transactions in-house rather than farming out production to outside companies.

Still, even in the nineteenth-century "gun quarter" in Britain, production took place inside firms, though some of these firms were very small (some being just one-person shops). What we call "the market" consists of firms competing or cooperating with each other, as rivals or suppliers or downstream customers. Some of these firms will become large and influential. Their founders will hire employees and obtain, combine, and assemble resources into an increasing variety of products and services. As these firms grow, they will do so under the watchful supervision of the managerial hierarchy, itself reporting to a board of directors representing investors.

This is now the normal growth path of a successful company, and it began with the transformation of business in the nineteenth century.

Alfred Chandler's landmark studies of managerial hierarchy, *Strategy and Structure* (1962), and his Pulitzer Prize–winning work, *The Visible Hand* (1977), showed how the large enterprise, with its layers of managerial hierarchy, had displaced smaller predecessors through superior efficiency and productivity. Chandler didn't say that large companies always and everywhere displace smaller competitors, as if by a natural law (although this is what Karl Marx believed, and the idea is still strong, mainly on the left side of the political spectrum). Big companies can certainly become lethargic, paving the way for typically smaller, more agile competitors to "disrupt" them, in innovation scholar Clayton Christensen's famous phrase. But large enterprises and their managerial hierarchies are not so easily dismissed; even those new firms that outcompete the dinosaurs are *themselves* organized as hierarchies.

Businesses grow by doing more. They may do more of what they are already doing, and they may do more new things that they haven't done before. Chandler described the emergence of the classical US industrial firm in terms of an initial expansion within one product line, assisted by the technological innovations of the nineteenth century, primarily the telegraph and the railway. As companies such as DuPont continued to grow, their managers gained experience handling the growth process. Operating procedures were established, production, logistics, sales, and even marketing and R&D were increasingly routinized, and excess resources were released in the management team. These resources could then be used for purposes of "diversification," that is, producing new products and services. One of Chandler's key contributions was explaining how the move from producing few products to producing many products changed how the big industrial companies structured their hierarchies. But as Chandler emphasized, hierarchy had been a part of the process all along. So hierarchy seems to be central for the understanding of what firms are and do and for the functioning of the economy.

WHY THE COMPANY WORKS

Interestingly, while the traditionally organized business has been under attack since at least the 1950s, most scholars, journalists, policymakers, and businesspeople until recently saw it as an important source of dynamism, wealth creation, and growth. The corporation helped to develop regions. It brought people from low-paying, low-productivity agricultural jobs in the American South into high-paying, high-productivity factory jobs in the North. It created much of the middle class and made blue-collar jobs not only a function but an identity. In the process,

American culture was decisively affected. For example, electric blues, the origin of so much contemporary pop music, emerged in response to the entertainment needs of industrial workers in Chicago and other big industrial cities.

Even critics of the corporation like John Kenneth Galbraith and Ralph Nader—who wanted the corporation regulated heavily to discourage its mischief-making—could not imagine an industrial economy without large companies. Developing countries and rural areas recruited factories, distribution centers, and other big firms to generate employment and kick-start their economies.

In his seminal treatise *The Wealth of Nations*, the Scottish economist and philosopher Adam Smith used the parable of a pin-making factory to drive home the advantages of the division of labor. In this factory (an imaginary one, as it turned out),

> one man draws out the wire, another straights it, a third cuts it, a fourth points it, a fifth grinds it at the top for receiving the head: to make the head requires two or three distinct operations: to put it on is a particular business, to whiten the pins is another . . . and the important business of making a pin is, in this manner, divided into about eighteen distinct operations, which in some manufactories are all performed by distinct hands, though in others the same man will sometime perform two or three of them.[3]

If, instead, each of the same eighteen workers performed each operation associated with making a pin, their total productivity would be much lower—by some calculations, 240 times lower! Smith's point was not about pins, but about the general benefits of specialization and the division of labor, namely, its massive boost to productivity. Smith thought the market and trade were the best ways to exploit the division of labor.

But as industrialization progressed and the big company emerged, Adam Smith's division of labor was gradually brought from the market into the modern industrial enterprise. Individuals and teams continue to specialize and trade, but much of this activity occurs within firms, where managers direct people to various tasks and oversee the process of linking and coordinating their activities. The Nobel laureate Ronald Coase argued that the division of labor is often best exploited inside firms because managerial coordination can reduce the "transaction costs" of putting all these pieces together (that is, the drawn wire has to be given to the worker who straightens it, and then to the one who cuts it, and so on, in the right amounts, at the right time, with the right speed, and so on).

In other words, bringing the division of labor inside the company often lowers costs, reduces the variability of the quality of the goods and services it delivers to the marketplace, guarantees relatively stable employment, may contribute to local community—and brings a regular paycheck! This explains the company's longevity.

Indeed, the traditional hierarchically organized company has remarkable staying power. The radically decentralized, bossless structure is sometimes seen as a natural outcome of a world facing rapid technological change, ongoing liberalization of world trade, and new attitudes in the workplace. But the hierarchically organized company actually emerged during a period in world history notable for radical changes in technology, a sweeping expansion of global trade, and increases in public education—namely, the period from the middle of the nineteenth century until World War I. The hierarchically organized company continued to spread in the interwar period and after World War II, first in the United States and then Europe and the rest of the world. This was a period of massive disruption of industries and technologies and a great deal of turmoil and change in politics, trade, and culture. If you think the conventional managerial hierarchy works only under stable, predictable conditions, think again!

To use lingo from evolutionary biology, the traditional company represents a successful adaptation to a fast-moving and unpredictable ecology. The evolutionary economist Sidney Winter at the Wharton School once referred to the company as a "hopeful monster," an allusion to the large and rapid transformations in biological evolution due to macromutations. To extend the metaphor, the major, long-lived, and successful lineage established by the traditional company should be modified only with caution!

CHANGING ATTITUDES TOWARD THE COMPANY

Some people see a dark side, socially and politically, to the traditional company. As we showed in Chapter 3, this perspective isn't exactly new: social critics have long identified the company as the central actor in the capitalist market system. Capitalism itself is—again—under scrutiny, particularly by millennials and Gen-Zs who find "socialism" (by which they often have in mind a more socially responsible capitalism) increasingly appealing. And the company is indisputably at the center of capitalism. Consider the recent book (and movie) by University of British Columbia law professor Joel Bakan, *The Corporation: The Pathological Pursuit of Profit and Power.*[4] Bakan analyzes the corporation the way a psychiatrist analyzes a patient. His conversations with The Corporation reveal the following character traits: extreme self-interest, deceitfulness, inability to admit guilt, lack of concern for the feelings of others, as well as other characteristics that we usually think of as characteristic of the psychopath. Who wants to work for an organization like that?

Bakan is part of a broader anticorporation movement whose adherents argue that the corporation has taken the place once held by the Church, the Monarchy, or the Party. The corporation is held in suspicion, however, across the political spectrum. It is seen as an often unaccountable concentration of power, and many believe that it is almost self-evident that such power must be curbed. An influential narrative holds that humanity is spiraling toward a consumption-induced ecological catastrophe—and that corporations, particularly the multinational ones, have brought us there. Hence, we get the calls for triple bottom lines, sustainability, environmental, social, and corporate governance (ESG) investing, restricting executive pay and perks, criminalizing "ecocide," the Earth Charter, and other more or less fanciful ways of constraining corporate power.[5]

Distrust of the corporation—and more broadly, the company—goes back a long time. You may know the hymn "Jerusalem," with music written by Hubert Parry and orchestration by Edward Elgar. The hymn lyrics are from an 1808 poem by the Englishman William Blake. It is inspired by the apocryphal story about Jesus visiting England as a child. Blake envisions the return of Jesus to England to create the "second Jerusalem," that is, to create Heaven on Earth, in contrast to the "dark Satanic Mills" of the industrial revolution.

Of course, Blake was picking up on a narrative that was already gaining ground during the industrial revolution: that the companies established to exploit the new advances initiated by the steam engine were destroying the fabric of English society. The model for those "dark Satanic Mills" seems to have been the Albion Mill Southwark (now part of London), the first big factory in England, capable of producing six thousand bushels of flour per week. It could have driven London's independent millers out of business but was destroyed in 1791 by fire, maybe caused by arson.

The narrative was reinforced by Karl Marx and his many followers and disciples. Marx, of course, was painting a picture of capitalism as a force that was simultaneously highly rational, creative, ruthless, and exploitative. The company-organized factory was where the exploitation took place concretely and where owner-capitalists siphoned off the "surplus value" created by workers. One step in this process was "deskilling" workers. In contrast to the precapitalist artisan, the industrial worker had no particular skills and was thus substitutable: what one worker could do, another could do equally well (if carefully supervised). Thus, a narrative took hold according to which industrialization, with its big corporations, had worsened the conditions of the ordinary person. This view is rejected by most serious historians of industrialization.

Marx also argued that capitalism would unavoidably be accompanied by increasing concentration of power as corporations killed each other off. In US politics, populist action taken against Big Business toward the end of the nineteenth century was based on similar ideas, though without the ideological underpinning. In one of the first works on what is today called "corporate governance," *The Modern Corporation and Private Property*, Adolf Berle and Gardiner Means argued that the US economy was essentially controlled by some two hundred corporations.[6] Moreover, they asserted that managers exercised this control despite shareholders' formal ownership.

These ideas are still very much in vogue. The big corporation is viewed with suspicion because of its supposed potential for exploiting its "market power" and overall dominance, as well as for paying its workers too little, taking advantage of small suppliers, jacking up prices to consumers, harming the environment, and so on. While Marx's critique of capitalism was directed at the factory system, not large corporations per se, many of Marx's admirers have taken up the argument and applied it to modern business.

Paul Adler, a prominent management professor at the University of Southern California and a past president of the Academy of Management, the world's leading association of management scholars, titled his most recent book *The 99 Percent Economy: How Democratic Socialism Can Overcome the Crises of Capitalism*. Adler charges capitalism with causing or exacerbating inequality, financial crises, environmental unsustainability, social disintegration, and political and international conflict, but also considers it responsible for what he calls "workplace disempowerment":

> Management is far too important to be left to managers. To overcome the crisis of workplace disempowerment, we need to democratize the management of our enterprises. We need to put these enterprises under the control of boards, representing workers, customers, and the broader community, and to replace top-down autocratic control with all-round participative management.[7]

Even those who support the capitalist system per se are wary of the social and economic power of big companies, especially in the tech sector. An October 2020 congressional investigation of Facebook, Google, Amazon, and Apple concluded that "these firms have too much power, and that power must be reined in and subject to appropriate oversight and enforcement. Our economy and democracy are at stake."[8] The use of antitrust and other regulatory measures to regulate and even break up the large technology companies is increasingly popular among legislators and the public.

More generally, much of the political turmoil of recent years has featured the company as an important actor, whether in the decline of smokestack industries and subsequent changes to communities or in the rise of the tech giants. As a central actor in society, companies have always been contested; the recent critique of hierarchy and managerial authority is just one more round in a long-standing debate about the role of the business company.

10

THE WORST FORM OF ORGANIZATION—EXCEPT FOR ALL THE OTHERS

The Case for Hierarchy

MANAGEMENT, EXECUTIVE AUTHORITY, AND HIERARCHY ARE RATIO-nal responses to the dilemmas and challenges of integrating complex activities and getting people with different motivations and interests to cooperate. However, an ever-growing perception that hierarchy is con-straining, old-fashioned, and out of step with the times, nothing but a command-and-control structure unsuitable for the knowledge economy with its empowered, educated workers and rapid technological and en-vironmental change, can lead managers astray. Better get in tune with the times by adopting the very flat management structures of companies like Valve and Zappos—especially now when many appear to believe that "the pandemic has changed everything," as we noted in Chapter 1.

If hierarchy is simply command and control, then we agree! Nobody wants to go back to the *Mad Men*–style office culture with its rigid roles and responsibilities, lack of spontaneity and creativity, and rooms full of bored and uninspired workers. That is hardly a model to emulate. Neither is the factory model popularized at the turn of the twentieth century by Frederick Taylor in which workers were treated as "data" in an engineering problem—giving rise to the word "Taylorite" to describe a rigid, hierarchical workplace.

From Laurence Peter's "Peter Principle"—that people in a hierarchy rise to the level of their own incompetence—to the criticisms of hierarchy of more recent gurus, consultants, and journalists, what is being described is often *dysfunctional* hierarchy. We laugh at Scott Adams's brilliant comic series *Dilbert* because we identify with the titular character, a smart but browbeaten engineer dealing with lazy coworkers, clueless interns, an evil feline HR director, and an incompetent (indeed, pointy-haired) boss. The 1999 Mike Judge comedy *Office Space* and TV series like *The Office* and *Parks and Recreation* poke fun at the mind-numbing boredom of cubicle culture. Yet we tend to overlook how the hierarchy, with its routines, chain of command, and job descriptions, is still extremely useful, indeed often enabling.

A well-designed hierarchy helps *coordinate* people and tasks. It lets the right hand cooperate with the left. It establishes routines, policies, and procedures—the *rules of the game*—to bring people together, exchange information, and resolve disputes. It provides structure without being overly constraining. It is flexible and can adapt; it bends but doesn't break. It is a complement to, not a substitute for, human freedom, creativity, and responsibility. This is the kind of hierarchy that has propelled the great civilizations, given rise to great companies, industries, and technologies, and made possible levels of health, wealth, and happiness that we can easily take for granted. Of course, like any social system, even well-designed hierarchies are not perfect.

Thinkers such as the German scholar Max Weber (the father of modern sociology, otherwise famous for linking the rise of Protestantism and the emergence of capitalism), US businessman and author Chester Barnard, the great business historian Alfred Chandler, and Nobel Prize–winning economists Ronald Coase, Herbert Simon, and Oliver Williamson harbored no illusions about hierarchy as a perfect system. They all realized that managers make errors, pursue their private interests, and sometimes simply mismanage. Still, to adopt the old saying about democracy, hierarchy is the worst form of social organization—except for all other forms of social organization. This is true even in the knowledge economy—perhaps more so than ever before.

THE CORE ARGUMENT FOR HIERARCHY

Hierarchy represents an effort to solve the universal twin problems of *coordination* and *cooperation* faced by any social group. Families have to deal with these problems, as do country clubs, neighborhood associations, and any parties entering a contractual relationship. So do political parties, labor unions or employers' associations, NGOs, mass movements, and even nations or systems of international collaboration like NATO or the European Union.

Social groups handle the problems of coordination and cooperation differently. Families often address them by consensus, inertia, or deference to an authority figure, without any formal negotiation or agreement and with nothing put in writing. Not so with the US Army or with Goldman Sachs. And that is as it should be. Different problems require different solutions. This goes for companies and their hierarchies as well.

Coordination means figuring out what should be done, by whom, when, how, and in what quantities. Think of coordination as a more or less detailed plan. A good plan clearly delineates people's responsibilities and how their roles and tasks are linked to those of other people. Coordination doesn't happen by itself; it requires deliberate forethought, motivation, review, and revision. In a well-coordinated project or organization, every part of the plan comes together.

While coordination is about figuring out what people should be doing, cooperation is about getting them to do it, even when doing so is not in everyone's self-interest. Cooperation typically requires incentives because what is good for each of us individually may not be what is best for the group. I may prefer to waste time at work watching cat videos, but when I do that I'm not working. A little shirking on my part may not be so bad for the firm (though of course, if everyone shirks, we have a problem). My boss may even allow me some time for rest, refreshment, or entertainment to keep me happy and make me more productive. But tensions over how people in the office spend their time, how they use the company's equipment, which tasks they choose to work on, and how they interact with others have to be addressed, and hierarchy provides an obvious means of doing so.

Coordination and cooperation problems are not issues specific to business or capitalism or Western societies or the modern age; they are common to any system of human activity. Sometimes we solve them among ourselves—peer-to-peer, to use contemporary jargon. Neighbors typically solve disputes about property lines, noise, stray pets, and the like by talking it out, following local custom, or asking for advice from trusted friends. Larger groups sometimes solve these problems by agreeing on common rules or standards, then letting each party do what it wants, subject to those rules. A common example is the shape of our AC adaptors, USB cables, headphone jacks, and other electronic connectors. Any US-style power plug can fit into any standard wall jack. Any USB memory stick can plug into any computer USB slot. A 3.5-millimeter headphone jack can plug into the headphone hole in any standard device. Of course, these standards are partial and local: electric adaptor plug shapes, holes, and voltage levels vary by country; there is both a regular USB and a USB-C standard; and Bluetooth devices often don't have headphone jacks. The point is that these standards are open, meaning that anyone can obtain the technical specs and make a product compatible with the other products using those same specs.

The market system itself, with prices determined by supply and demand, is a kind of coordination and cooperation mechanism. The Covid-19 pandemic led to reduced demand for personal grooming products. Retailers finding themselves with unsold hair gel, lipstick, and deodorant lowered their prices, and finding customers hard to come by because of lockdown conditions, they reduced their inventories and the amount they paid suppliers. Essentially, falling prices suggested to producers that they should put their resources elsewhere.

As F. A. Hayek famously argued in a 1945 article, prices help coordinate the best use of resources.[1] The lack of prices is why economy-wide central planning inevitably fails. Hayek's teacher Ludwig von Mises put it this way: "To the entrepreneur of capitalist society a factor of production through its price sends out a warning: Don't touch me, I am earmarked for the satisfaction of another, more urgent need. But under socialism these factors of production are mute."[2]

Prices also help solve the cooperation problem. If, as a retailer, you can get the product (say, lipstick) at a good price, you have a good chance of benefiting from selling it to consumers or customers at a profit. Of course, the lure of that profit motivates you to buy the product and put effort into selling it. The profit emerges when there is a difference, to your advantage, between what you paid and the selling price that you correctly judged. Again, prices provide motivation and make people (the lipstick producer, you, your customers) cooperate in activities that create value.

Coordination and cooperation cannot always be achieved, however, by arm's-length interactions among firms and between firms and customers; sometimes an entrepreneur can increase the level of coordination and co-operation by bringing activities *inside* a firm. To see why, let's look further into the work of historian Alfred Chandler and economists Ronald Coase and Oliver Williamson.

ALFRED CHANDLER: THE VISIBLE HAND

A Harvard Business School professor from 1970 until his death in 2007, Alfred Chandler is the foremost historian of the corporation. His well-deserved reputation is based on his careful, painstakingly detailed tomes on how the big US industrial firms emerged, consolidated, and changed—and the essential role of hierarchy in these transformations.

Chandler's first major work was *Strategy and Structure: Chapters in the History of the Industrial Enterprise*, published in 1962.[3] Relating the company histories of DuPont (Chandler himself was part of the Du Pont family), Standard Oil of New Jersey, General Motors, and Sears Roebuck, Chandler made the case that structure follows strategy. Each of these firms started with narrow product portfolios and a simple managerial hierarchy organized along functional lines (in other words, the major subunits, such as production, finance, sales, and marketing). As these firms began to diversify, however, they embraced a structure of product-line divisions, each with its own functional subunits underneath it—the "M-form" structure mentioned in Chapter 6. The M-form structure makes more sense for a diversified firm, as it gives the subunits more autonomy, makes them directly accountable and easy to monitor (because they have their own divisional profit-and-loss statements), and allows the corporation executives to focus on longer-run strategic issues.

Chandler's later work shows that the managerial hierarchy itself was crucial to the emergence of the large corporation.[4] What the political theorist James Burnham called the "managerial revolution" made mass production and mass prosperity possible by persuading employees to cooperate with each other and with management and by tightly coordinating productive activities. As even critics such as John Kenneth Galbraith admitted, the classical corporation was a highly effective machine that was part and parcel of the growth-and-wealth miracle of the post–World War II years.

Chandler's big lesson is that hierarchy is an unbeatable machine when it comes to coordinating a flow of activities at the lowest cost. Hierarchy is an instrument of efficiency rather than the opposite. Note that, in making his case by detailing the history of firms that embraced the M-form structure, Chandler was not cherry-picking a few extreme examples, as bossless company fans are prone to do. Rather, he observed a general, economy-wide trend and illustrated it with a few well-chosen company histories, each highlighting a different version of the M-form structure.

COASE AND WILLIAMSON: TRANSACTION COSTS AND HIERARCHY

How are entrepreneurs and managers able to realize these efficiencies? Put differently, why can't the cooperation and coordination organized by managers inside the large firms studied by Chandler happen outside the firm—say, in partnerships or spot-market transactions between individuals or smaller firms? Why do we need to create companies in the first place?

This basic question—why do firms exist?—was posed by a young English economist named Ronald Coase in 1937. At the tender age of

twenty-one, Coase wrote what would turn out to be one of the most famous papers in economics. Why, Coase asked, do we organize firms in the
first place, in light of the elegant model of the market economy provided
by thinkers like Adam Smith and F. A. Hayek in which coordination and
cooperation are driven by the invisible hand of anonymous price movements and the free interactions of small entrepreneurs? If we take this
model of the market seriously, then why do we see the emergence of big
firms with their multilayered hierarchies? When are anonymous prices
alone not up to the job? And if firms are sometimes better than markets,
then why aren't they better all the time? Why isn't all production carried
out in one big firm?

Coase's answer starts with the recognition that the invisible hand does
not do its job costlessly. Trading can be difficult. You need to know the
offerings. You have to bargain with vendors or entrepreneurs. Contracts
must be made and enforced. Disputes arise. It is difficult to know the
quality of many products and services. Remember "lemon," the now
somewhat dated word for a low-quality car? No one wants to end up with
one, but that might be difficult to avoid for potential buyers who can't
figure out a car's quality. The same goes for finding good repairpeople or
contractors, or even choosing a restaurant for dinner. Without full knowledge of the available options and the ability to make sure you always get
what you think you paid for, you might go home unsatisfied.

These challenges are examples of what Coase called the "costs of using the price mechanism," or what we would nowadays call "transaction
costs." One of the key breakthroughs of modern social science is the recognition that these costs are found pretty much everywhere and that they
influence how we arrange and organize things. Indeed, some professions
would not exist if not for these costs. Take lawyers. They are basically in
business because people don't always honor agreements. If transaction
costs were truly zero, there wouldn't be any conflicts over agreements.
(Maybe blockchain technology will enable this!) Or consider real estate
agents. If people always knew what properties were available, intermedi-
aries like real estate agents would be superfluous. Coase's big insight was
that, absent transaction costs, there would be no firms either.

In fact, one way to understand the revolutionary power of the internet is that it has sharply reduced many of the transaction costs described by Coase. We can avoid buying a lemon by using an online service like Carfax to check out the maintenance and repair history of a car we're interested in. We don't even have to haggle over the price—we can search for the make and model we want across many sellers using one of the many car-buying sites, most of whom advertise "no-haggle" pricing. We no longer need brokers or agents for buying and selling stock or making airline reservations (though we still need them for real estate and some other transactions). And restaurant reviews are everywhere, taking the guesswork out of choosing a place to eat.

At the same time, other kinds of transaction costs—figuring out who owns what, writing and enforcing contracts, negotiating deals, bringing new goods and services to market, and resolving other kinds of disputes— have hardly gone away. Lawyers don't seem to be hurting for business in our modern era! Coase's argument isn't about a specific kind of transaction cost that can be lowered by technology, but about the challenges of transacting more generally.

What, then, is the role of the firm? Think of a simple firm with one boss and one employee. Coase reasons that, in principle, the boss and employee could negotiate and write a contract for each thing the boss wants the employee to do. But there are practical challenges here. First, it is costly and annoying to set up a new contract for each new task or activity the employee is supposed to do. Second, employers partly think of employees almost as "reserves": we don't know what exactly the future will bring, so we keep employees on hand so we can deal with new situations as they arise. If you like, employees have "option value."

For this reason, the typical employment contract is open-ended, including a general job description but not a listing of every possible task the employee might need to perform. This gives the boss the flexibility to direct employees to do things in the future that cannot be anticipated now. Thus, the firm reduces transaction costs and allows for flexibility. And yet, managers can only do so much, so this argument does not scale infinitely. There are "diminishing returns" to the transaction cost–reducing properties of firms.

Oliver Williamson, an economist who, like Coase, won the Nobel Prize for theorizing about firms and managers, built on Coase's ideas to develop what he called "transaction cost economics." Williamson pointed out that the law makes a huge difference in the choice between markets and firms for organizing transactions. There is one body of law, mainly employment law, that relates to those transactions that are "inside" hierarchies. And there are different bodies of law that regulate transactions between hierarchies or between hierarchies and consumers.

Recent controversies regarding the status of Uber and Lyft drivers provide a stark example. Legally, these drivers are independent contractors. They own their cars, and they use the ride-sharing service's app to arrange bookings. The riders pay through the app, which keeps a percentage of the fare. From Uber's and Lyft's point of view, they are logistics companies producing apps that allow drivers and riders to connect. In this business, the "boundary" of the firm encompasses the hardware and software needed to run the system plus the employees who write and maintain the code. Drivers, just like riders, are outside this boundary, and the company has no legal responsibility to them beyond what it provides to any other supplier or customer.

This arrangement, of course, is different from the organization of the traditional taxi and limo industry, in which drivers are employees and are protected by labor law, such as those that mandate minimum wages, maximum hours, and health and retirement benefits. In 2019, California passed a controversial law requiring that Uber and Lyft drivers, along with other "gig economy" workers, be classified as employees for the purposes of labor law, even though they choose how much to drive and can use multiple services concurrently. Uber and Lyft promptly threatened to exit the state, and the law was revised the next year (after a successful voter petition) to exempt ride-sharing and food delivery services from the employment requirement. (It probably helped that the law seemed to prohibit journalists from working as freelancers—after freelance journalists had been its strongest supporters!)

Without the technological innovations (smartphones, GPS, widespread internet access) that allowed ride-sharing platforms, food delivery services, and other on-demand services to be produced and to become commercially viable, all these operators would be employees of a company, with loosely defined roles and responsibilities (for example, pick up customers and take them to their destinations between the hours of 8:00 a.m. and 5:00 p.m.). It would not be feasible for drivers, passengers, and the taxi company to negotiate routes, fares, wages, and the like for every potential ride—the transaction costs would be prohibitive. But with ride-sharing apps, transaction costs have plummeted, such that these moment-to-moment negotiations do, in a sense, take place (via the app). Technology and the law thus shape transaction costs, and hence what goes on inside the firm and what goes on outside the firm.

Williamson adds a profound dimension to the point about the role of the law. He argues that hierarchies create their own internal law systems based on "forbearance." These systems are necessary because most firms lack the autocratic top-down hierarchy of the caricature. Conflicts within the firm are often solved by negotiation, through convention ("corporate culture"), and sometimes even with reference to formal written agreements. Courts rarely intervene in the interpretation or enforcement of these internal agreements but instead allow the parties inside the firm to figure it out.

In other words, a big difference between firms and markets is that conflicts between firms and outside parties (customers, suppliers, competitors, community members) are usually resolved by courts, while conflicts inside the firm are settled by the firm itself, with the board or top executives serving as a sort of supreme court. Firms at which this internal dispute resolution system works better than the external legal system—for example, firms where it is faster, more efficient, or more accurate—have an additional advantage compared to markets. We see this dynamic at play in emerging markets, where poorly performing formal institutions (courts, police, regulatory bodies, and the like) create what the Harvard economists Tarun Khanna and Krishna Palepu call "institutional voids," which make it difficult to do business.[5] In response, firms become larger and more diversified so that more transactions are taking place inside firms than between firms; the firm's managers fill the voids by performing contracting, negotiating, and dispute resolutions services that would otherwise take place in the market.

WHAT MANAGERS DO

According to Coase and Williamson, then, hierarchy makes economic sense, under certain conditions, essentially because it makes the best possible use of human effort (including cognitive effort) and, when necessary, can sometimes make people expend more effort than they are "naturally" inclined to. This understanding leads to the idea of the manager as a *monitor*—someone who makes sure that the right effort is expended at the right time in the right amount, that schedules are followed, and that work takes place according to the rules. As a practical matter, this role is what most people associate with "management," and so it's hardly surprising that management gets a bad rap: few people like to be monitored, controlled, and sanctioned. In fact, we think that too much focus on this aspect of the managerial role may have contributed to the popularity of the bossless company narrative. Focusing on the monitoring role of managers seems to assume that Frederick Winslow Taylor was the only management thinker of note. However, not long after Taylor's ideas had become influential in US business, a different approach to thinking about management became influential as well, one that in some ways was "softer" or more "humanistic."

Chester Barnard, a businessman who studied economics at Harvard, sold pianos, and led a dance band, was a key early thinker on the corporation. He was president of the New Jersey Bell Telephone Company, served in the First World War, and later headed the Rockefeller Foundation.

Barnard's classic 1938 book, *The Functions of the Executive*, about what CEOs *essentially* do, is rooted in a deep understanding of companies as social systems facing the twin problems of coordination and cooperation. In this context, the executive defines the company's purpose and objectives, giving everyone a sense of direction and adding meaning to work. But efforts also need to be coordinated, so establishing and maintaining the company's system of communication is a key executive task. Once the coordination problem is addressed by defining objectives and securing information flows, the remaining cooperation problem is handled by managing employees so that they carry out their jobs in the right way.

To anyone who thinks of all traditional visions of hierarchy as being about crude top-down control, Barnard's book is an eye-opener. He insists on the overriding importance of good communication, which he sees as not just a matter of having well-defined communication channels but also ensuring that every employee knows about and has access to these channels. Moreover, lines of communication should be short and direct, and every communication must be authenticated. Similar ideas had been disseminated even earlier in the pioneering thinking of Mary Parker Follett. Both Barnard and Follett essentially argue that authority partly depends on communication as well as on the "buy-in" of subordinates. To get such buy-in, managers need to treat employees with respect.

This theme resurfaces when Barnard discusses getting employees to contribute to the workplace. He recognizes the role of tangible rewards (the paycheck) in motivating employees, but he also understands the importance of persuasion and the rhetorical aspects of the manager's job. A manager must convince employees that what they are doing is meaningful and appreciated.

Remember, this was thinking about companies that went back to the 1920s and 1930s and was a far cry from the *Modern Times* view of the corporation of that day as a soulless, dehumanizing, authoritarian machine.

Chester Barnard has many "big lessons" for managers. The most important is the idea of authority as an *exchange relation*. Employees offer their time and talents to help the firm create value and must receive some inducements to provide these efforts. But those inducements can go far beyond monetary rewards. Barnard, one of the first thinkers to highlight the "soft" aspects of the rewards system in a managerial hierarchy, anticipated the idea of an implicit or unwritten contract between employees and managers.

The key thinkers on management have always known that management involves much more than controlling, monitoring, and sanctioning employees, roles that tend to decline as economies grow and become more complex. Increasingly important for managers is their role of *coordinator*.

A coordinator designs rules, procedures, and plans. Sometimes that involves detailed, forward-looking contingency planning, but sometimes it also includes *adaptation*—putting in place systems that allow the firm to change what it is doing in response to unanticipated changes. It goes without saying that such coordination is particularly critical when things are moving fast. People with particular insight into how best to respond to changes (in regulation, competition, technology, customer preferences) should be given authority to decide. Those at the top often know best what should be done, but we should not assume that they always or exclusively do. When things move fast, decisions must be made *quickly*, and when there is no time to fully explain the reasons for why something should be done, it is often better to simply let the person with the relevant insight decide on the course of action.

A hierarchy is simply an arrangement in which someone holds authority over others for the reasons described here. Of course, hierarchy is by no means a panacea for every problem that an organization faces. Still, it is there for a reason: it helps get activities coordinated and people cooperating.

MANAGEMENT MATTERS

If a hierarchy of managers helps to get things done, that should show up in the numbers. After all, we expect CEOs to make the big decisions about big investments that determine the fate of their company hard to undo. A basic purpose of hierarchy, then, is amplifying and executing such decisions and making sure things proceed in a way consistent with keeping the company a going concern, that is, one that creates enough value and has enough resources to continue in operation. Because leadership seems to be an important factor in the success and survival of companies, we tend to associate successful big companies, past and present, with their best-known leaders: Jack Welch at GE, Sam Walton at Walmart, Steve Jobs at Apple, Jeff Bezos at Amazon, Elon Musk at Tesla and SpaceX.

Pinpointing the importance of CEOs in the data, however, is tricky. One reason is luck. One of the most provocative things we can say in our executive courses is that a large part of corporate performance is driven by luck. Executives naturally (and understandably) balk at this assertion. When challenged (for the purposes of discussion), the more thoughtful executives will point to the (few) persistently successful CEOs and presidents. Think of Jobs after his return to Apple, Welch during most of his time at the helm of GE, or, for those with a historical orientation, Alfred P. Sloan or Henry Ford. Surely these leaders weren't simply lucky year after year!

Of course, it is theoretically possible that high performers are consistently lucky: even if performance is 100 percent driven by luck—as in, for example, flipping coins—there will still be some persistently successful (that is, very lucky) performers.[6] The "random walk" theory of stock prices holds that no investor (without inside information) can systematically beat the market, suggesting that Warren Buffet is no more skilled than you or me at anticipating future market conditions—just luckier!

Although it is surely incorrect to attribute all differences in firm performance to luck, it would be hard to deny that luck does play some role. Top managers have to make decisions in conditions of high uncertainty. Sometimes it's hard to pick the "best" action using careful, rational analysis, which is where instinct, intuition, or gut feeling comes into play. When things work out well, it looks like the manager had excellent judgment. But sometimes you just roll the dice! The Apple board's decision to bring back Steve Jobs as CEO at the end of 1996, following Apple's worst financial quarter ever, looks in hindsight like a genius move. But it was a controversial move at the time; after all, Jobs had left Apple in 1985 after losing a power struggle with John Sculley, and he had gone on to found NeXT, a company that seemed to have a bright future. For many people, Jobs's return to Cupertino as interim CEO (iCEO!) was a huge surprise. Was Apple just lucky that Jobs was available and willing to return, and that he went on to reboot the company completely? Was Jobs's belief that the future lay in mobile devices connected to a proprietary ecosystem of apps and media (first the iPod, then the revolutionary iPhone) a brilliant insight or a lucky guess? Sometimes it's hard to tell the difference between brilliance and luck.

THE ROLE OF THE CEO

How, then, do we demonstrate the most salient point of the argument that bosses matter—that the CEO is important? It would be wrong simply to look at financial performance, not only because some firms perform well despite having an average (but lucky) CEO, but also because high-performing firms may attract good CEOs, in which case the CEO is not the cause of the firm's high performance.[7] Leaving luck aside, superior financial performance can also be driven by the company's particular industry or market. Perhaps the industry is experiencing particularly high growth, customers love the products, prices are high, and costs are manageable. Indeed, one of the most famous models for studying firm performance, Harvard Business School professor Michael Porter's "Five Forces" framework, is mainly about industries, not firms. (Since barriers to entry, customer and supplier bargaining power, and intense rivalry are common to all firms in an industry, strategy researchers look for alternative factors, such as a company's unique "competences" or "resources," to explain differences in performance *between* firms in an industry.)

To tease out cause and effect in the relationship between the CEO and firm performance, researchers have looked at cases where the CEO changed for reasons beyond anyone's control—unexpected death, for example—and found that the CEO matters a lot. In one study, the unexpected death of a CEO resulted in a decline in operating returns on assets by almost a full percentage point—a significant difference when returns in the millions of dollars are involved.[8] Another study attributed 13 percent of the variance in firm performance in the 1950s and 1960s to the quality of the CEO, with this figure rising to 25 percent for the 1990s and 2000s.[9]

THE MISUNDERSTOOD MIDDLE MANAGER

Clearly, the person at the top of the hierarchy matters a lot—even more so today than in decades past. What about those at other levels of the hierarchy? After all, radically flat hierarchies are still hierarchies, just ones without the middle managers between the boss and the employees. What do middle managers do? Are they really necessary?

Middle managers get a bad rap. Often they are seen as impediments to getting things done, as exemplified by Elon Musk's email quoted earlier about the imperative of every employee being able to contact anyone above them with one email or phone call. Still, as we noted in Chapter 7, middle managers play an important buffering role. Let's flesh out that argument in more detail.

Middle managers are conventionally viewed as having operational, not strategic, responsibility. They make the trains run on time, but they don't decide the routes. Middle managers' role of translating "strategies defined at higher levels into actions at operating levels" involves "(1) defining tactics and developing budgets for achieving a strategy; (2) monitoring the performance of individuals and subunits; and (3) taking corrective action when behavior falls outside expectations."[10] In a traditionally organized managerial hierarchy, decision-making authority flows from top to bottom, with each layer faithfully implementing commands from above. When lower levels of the corporate hierarchy initiate change, it is normally for the purpose of implementing more effectively a general directive from the top management team.

Nevertheless, there are many ways in which middle managers can influence decision-makers at the top, even in a more centralized structure. One is by bringing to the attention of executives new ideas or projects or strategies that they might not otherwise have considered. Another is by shaping the perceptions of top managers in how they frame options or in the ways they present and interpret information.[11]

These essential middle management functions are known as *brokerage* and *bridging*. Brokerage is the art of "making deals"—getting people at higher and lower levels of the organization to cooperate by passing information up and down and negotiating. Bridging is the use of one's networks to bring people together. In both cases, middle managers are helping to shape the company's strategy as well as execute it. This role is especially important when top executives are uncertain, unprepared, or unable to deal with particular issues; letting middle managers take the lead also gives top executives plausible deniability![12] For example, senior executives have largely delegated diversity, equity, and inclusion training—a sensitive topic in which top managers have little expertise—to human resources departments, which organize, promote, and implement these programs on behalf of the company.

In short, far from being useless, middle management is an essential part of a well-functioning managerial hierarchy. Still, particularly in highly regulated industries or those subject to substantial social pressure, there are many middle managers engaged primarily in regulatory compliance, public affairs, and other forms of stakeholder engagement who may not contribute directly to creating value. This is the main point of classic critiques of bureaucracy from James Burnham, Joseph Schumpeter, and Ludwig von Mises. And the increasing emphasis on social justice, corporate social responsibility, and stakeholder capitalism is likely to increase the number of middle managers whose work is devoted to maintaining a particular corporate image.

"I FIGHT AUTHORITY, AUTHORITY ALWAYS WINS"

Being subject to authority, from any level, can be unpleasant, yet it seems inevitable. As pop crooner John Cougar Mellencamp suggested in his "Authority Song," when you fight authority, it always wins. But must we be subject to authority in the workplace? Management, executive authority, and hierarchy are permanent features of organizing work, but for many everyday business activities, employees no longer need a boss to direct them to tasks or to monitor their progress. Such involvement can be demotivating. In a networked economy characterized by dispersed knowledge residing inside the heads of highly qualified specialists, leaders should let go of the notion that good management means everything should be managed from the top. Rather than telling people what to do, it is often better for managers to define the principles they want people to apply or the goals they want people to meet. In other words, they can design the rules of the game without specifying the actions of the players.

To see how this is done, let's meet another great thinker in the pantheon of management, Herbert Simon.

SIMON: HIERARCHY EVERYWHERE

Herbert Simon was a towering figure whose work included pathbreaking contributions to artificial intelligence, mathematics, statistics, economics, systems theory, political science, and organization theory. His views on hierarchy and authority resemble Coase's. Both would formally define authority as the right to choose an action for another person, out of the set of that person's possible actions. In simpler terms, when we say that a boss has authority over an employee, we mean that the boss can tell the employee what to do among those things that the employee has previously agreed to do.

Like Coase, Simon also says that authority works by reducing transaction costs. The employment relation is flexible and partly open-ended. It's too costly to figure out in advance exactly what the employee will need to do on a day-to-day basis, so the boss and employee simply agree ahead of time on a set of possible activities, tasks, or projects, and the boss then directs the employee to do specific things on a given day as needed.[13]

Simon's fundamental thinking on the nature of "hierarchy" led him to argue that hierarchy is ubiquitous and not just a characteristic of human organizations. We see hierarchy everywhere we see complex systems, whether human systems like the bureaucracies of organizations or the hierarchies we observe in the natural world—for example, elementary particles, atoms, molecules, and so on.[14]

Hierarchies, according to Simon, are stable, which is the reason for their longevity. They are favored by evolutionary processes.[15] This claim may run counter to our immediate intuition (further explained in the following chapter) in light of the steady number of big companies being dissolved by market forces. The fate of Kodak, Xerox, Blockbuster, Nokia, Segway, JCPenney, and many others is fresh in our memories. But the rise and fall of particular firms doesn't disprove the great staying power of the hierarchical form. Moreover, the big companies of the past, like those of today, created a lot of value for their hundreds of millions of stakeholders for a very long time.

MODULARITY AND ADAPTATION

In seeing how hierarchy can help a company adapt to a changing environment, recall our earlier discussion of "modularity"—using standardized parts to build products that can be produced by many suppliers. Modular systems are more robust against outside disturbances than nonmodular ones. And hierarchies are good at establishing and maintaining modularity.

Simon tells a story of two imaginary watchmakers, Hora and Tempus. Their skills at watchmaking are exactly identical, but only one succeeds. The difference between the watchmakers lies in how they design their watches. Each watch has one thousand components. Tempus assembles his watches one component at a time, taking what Simon considers a nonhierarchical approach. Hora combines ten elementary components into small subassemblies, then combines ten subassemblies into larger subassemblies that he finally puts together to make complete watches. Simon thinks of this as a hierarchical way of producing watches. The analogy is clear: each subassembly is handled, in effect, by a different organizational unit.

Simon then introduces disturbances, imagining that Hora and Tempus are frequently interrupted by phone calls from customers. In Simon's fable, watchmaking is a process in which a large number of tiny parts have to be kept in delicate balance, so each time Tempus puts down a half-finished watch to answer the phone, it falls apart and he has to start over after he finishes the call. When Hora takes a call, however, he loses only the subassembly he was working on; the rest of the unfinished watch is undisturbed. Thus, despite the equal skill of the two watchmakers, Hora can produce many more watches per day, as his "hierarchical" assembly method is more robust when it comes to dealing with interruptions.

It is easy to see that Simon's parable uses the concept of modularity. Modules are smaller pieces of a larger system that can be combined in different ways. In the construction industry, modules are project components with different functionalities; produced in huge numbers before installation, they can be mixed and matched, depending on standards. In manufacturing, the automobile industry has perfected modular designs in the use of exchangeable parts or the design and manufacture of modular components. In industrial design, modular engineering techniques are used to build large systems from smaller subsystems, much like a child's constructions from a Lego set. In such models, modularity is supported by sharing components (perhaps the same machine can be used for producing different components, or the same legal language about terms and conditions can be repeated over and over again) and by defining the modules and the relations between them (the "interface standards"). For example, Lego bricks are based on a particular standard, as are USB cables, computer circuit boards, screws and screwdrivers, railroad tracks, cell phones, and cell towers.

Modularity drives down costs, allows for flexibility, and encourages innovation by making it easier to combine components, services, and ideas. Components in a modular system can be separated and combined and recombined. Think of the many apps we can add to our phones, usually with little effort and at no or low cost. As consumers, we can easily see the benefits of apps, but there is also a huge advantage for producers, who can focus on what they are truly good at, namely, the specific module (app) they handle as part of the bigger system. They can make their own module better without worrying about other modules. For example, by outsourcing their payment processing to PayPal or Alipay, online merchants can focus on product design, marketing, and procurement without wondering whether changes to their website will require redoing the checkout section.

From the perspective of systems, modularity also has the advantage of not presenting the system with a big adjustment to make if a local module is somehow disturbed (for example, if one of Hora's subassemblies falls apart). The disturbance is handled locally, and after a brief interruption, the system continues to function. Work can even proceed on the other modules while the broken module is fixed.

A further advantage of modularity is the huge possibilities it offers for remote and asynchronous work. Consider GitLab, the world's largest remote company with more than thirteen hundred employees across sixty-nine countries.[16] GitLab isn't just remote—it is *all*-remote. It has no headquarters, no company-owned offices anywhere. Not only is its approach to work based on modularity, but it uses its own product while building software tools that help other companies achieve modular production. Specifically, GitLab's main product is a continuous integration tool that allows coders to take a complex development project and "cut it up" by defining modular chunks of software, enabling continuous, parallel development efforts, *and* making it possible to put all the modules together into a coherent whole. GitLab's use of this tool enables its heavily dispersed and asynchronous approach, which is further supported by heavy reliance on shared code, document repositories, and communication tools such as Slack. This workflow process is very rigid in that it includes no other way to modify code. Essentially, it works by first placing constraints on the kind of code edits that a user can perform and then leaving it to a "maintainer" to decide whether to accept the changes.

The modularity revolution is sometimes described as a reversal of hierarchy, as a move away from Chandler's visible hand of hierarchy to the vanishing hand of a more flexible, egalitarian system, perhaps all the way back to Adam Smith's invisible hand of the market, with small, specialist producers interacting through standards and prices.[17] But modularity is used in hierarchical firms as well; for example, the big auto producers have led much of the modularity revolution with their platform-based production methods, all taking place under the supervision of their corporate hierarchies.

Moreover, the modular system itself has to be *defined*. GitLab sells software that does this for software development projects, and it is conceivable that these tools will be extended to other kinds of development and production tasks. But until then, managers have an important role in defining system architecture, which means first and foremost setting module and interface standards. Modularity works only where clear interface standards ensure that the modules fit, and somebody has to specify these interfaces. Modularity also requires gatekeepers; low-quality producers or fly-by-night operators will give the system a bad name, so somebody has to control membership. Disputes about sharing income may arise, as in the recent dispute between Apple and Fortnite when the latter refused to share the revenue from in-game purchases with Apple, as mandated by Apple's App Store rules.[18]

While these definition, monitoring, and dispute resolution functions can be shared, they are typically driven by a few large, core firms. These "big players" are at the center of ecosystems in automobiles, aircraft engine control systems, contract manufacturing computing, and mobile phones. These ecosystems have independent players, so it is not exactly Chandler's visible hand at work here. But it is not the fully decentralized, purely invisible hand of the market either. Rather, the big core firms are lending a coordinating hand to serve the overall system. Ecosystems of firms need a central, coordinating hub because standards cannot solve all coordination problems, just as standard operating procedures and routines cannot solve all coordination problems inside companies.

The other side of the coin is that bottom-up systems work best where things are tranquil and rather predictable—where technology doesn't change too quickly or abruptly and what customers and consumers want is clear and easy to anticipate. In other words, hierarchy isn't as valuable where few interdependencies exist among people, resources, and tasks, uncertainty is low, and there is plenty of time to make decisions. To see this, we will consider the tomato producer Morning Star, one company frequently cited as a paradigm of a business without bosses.

MORNING STAR: MAKING TOMATOES, PEER-TO-PEER

Morning Star, a food processing company based in Woodland, California, has garnered praise as a company with employees who are "ridiculously empowered," yet who also work together "like members of a carefully choreographed dance troupe."[19] Founded in 1970 by Chris Rufer, who remains sole owner, it is a big company, totaling close to $1 billion in annual revenues. Interestingly, that huge revenue is produced by a workforce of only six hundred employees, which is extremely small for a commodity production firm (and which, admittedly, is boosted by the addition of four thousand seasonal workers during the harvesting season).

Morning Star has become famous for a radical employee self-management model. Ostensibly, the company has done away with hierarchy, managers, and titles. Holding a certain position in the hierarchy confers no authority to tell colleagues what to do. In principle, all activities are a matter of voluntary agreement between individual employees.

Of course, employees are not entirely free to choose; most generally, what they can do is limited by the corporate mission of Morning Star: "To be a full-service tomato ingredient supplier providing unequivocally superior services and supply-chain solution to specialty, and geographically unique customers." This mission statement is broken down to the department level, shaping what employees can do and agree upon.

Morning Star's main innovation, according to its admirers, is doing everything by contract.[20] All companies use contracts, written or implied; indeed, if you're an employee, your relationship with your company is fundamentally contractual. You have an employment agreement that provides general information on what you are supposed to do and what you will get in return. Sometimes the contract is implied and informal rather than written out in detail. Moreover, most employment agreements are "incomplete" or open-ended: they don't specify exactly what you will do and what will happen in all possible circumstances. These agreements are left open-ended by design, since employers can't anticipate and write down all of the specific things they will want their employees to do. They don't know exactly what will happen in the future, so employment contracts have a lot of gaps.

In the traditional hierarchy, these gaps are filled by the boss; managers direct employees to do certain tasks as needs arise, or employees follow some operating procedure that tells them what to do in the new situation. For instance, when a sales order comes in, the boss in a small company may direct everyone to work to meet the order. In a larger firm, so many sales orders arrive at regular intervals, looking sufficiently alike, that it makes sense to design a procedure for handling them. If the order is unusual, employees involve the boss.

Morning Star ostensibly has no bosses. There is no one telling employees exactly what to do when a new order for tomato pulp arrives. Does chaos ensue? No, because Morning Star has a substitute for managers. As Chris Rufer reasoned, this could be accomplished by reversing the traditional contractual logic: make contracts more detailed! And because what one employee does affects the activities of other employees, let them make contracts *between themselves* to handle those interdependencies.

CONTRACTS, CONTRACTS, AND MORE CONTRACTS

Each contract is called a CLOU, standing for Colleague Letter of Understanding. "Clou" in English means the main point of interest. In French, a *clou* is a nail. The CLOU is indeed the main point of interest in the organizational design of Morning Star because it is literally the nail that keeps everything together.

The (digital) CLOU governs relationships among employees but looks more like a job description. It includes a personal mission statement, a set of key activities associated with that mission, performance indicators, a time commitment, and a list of the colleagues (typically ten) to whom the CLOU applies and who must sign the contract to indicate their agreement. A mission statement for a person who sorts tomatoes might be: "to ensure that our customers receive pristine tomato products free of foreign material." The performance of a forklift driver might be measured in pounds of product shipped per person-hour.[21]

Other companies also typically use job descriptions that describe activities and performance goals, and most jobs feature annual reviews with goal-setting, assessment, and revision of tasks and objectives. The Morning Star model is different, however, in several respects.

First, employees write their own CLOUs, in consultation with their colleagues. Most of us "choose" our job description by choosing the job. Second, CLOUs change frequently: each (permanent) Morning Star employee negotiates a new CLOU every year, and as noted earlier, some CLOUs are modified even more frequently. Job descriptions in a traditional company are more stable. Most people change their job description by changing jobs.

Second, a CLOU is a contract between the employee and the set of colleagues most influenced by her work—not between the employee and the company. All companies feature contracts, but usually the firm itself is the hub, contracting with its employees, its suppliers, its capital providers, its distributors, and its customers. An employee doesn't negotiate with each customer; the employee negotiates an employment contract with the firm, and the firm negotiates the purchase agreement with the customers. The firm itself has been memorably described by the economists Michael

Jensen and William Meckling as a "nexus of contracts." If drafting, negotiating, and enforcing contracts takes time and effort, then letting the firm act as a hub—thus reducing the number of contracts needed for production—saves money. This is a basic rationale for establishing firms in the first place.

Morning Star flips this logic on its head. It is a firm, yes, but a firm that operates internally like a market. Each employee contracts with each other employee (or, at least, the employees with whom she works most closely). If drafting, revising, and enforcing these lateral agreements is costly, however, problems can arise, as we demonstrate later.

Third, CLOUs specify deliverables, goals, and performance metrics in detail. Job descriptions in traditional companies often feature such details, but they are not usually included in the employment contract, which is typically more general and open-ended.

MOTIVATION AND COORDINATION

Can such a system work? One of its advantages is that the Morning Star model attracts a particular type of employee, one who is self-motivated, independent, and committed. Moreover, the emphasis on horizontal relationships among employees rather than vertical relationships with the company can have some psychological benefit: commitments become commitments to other colleagues rather than to the company or a boss. Research has shown that soldiers are much more committed to their comrades than to an officer, a nation, or a cause, and thus more motivated to fight for them. Morning Star employees may resemble soldiers in this regard. Moreover, employees understand their jobs clearly, they know what their colleagues are doing, and they can hold each other accountable. Sometimes conflicts are best handled locally, among employees, without the intervention of management.

At the same time, this model has a lot of potential problems. As already noted, the costs of writing and enforcing so many contracts can be high. If workers are really autonomous and can negotiate and deal easily with each other, then why have a firm at all? Why not just produce tomatoes, or anything else, through a network of independent contractors or entrepreneurs? Of course, Morning Star is not literally a network of independent actors; the employees are legally employees, subject to (potential) managerial authority, at least from a legal perspective. But with the CLOU model, they have to resolve conflicts on their own; without a conventional hierarchy, there are no supervisors to step in and help solve problems. The firm does have a system with layers: if employees cannot resolve a conflict, they turn next to internal mediation. If mediation can't resolve the conflict, an internal board of employees with supposedly different perspectives provides advice. Any conflict that remains unresolved at this point is appealed to the internal supreme court—namely the founder, Chris Rufer.

Despite supposedly abolishing titles, management, and hierarchy, Morning Star is not completely flat, and it is certainly not bossless. Its workers are arranged in departments, the building block of most hierarchies, and it does have titles and managers. While Morning Star gives its employees considerable freedom, that freedom is constrained by the firm's mission and the derived missions for the individual departments and the CLOUs.

CAN THE MORNING STAR MODEL WORK FOR YOU?

Morning Star seems bossless and it has certainly done away with a lot of the middle management functions we would normally see in a six-hundred-person company. But that is because the company has skillfully delegated managerial tasks to employees themselves through the CLOU system. In effect, those who can manage best, because they are closest to the action, do the managing. The management task doesn't disappear just because the company decides to go "bossless."

What has made it possible for Morning Star to delegate the management task? The answer is simple: the firm operates in a traditional industry doing traditional things that don't involve a lot of changes of processes and technology. Productive activities can be highly divided and can be described in great detail. Many of those activities can be automated. There are interdependencies, but growing and processing tomatoes is a mostly linear process with little feedback between the stages of the overall production process. There may be seasonal variations (although this is California!), and there may be new environmental demands and corporate social responsibility concerns to be met. At the end of the day, however, things at Morning Star are straightforward and predictable.

In sum, it is not too surprising that a company like Morning Star can succeed with a very flat structure that involves lots of delegation and little intervention from bosses. Morning Star operates under particular or special conditions: it makes a simple product (basically a commodity), uses simple production processes, and benefits from being in a relatively stable industry. Under these conditions, it is easy to look ahead. It's not too hard to draft those CLOUs.

We don't wish to trivialize Morning Star's practices. After all, the company is quite successful and enjoys considerable employee loyalty. The thinking that gave rise to CLOU is probably sound. But most companies operate in very different circumstances.

The CLOU system and other aspects of the Morning Star organization are not likely to work if you run a more complex company in a more dynamic environment where things happen that no one can anticipate. There is nothing in a CLOU contract that will tell you what happens next. Your productive activities may not be linear and predictable but rather intertwined and highly variable, requiring iterations and feedback loops, as in development work. You inevitably make revisions as new prototypes, beta versions, and so on, are put together, assessed by people in production, and tested by focus groups or testers. Or think of the activities that involve a team of consultants, or a team of engineers in an engineering consultancy, or a group of architects in an architectural company. Because of the unpredictability and complexity of events in such environments, making CLOUs would be pointless because only very general aspects of the interactions could be meaningfully specified.

The bottom line is that Morning Star, though a highly decentralized firm featuring coordination by lateral contract instead of managerial intervention, is still a firm with bosses. This kind of organization seems to work pretty well in tomato production and processing, an industry where the technology is well known, there are few disputes to resolve, contracts are not too costly to write and enforce, and conditions don't change radically enough to require central coordination. This model will almost certainly fail, however, in most other contexts.

HIERARCHY AND TURBULENT ENVIRONMENTS

Most companies don't operate in "stable" environments. Technology changes, customers decide they want different things, suppliers go broke, a social media campaign rocks the industry, the government changes its rules, and new competitors are always lurking on the horizon. Then there are the internal challenges: business units fighting over corporate resources, employees acting out, key personnel leaving for better jobs, and so on. Not that managers should be complaining; handling these kinds of frequent, unpredictable issues is in the job description!

If internal challenges are unsettling just one part of the company, no problem. Microsoft could never crack the phone market and eventually shut down its Windows Phone division without affecting the profitability of its desktop operating system or its productivity software businesses (which are booming to this day). Maybe your company loses a key customer, but you have enough untapped demand that you can still grow the business. A milling machine unexpectedly breaks down in production, but the engineers fix it quickly, without interrupting your production schedule. Congratulations! You have a system with modular properties.

What if the problem affects the whole firm? For example, suppose the company is accused of ethical violations. In the 1990s, Nestlé was accused of aggressively pushing infant formula in developing economies even though it knew that mothers often mixed the formula with polluted water, putting their children at risk. A business unit or a key account manager alone could not have handled such an accusation, since problems associated with one product spilled over to others, leading to a firm-level crisis. Or imagine that the milling machine supplies an essential input to the rest of the company, and everything grinds to a halt until it can be fixed. What happens if the machine isn't easily replaceable or takes a long time to repair? The company has a serious problem.

In other words, hierarchy is especially useful when production involves interdependencies, close ties between people, things, and business units. As we have seen already, flat modes of organization such as Holacracy can work when activities are highly modular (or simple and well understood), but they tend to break down when interdependencies arise, especially as firms grow. When activities are interdependent, a change to one has ripple effects on the others, and some central coordination is necessary to make sure the system as a whole continues to run smoothly. A key function of hierarchy is having procedures that describe how interdependencies are to be handled. When things change in a way not anticipated by those procedures, managers are needed to handle interdependencies. Otherwise, things can go very wrong.

Remember the spaghetti organization from Chapter 6? The brilliance of Oticon's Lars Kolind lay not just in his daring vision of a radically decentralized organization, but also in his understanding that too much decentralization could make everything fall apart. With most of middle management eliminated, Oticon's structure needed something else to keep things together. A new culture, a new reward system, and a detailed performance management system worked together with the decentralized structure to handle interdependencies; all elements of the firm's organizational design were parts of a whole, intended to be mutually supportive and reinforcing—or "complementary." As we will see in Chapter 12, failure to incorporate all elements of a complementary system can lead radically decentralized organizations astray.

Kolind was clearly alert to the importance of designing incentives—the formal (or "hard") and informal (or "soft") elements that motivate employees and that need to be designed in such a way that they work together. For example, a "soft" culture that encourages employees to collaborate may be hard to align with strong performance incentives. Finding the right mix is crucial. Flexibility may be limited by culture. When people say that "culture eats strategy for breakfast," what they mean is that a strategy that runs counter to a firm's culture won't work. The same holds for incentives. So, at least in the short run, rewards need to be attuned to culture. Rewards attuned to a longer-run perspective can be more flexible because company culture can be changed over time.

In a fast-moving economy, managers must frequently revisit the design of the company's incentive instruments as work and organizational structures change and new employees with different values come on board. Lincoln Electric has relied on its elaborate system of performance incentives for more than eighty years. Analysts argue that the system is the main reason for the company's continuing profitability. (It hasn't had a single year with red numbers.) It may seem that Lincoln's reward system is so well designed that it "runs itself," but it has actually been tweaked continually.[22]

The tweaking is, of course, done by managers. But suppose that teams were allowed to set their own rewards. Teams at Valve have some discretion over pay. In the Oticon spaghetti organization, decisions about employee salaries and bonuses were largely delegated to team leaders. This may make sense because team members can better observe performance than an outside manager. It is not difficult, however, to see the perils of such a system.

Teams may set different standards for normal effort, or they may reward extra individual effort differently. This becomes a problem when teams carry out the same activities. Rewards then stop accurately reflecting productivity. Members of badly paid teams may depart for a team with more generous awards. Envy could come to dominate the workplace, poisoning it.

Incentive design is usually left to managers for good reasons. When Oticon abandoned the spaghetti organization, the right to negotiate salaries and award bonuses was centralized again. Managers can impose uniform principles in rewarding employees. Because they reward many employees, teams, and units, they learn about what works and what does not. In other words, they become familiar with the "economies of learning" as they design incentives for employees. Concentrating the design of incentives in the hands of a few managers or in a central function also reduces the costs of arranging the rewards per unit (whether employees or teams), thus achieving economies of scale in the task of designing and adjusting incentives.

Like everything else associated with doing business, a company's structure needs to change with the times as well as in response to unanticipated shocks. The Covid-19 pandemic changed much about how we work: bosses had to change how they measured and monitored performance as many employees went remote; production methods had to change as supply chains were disrupted and distribution channels moved toward remote delivery; and flexible hours replaced regular work schedules. More mundane changes happen even more often as companies accept (or turn down) new projects that require a change of the organization or as changes in strategy, the customer base, technology, markets, the composition of the workforce, and other changes require adjustments to the company's organizational setup.

Finally, note that even radically flat structures with maximum delegation are a product, like Wikipedia, of someone's decision to design the firm that way. A flat hierarchy is still a hierarchy, and a company's owners continue to bear the ultimate responsibility for determining what they alone will decide and what decisions they will delegate to others.

THE BOTTOM LINE

The message of thinkers from Max Weber to Chester Barnard, Ronald Coase, Alfred Chandler, Herbert Simon, and Oliver Williamson is that hierarchy and skilled managers coordinate work better than can be done with any other method, including unstructured, bottom-up, spontaneous coordination. But this conclusion does not lead to a call for superpowerful managers or micro-management. On the contrary, the basic thrust of these classic works is that the level and kind of management needed depends on various contingencies. The ability to figure out these contingencies and how best to respond by incentivizing and evaluating employees, delegating (or centralizing) decisions, making people work well together, and deciding whether to rely on fixed procedures or go with the flow, is what separates the good managers from the bad ones.

11

HIERARCHY ISN'T
A DIRTY WORD

HIERARCHIES, WE HAVE ARGUED, ARE ESTABLISHED BECAUSE MOST of the time they work better than the alternatives. Entrepreneurs routinely, almost instinctively, set up hierarchies when they start and grow companies. When companies reorganize, they look for ways to rearrange their hierarchies; they usually don't abolish them. The bossless company narrative, if taken to its logical extreme, says that this is all wrong, that the preference for hierarchy is naive, perhaps even a superstition that we inherited from our forebears and practice without thinking. Or even worse, these advocates say, those in power establish and maintain hierarchies to keep their power, even at the expense of the economy and the community. Companies, and even society as a whole, are better off without bosses.

In our contemporary culture, "hierarchy" has become almost a dirty word, as have "bureaucracy" and "authority." (For some reason, the word "leader" has escaped this fate, though leadership, both formal and informal, is itself an aspect of hierarchy.) The word "bureaucracy" carries the most negative connotation and is usually taken to mean an "excessively complicated administrative method of making decisions" (or not making them). Historical experience has also shown us that a well-functioning bureaucracy can be an instrument in the service of the worst atrocities. The philosopher Hannah Arendt, reporting on the 1961 Adolf Eichmann trial, found Eichmann to be not a roaring monster but a little ordinary bureaucrat who had committed his terrible deeds mainly to advance his career within the Nazi bureaucracy.[1]

Hierarchy also carries a negative connotation—though it may not be as strong as bureaucracy's—and authority is frequently mocked. (Remember the *South Park* episode in which the antagonist Eric Cartman, playing a police officer, says, "You will respect my authoritah!") Although people still accept the informal authority ascribed to parents and grandparents, religious leaders, and public figures like Nelson Mandela (before he became South Africa's president), bureaucracy, hierarchy, and authority continue to carry a lot of negative reputational baggage and advocating for them can seem like a steep uphill climb.

But consider the great German sociologist Max Weber, whose life was cut short in 1920 by that era's equivalent to Covid-19, namely, the Spanish flu. Weber was a student of bureaucracy. He defined bureaucratic organization as a system with defined roles and responsibilities, fixed rules and written procedures, expert personnel, promotion based on performance, and clear lines of authority. He thought the best way to organize all human activities was bureaucracy, which would have looked to Weber like the traditional, rigid bureaucracy of Imperial Germany with which he was familiar—or like a well-functioning military company, a Taylorite factory, or even to some degree an office filled with men in gray flannel suits.

Weber's idea of bureaucracy sounds pretty good, especially for the public sector. Who would want public officials *without* "expert training in their fields," career advancement *not* based on qualification, and an *absence* of accountability? In fact, much of what can go haywire with the public sector results from lack of adherence to Weber's ideal type. Wouldn't we like, for instance, to have public-sector hospitals that conform to key elements of Weber's ideal? And though we often admire politicians and government officials who "think outside the box" and come up with new and different ways of doing the people's business, we also like to think that these bold and daring officials are kept in check by a cadre of professional, career civil servants with their own set of rules and a longer-term perspective.

Weber's metaphor of the "iron cage" of bureaucratic rules and control reveals his understanding that bureaucracy can threaten human creativity and indeed liberty. For example, a well-functioning bureaucracy can become an "acquisitive bureaucracy"—one mainly interested in growing and protecting its influence and power.

The same considerations apply to authority and hierarchy. We typically understand authority as the power or right to give orders and enforce obedience. Most of us dislike being given orders or having to be obedient. Indeed, people choose certain occupations partly to avoid being subject to authority—the ostensibly free life, for instance, of the writer or entrepreneur. Some observers view much of what has been going on lately in the political realm through the lens of "the crisis of authority"—that is, the authority of the media, the political parties, the government, and academia is being increasingly questioned and rejected.[2]

Mistrust of authority goes back much further and in fact is likely to arise during any major conflict or change in power. Not long ago, the awful misuses of authority witnessed in the Second World War were part of the soil from which the "anti-authoritarian" counterculture grew in the 1960s. The Milgram experiments, which began just a few months after the start of the Eichmann trial, have found a place in popular culture. They are good entertainment, and various national TV shows across the world have replicated them. They are supposed to show how easily people can be manipulated by authorities to administer lethal electrical shocks to innocent, protesting victims. In reality, the Milgram experiments have been misinterpreted; many participants actually knew that the whole thing was staged, and many even disobeyed the instructions of "the teacher."[3]

The power that authority confers can certainly be misused. But as we have seen, authority can be highly functional, including layered authority in hierarchies. We want to put the most capable people at the top of companies to magnify the effects of their decisions. That's what a well-functioning hierarchy does. The layering of authority can be an instrument in service of what the Swedish economist Magnus Henrekson calls "good power"—authority bestowed on those who are best able to contribute to the group's (including the company's) success.[4] We may be willing to give power to someone we see as more capable and to see her exercise of authority as legitimate. Our willingness to recognize authority may extend not only to a specific person but also to the embodiment of authority in a hierarchy.

In this chapter, we further build the case for hierarchy by showing that it is quite natural: hierarchy has been around for a long time, it has adapted to changing circumstances, and its response to a variety of challenges has been robust. In short, hierarchy has high survival value. At the same time, many of the criticisms levied at hierarchy—that it is overly rigid and controlling, stifles creativity and innovation, and is fundamentally unfair and unjust—are based on misunderstandings.

HIERARCHY IS NATURAL—LITERALLY

Hierarchy is as old as human history. For obvious reasons, we can only speculate on the form that hierarchy took among the small bands of hunters roaming the savannas in Africa thousands of years ago. But for as long as we have had some kind of recorded history, there has been hierarchy.

The word "hierarchy" comes from *hierarkhia*, the ancient Greek word for the "rule of a high priest"—an ancient form of governance found in the earliest societies that we have detailed knowledge about, such as Ur and other Sumerian city-states established almost six thousand years ago. In line with these religious origins, the term first appeared in English in 1881, when "hierarchy" was used—wait for it—"in reference to the three orders of three angels as depicted by Pseudo-Dionysius the Areopagite (5th–6th centuries)." (The original Dionysius was apparently a Christian Neoplatonist who wrote around the late fifth century.)

However, Pseudo-Dionysius also used the word to refer to the structure of the Catholic Church. That the Church is a conventional example of hierarchy should give us pause: the world's oldest surviving organization,

and therefore a very successful one in terms of longevity, is also very hierarchical. Incidentally, the call for a much less hierarchical organization—
one more like the Church of the first few centuries—issued during the
Protestant Reformation and Martin Luther's "Principle of Christian Liberty" ("A Christian man is a perfectly free lord, subject to none") sound
very "bossless." Of course, the Reformation soon got tangled up with the
hierarchies of the kings and princes, and the Catholic Church, despite
having taken a few very hard blows recently, is very much still around. As
Herbert Simon argued, hierarchy may have survival value.

Hierarchy, the dictionary tells us, is "a system in which members
of an organization or society are ranked according to relative status or
authority." Our immediate association with the word "hierarchy" may
indeed be with the hierarchy of the Catholic Church, the military, the
courts of Louis the XIV, the hierarchically structured society of the
seventeenth- and eighteenth-century Edo period in Japan, or indeed
the hierarchy of the corporation for which we work. But hierarchies are
ubiquitous, and hierarchy may even be an anthropological constant—
something that is pretty much everywhere, in one form or another. It
has always been present, in one form or another, for as long as there
have been humans.

ARE HUMANS HARDWIRED FOR HIERARCHY?

The basic view among anthropologists is that early humans lived in small,
egalitarian groups of hunter-gatherers and developed more complex and
hierarchical societies much later as they developed agriculture during the
Neolithic period, around 12,500 years ago.[5] This view has been embraced
by philosophers and social critics from Jean-Jacques Rousseau to Francis
Fukuyama and Jared Diamond. As Fukuyama wrote in his book *The Origins of Political Order: From Prehuman Times to the French Revolution*:

> In its early stages, human political organization is similar to the band-
> level society observed in higher primates like chimpanzees. This may be
> regarded as a default form of social organization. The tendency to favor
> family and friends can be overridden by new rules and incentives that

mandate, for example, hiring a qualified individual rather than a family member. But the higher-level intuitions are in some sense quite unnatural.

Band-level societies are highly egalitarian. The major social distinctions are based on age and sex; in hunter-gatherer societies, the men hunt and the women gather, and there is a natural division of labor in reproductive matters. But within the band, there is relatively little differentiation between families, no permanent leadership, and no hierarchy. Leadership is vested in individuals based on qualities like strength, intelligence, and trustworthiness, but it tends to migrate from one individual to another.[6]

In contrast, once tribes became settled, they began competing with other tribes for scarce resources—and for land in particular. As populations grew and conflicts became more frequent, chiefs, governors, and eventually kings emerged, along with the other trappings of the state. As Jared Diamond put it: "Large populations can't function without leaders who make the decisions, executives who carry out the decisions, and bureaucrats who administer the decisions and laws."[7]

We might be tempted to conclude, as do proponents of the bossless company narrative, that hierarchy is a fairly recent innovation in the broad sweep of human history—a social structure necessary to accommodate larger, settled populations who expect to have property rights, technology, and modern forms of production, even if these are "unnatural" for the species. This view is almost certainly wrong. We actually know little about prehistoric societies, but the archaeological evidence suggests that they featured significant inequality, had wealthy political or priestly castes, and built large buildings and monuments with complex designs that would have needed prior planning and a division of labor to create. As the anthropologist David Graeber and archaeologist David Wengrow suggest, these early human communities "had nothing in common with those blissfully simple, egalitarian bands of hunter-gatherers, still routinely imagined to be our remote ancestors."[8] That these prehistoric societies were sometimes organized in complex hierarchies indicates that there is nothing "unnatural" about modern forms of social organization.

Graeber and Wengrow argue that the big difference between these prehistoric communities and later civilizations was seasonality:

> Most of the Paleolithic sites discussed so far are associated with evidence for annual or biennial periods of aggregation, linked to the migrations of game herds . . . as well as cyclical fish-runs and nut harvests. At less favorable times of year, at least some of our Ice Age ancestors no doubt really did live and forage in tiny bands. But there is overwhelming evidence to show that at others they congregated en masse within the kind of "microcities" found at Dolní Věstonice, in the Moravian basin south of Brno, feasting on a super-abundance of wild resources, engaging in complex rituals, ambitious artistic enterprises, and trading minerals, marine shells, and animal pelts over striking distances.

In other words, according to this analysis, our remote ancestors were "shifting back and forth between alternative social arrangements, permitting the rise of authoritarian structures during certain times of year, on the proviso that they could not last; on the understanding that no particular social order was ever fixed or immutable. Within the same population, one could live sometimes in what looks, from a distance, like a band, sometimes a tribe, and sometimes a society with many of the features we now identify with states."[9]

Moreover, the proclivity for hierarchy may be more deeply rooted in human nature. Several studies have used magnetic resonance imaging to study how the human brain responds to different cues about social hierarchy. They show that the brain reacts to how we perceive our place in the hierarchy—we pay more attention to people we perceive as "above" us than those we see "below."[10] Our brains also perceive and remember hierarchical social relationships more easily than less hierarchical ones.[11] Lab experiments also find that groups of people solve problems involving interdependencies more effectively when one person is designated the "boss" and given authority to direct the others. One such experiment measured testosterone levels (in both men and women), which is commonly used to measure aggression and the will to dominate. Groups with some high-testosterone and some low-testosterone members out-performed groups in which all members were high in the hormone (too many coaches, not enough players) or all members were low (nobody willing to take charge).[12]

Hierarchy may also emerge in groups as an instrument of exercising power. "The Will to Power" that the philosopher Friedrich Nietzsche made central to his thinking may also derive from the benefits of power: status, recognition, material goods, easier access to sex, and, for some, the joys derived from determining the outcomes of others. A recent experiment found that a substantial fraction of individuals accept less income in exchange for power over others.[13] That is, they are in effect willing to pay for the opportunity to exercise control. Those who seek political office or strive to make it to the top of the corporate hierarchy may be driven as much by such "preferences" as by the desire for financial rewards.

All these experiments, theories, and stories explain how hierarchies and leaders emerge organically in groups. "Natural leaders" are also instrumental in the creation of groups in the first place. As discussed throughout the book, hierarchy is a means for solving coordination and cooperation problems. But which coordination and cooperation problems are worth solving? If everyone in a community has equal social standing or stature, then everyone has to talk to everyone to persuade people to come together into groups (teams, ventures, or companies). Leadership alleviates this problem by creating a sort of marketplace in which leaders propose problems or tasks that can only be solved in groups, and followers decide which groups they want to join. Hierarchy thus solves the "meta-coordination" problem of "coordinating with others about what to coordinate about."[14]

These and similar findings suggest that hierarchy in human societies and communities is not simply a product of culture or the environment— it is not a "social construct"—but rather that hierarchy is built into our biology. Certainly, none of the creation accounts of the major world religions feature an egalitarian original state. Adam was the original inhabitant of the biblical Eden, and Eve was created as his companion and helper; children followed soon after. The first human society in Hebrew and Christian accounts was a nuclear family, not a hippie commune. The Koran offers a similar account featuring Adam and Eve, while most Hindu creation stories also include a man and a woman.

Evolutionary anthropology provides evidence that hierarchy is highly useful and has basic survival value. Much work on the evolution of humans assumes that human brains evolved to assist humans as they cooperated in small nomadic hunting bands that roamed the African savanna. In a sense, the brain is just an evolved organ that helps us solve certain problems. Our particular human ability to recognize activities that require a joint, coordinated effort and specific ways of cooperating was shaped by these early environments.

Those early environments also shaped hierarchy and leadership. Of course, many other animals have hierarchies, namely dominance hierarchies that keep the level of conflict at a minimum. Any dog owner knows this: the weaker animal quickly submits, avoiding violence from the stronger one. But human hierarchies are different. Because it is so important for us to cooperate, too overt an exercise of domination usually backfires! Even in the prehistoric hunting bands, it may not have been the physically strongest human who became the leader, but the one who was best at keeping the band together and who perhaps had the advantage of some other knowledge (for example, knowing the most likely position of prey). In fact, the evidence from so-called primitive cultures seems to point to consent as an important basis of de facto leadership. People will consent to being led by someone they respect. This explains why there is often a close correlation between hierarchical rank and status and why, again, we see the influence of biology: managers, certainly top managers, are usually male, and they are also taller than subordinates on average.[15]

DOES HIERARCHY HAVE AN UGLY PAST?

Something may have existed for a very long time, but that is no reason to accept it. Slavery has been practiced for most of human history, but it is now universally condemned and has become abhorrent to us. Historically, hierarchy has sometimes been a vehicle of domination and an instrument of oppression. If you were a peasant in Louis XIV's France—and after all, most French people in that day were just that—you may have grudgingly accepted your place in what you were told was a natural, God-given hierarchy. But you may also have thought that there really wasn't much in it for you, and you probably didn't celebrate your status.

Similarly, while corporations have been for most people the best chance at a steady income and a successful career (outside of government bureaucracies), it has not been hard for critics, such as labor organizers and even socialist agitators, to push back at the desirability, and inevitability, of the hierarchical corporate system. More generally, the idea that hierarchy benefits not only those at the top of the hierarchy but also those at the bottom has not always been commonly accepted, even among scholars of the corporation.

As we mentioned in Chapter 7, in the late 1960s a view began to develop among some "radical" historians and economists, picking up on Marx's ideas, that the purpose of hierarchy is to create a kind of soulless machine to carry out capitalist exploitation. In this understanding, the hierarchy of the corporation assists capitalist exploitation by making workers extremely specialized. A worker who does only one thing over and over again needs very little training and very few skills. In fact, these historians and economists provocatively argued, the corporate hierarchy deliberately "deskills" workers. People without skills may have less self-respect and identity. They will find it more difficult to collectively resist the exploitation to which they are subject. They are also fully substitutable.

This theory smacked of conspiracy thinking (how exactly did those capitalist pigs coordinate the deskilling?), and it just didn't square with the historical evidence. In fact, firms and "capitalists" invest in training because it's an important way to make workers more productive, and higher productivity is in the interest of both capitalist-owners and workers themselves.

A more recent critique of business hierarchy comes from a scholarly movement that identifies as the "New History of Capitalism." A central theme of this critique is that modern business practices such as accounting techniques, quantitative performance measurement schemes, group-based outcome assessments, and standards that are ratcheted up over time originated in coercive, power-based relationships—particularly those of the antebellum slavery period of the American South.

The historian Edward Baptist claims in his influential book *The Half Has Never Been Told: Slavery and the Making of American Capitalism* that productivity increased fourfold in the US cotton sector in the first half of the nineteenth century not because growers were using improved cotton varieties (the generally accepted explanation among economic historians), but because of innovations in the brutality of the slave system.[16] Baptist claims that slave masters developed a system of individual quotas that he calls the "pushing-up" system. "If a slave failed to meet the daily quota, he would be whipped; if he exceeded the quota, that day's production would become the quota for the next day. In this way performance expectations could only be ratcheted up."[17]

According to Baptist, the use of production or sales quotas in modern companies is the descendant of these practices: "Most of us are managed by techniques that enslavers first invented—for instance, the now-ubiquitous workplace surveillance or the computer-generated measurement of people's daily output. The management of work today derives directly from the methods and skills enslavers developed for managing and coercing human beings."[18]

Fortunately for modern management, Baptist's account of the pushing-up system turns out to be fictitious.[19] Although increases in cotton productivity were likely to be related to management practices like better record-keeping, improvements in capital equipment (tools, more efficient farm animals), and the use of more productive inputs (seeds, fertilizer), there is no historical record of the individual quota system he describes.

The pushing-up system, what management scholars call the "ratchet effect," is actually well known and has been studied since the 1930s, when it was observed that workers in piece-rate production schemes (which link payments to the number of "pieces" produced, that is, to output) often limited their production, even though producing more would have yielded a higher payment. These workers reasoned that a burst of productivity might provide a short-term gain but would hurt in the long run because it would raise their supervisors' expectations, causing them to fall short in the future. The ratchet effect can also lead workers to misreport their performance: imagine a salesperson who has met expectations for the current year but then gets a big sale in late December; he might choose to report the sale in January so that, by not appearing *too* successful, the current year doesn't set an unrealistic target for the next year. Call it the "'what have you done for me lately' effect." Successful athletes and coaches sometimes worry that their fans will come to expect a championship every year and be disappointed by only a "very good" performance![20]

The sociologist Matthew Desmond echoes Baptist's language and imagery in seeing modern managerial and accounting practices as direct descendants of techniques developed to manage antebellum American slave plantations.

> Perhaps you're reading this at work, maybe at a multinational corporation that runs like a soft-purring engine. You report to someone, and someone reports to you. Everything is tracked, recorded and analyzed, via vertical reporting systems, double-entry record-keeping and precise quantification. Data seems to hold sway over every operation. It feels like a cutting-edge approach to management, but many of these techniques that we now take for granted were developed by and for large plantations.
>
> When an accountant depreciates an asset to save on taxes or when a midlevel manager spends an afternoon filling in rows and columns on an Excel spreadsheet, they are repeating business procedures whose roots twist back to slave-labor camps.[21]

As many critics have pointed out, double-entry bookkeeping emerged in the Italian city-states during the fourteenth century. Goethe called it "among the finest inventions of the human mind."[22] Depreciation methods were developed by the railroad industry in the 1830s and 1840s as a way of dealing with long-lived physical assets. To be sure, as Caitlin Rosenthal points out in her book *Accounting for Slavery*, slave owners and plantation managers adopted the managerial and accounting techniques used in other industries at the time for managing cotton production, including the directing of slave labor and estimating the value of slaves (as durable assets).[23] But this observation simply shows that cotton and other slave-intensive industries were industries, and that just like other industries, they were managed to generate financial returns to owners. There is no evidence that slave plantations invented new techniques that were specifically intended to manage slaves and somehow were carried over into the managerial hierarchies of the modern era. As Rosenthal notes, her book "is not an origins story. I did not find a simple path where slave-holders' paper spreadsheets evolved into Microsoft Excel."[24]

IS HIERARCHY UNJUST?

The last few years have brought forth a spate of works by philosophers, historians, sociologists, and others critical of capitalism, hierarchy, and authority itself. The philosopher Elizabeth Anderson's 2017 book *Private Government: How Employers Rule Our Lives (and Why We Don't Talk About It)* argues that the authority of bosses over workers is per se unjust and unfair—akin to the power of governments over citizens, but without democratic accountability.[25] Unfortunately, she confuses government (the state and its legal monopoly on violence and coercion) with *governance*, the set of rules, policies, and procedures that coordinate behavior in private organizations. Corporations per se cannot coerce you to do anything. Of course, the boss can "make" you do work you don't want to do, or the store can "make" its customers pay prices higher than what they want to pay. But this kind of pressure is not like the government's power to make you pay your taxes or obey certain rules. The employee can quit and work for someone else or start his own company (or team up with other workers to start a worker-owned cooperative). The customers can shop somewhere else or find a substitute product. The taxpayer or citizen, on the other hand, can't choose not to do business with the state!

Of course, your employer can certainly have substantial *influence* over your life. A job can pay better or worse, be more or less pleasant, offer steady employment over many years or frequently hire and fire employees, provide or withhold important fringe benefits (like health insurance or child care), provide promotion opportunities or not, and generally be more desirable or less. But this is not the same as having coercive power.

In a famous 1972 article, the UCLA economists Armen Alchian and Harold Demsetz objected to the terms "hiring" and "firing" because they make these transactions sound one-sided, as if companies unilaterally decide who agrees to provide labor (or to provide other inputs, or to buy the firm's products).

> The firm does not own all its inputs. It has no power of fiat, no authority, no disciplinary action any different in the slightest degree from ordinary market contracting between any two people. I can "punish" you only by withholding future business or by seeking redress in the courts for any failure to honor our exchange agreement. That is exactly all that any employer can do. He can fire or sue, just as I can fire my grocer by stopping purchases from him or sue him for delivering faulty products.[26]

This has become a famous passage in the literature on organizations, partly for its shock value. But Alchian and Demsetz are not just indulging in a rhetorical flourish—they are making an important philosophical point. The employer has no power of *compulsion* or *coercion* over the employee but can only seek to persuade the employee to accept the job and not to quit. The employer cannot tax, imprison, draft into military conflict, or execute an employee, as a government can do to its citizens! Anderson seems to simply gloss over these fairly fundamental facts. Of course, employees are not always "free" to accept or reject any job offered; in a tight labor market, people may feel that they have to accept whatever jobs are available. But this is a different "compulsion" than the literal compulsion exercised by states, even democratic ones.

As for the claim that the corporation has no democratic accountability, it is true that managers are not directly accountable to employees. But managers are accountable to other parties. First, the corporation is a "capitalist cooperative," to use the words of Yale Law School professor Henry Hansmann.[27] It is owned jointly by those who have invested capital, and it has fiduciary duties to them (and in some cases to other stakeholders).

This is not democracy in the sense of one-person-one-vote, but the corporation is similar to democracy in that it is usually accountable to many individuals and corporate persons.

The journalist Sarah Jaffe offers another critique of the corporate hierarchy: it pretends to make us happy! Her 2021 book *Work Won't Love You Back: How Devotion to Our Jobs Keeps Us Exploited, Exhausted, and Alone* offers a series of colorful accounts of the challenges that people find at work, describing them in the language of power, oppression, and even "violence."[28] She is particularly exorcised by employers' use of positive language to motivate their workers (for example, describing the workplace as "like a family"), which, she argues, is just sugarcoating a system of coercion.

Jaffe is right, of course, that the workplace is not a literal family (just as the private company is not a government with coercive power). And while a pleasant work environment, greater autonomy on the job, and higher pay are certainly desirable, those who have these benefits are still working—that is, they are still engaged in a contractual relationship in which they provide services in exchange for compensation. As Alchian and Demsetz point out, we already have the powers that Jaffe names, in that we can choose among jobs and employers. Of course, we cannot all have our dream job, any more than we can all have our dream house or dream car. But such is life.

HIERARCHY HAS NEVER BEEN 100 PERCENT TOP-DOWN

Another common misconception about hierarchy that doesn't survive scrutiny is that only those at the very top can exercise judgment, be creative, and have autonomy; the rest of us are just drones, doing what we are told. The idea that hierarchy requires top-down, authoritative decision-making by a single boss is largely a fiction. The historical reality is more subtle. The role of the followers' consent is important—hence the many historical references to a kind of contract. One explicit example is the feudal pledge that kings had to make upon being crowned in which they promised to protect and provide for their vassals in exchange for the vassals' taxes and military service.

What does a more subtle, contractual, consent-based hierarchy look like in business? Not that different from a traditional hierarchy. For example, the first formal organizational chart, designed in 1854 for the New York and Erie Railroad, reflected a highly decentralized structure, with operational decisions concentrated at the local level. Caitlin Rosenthal describes it as an early attempt to grapple with "big data," another of today's buzzwords.[29]

Like all organizational charts, the railroad's chart depicted, albeit loosely, roles and responsibilities, lines of reporting, and a basic structure for decision-making. Decisions that were best made at the local level were decided there, while decisions requiring coordination across local levels were made at the next highest level. The design was the brainchild of Daniel McCallum, the New York and Erie's general superintendent and a pioneer of management theory. As Rosenthal explains:

> In crafting the organizational plan, McCallum sought to improve the way the railroad used information. Through 21st-century eyes, the chart looks both antiquarian and surprisingly modern. Far from the static, hierarchical pyramids that we today associate with such charts, his was modeled after a tree. McCallum drew the board of directors as the roots, himself and his chief officers as the tree's trunk, and the railroad's divisions and departments as the branches.
>
> Critically, McCallum gained control by giving up control, delegating authority to managers who could use information in real time. He put what we would call the organization's C-level at the ground level, supporting the railroad, not directing its operations. Following one of McCallum's key precepts—"a proper division of responsibilities"—authority over day-to-day scheduling went to the divisional superintendents down the line.[30]

This illustrates the basic claim we have made in preceding chapters, namely, that delegation of responsibility makes perfect sense when lower-level managers or employees possess the specific knowledge needed to make good decisions. However, delegation brings costs as well as benefits:

loss of coordination, discretionary behavior, slow decision-making, and so on. Indeed, McCallum's design emphasized not only delegation but also reporting from divisional superintendents back to the board, which monitored closely the performance of these empowered decision-makers.

McCallum was a pioneer in developing almost real-time reporting of important metrics (what we would now call "key performance indicators" or KPIs), such as cost per ton-mile and average load per car. In other words, the goal of this model was not delegation or worker empowerment per se, but the separation of day-to-day operational responsibility (held by the local operators) and performance monitoring, strategy, and long-term planning (held by the board). McCallum's chart was an attempt to make the board more productive—not to eliminate the board altogether.

A well-designed hierarchy, in other words, is a blend of centralization and decentralization: it delegates activities best performed by those "on the ground," who possess the relevant local knowledge, while expecting coordination, evaluation, and strategic planning to be conducted by higher-level managers.

Hierarchy takes a variety of forms, and managerial authority is exercised within a great diversity of organizational types. The exact blend between centralization and decentralization varies over time and according to the circumstances. Managers should seek to balance the advantages and disadvantages of each approach, finding the blend between centralization and decentralization that works best in their situation.

What happens if this blend is not achieved? Both the scholarly and popular literature are full of warnings about overcentralization and its tendency to demotivate employees, stifle creativity, cause burnout, and leave companies unable to adapt to change. But what happens if a firm is not centralized enough? What can go wrong with extremely flat organizations? The next chapter looks at some of the drawbacks of flatness that have been mostly ignored in conversations about organizations—especially in the bossless company narrative.

12

WHY YOU (MAY) NEED MORE HIERARCHY

The Al-Qaeda attack on the United States on September 11, 2001, was the deadliest act of terror in US history. Almost three thousand people were killed, nearly ten times as many were injured, and infrastructure and property damages came to more than $10 billion. The string of attacks by Islamic terrorists included Richard Reid, the "shoe bomber" who attempted to detonate a bomb during a flight from Amsterdam to Detroit on Christmas Day 2009, and a suicide bombing at a CIA base in Afghanistan by a double agent.

Figuring out the cause of these attacks, and why the authorities failed to prevent them, has been difficult. Each case is different. In the 9/11 attacks the obvious direct causes were the planning of Osama bin Laden and the terrorists who flew the planes into the Twin Towers and the Pentagon. But the indirect cause was the lack of an intelligence capability to detect and deter such an attack, despite the giant intelligence and security operations in the United States and elsewhere designed to do just that. Was the intelligence community hampered by a lack of hierarchy?

The 2002 *9/11 Commission Report* made the point that the "9/11 attacks revealed four kinds of failures: in imagination, policy, capabilities, and management."[1] Instead of "management," they might have used the word "organization," at least according to economist Luis Garicano and legal scholar Richard Posner:

> The national intelligence apparatus of the U.S. . . . consists officially of 16 separate agencies, and unofficially of more than 20. Each of these agencies is protected by strong political and bureaucratic constituencies.
>
> Five and a half years after the report of the 9/11 Commission identified the cascade of intelligence failures that allowed the 9/11 attackers to achieve total surprise, the problems it highlighted persist: We learn of multiple, separate and unshared terrorist lists; of multiple agencies (State Department, CIA and the National Counterterrorism Center) unable to combine the tips they receive; . . . and of terrorists released from American custody to become leaders of al Qaeda abroad. There is the sense that nobody is in charge.[2]

"There is a sense that nobody is in charge" is a damning indictment. And lack of coordination is a huge problem for sprawling bureaucracies like intelligence and defense agencies. Decentralized intelligence gathering may be effective when different agencies are given different missions. For example, many countries have a branch dedicated to internal intelligence and one to external (foreign) intelligence, such as Britain's MI5 and MI6 (home of James Bond), respectively. These missions are sufficiently different that it makes sense to keep them separate. And sometimes intelligence information can be extracted and shared "by the crowd," as with anonymous, bottom-up document reporting and dissemination sites like Wikileaks. The economist Armen Alchian figured out in 1954 that the United States was using lithium as the fissile material for the hydrogen bomb simply by observing the stock prices of the companies mining and selling various rare metals.[3]

But in general, eliciting useful information from the crowd of the market is tricky. And having more than a dozen partly overlapping and competing agencies is likely to harm intelligence efforts. There will be duplication of effort, turf wars, and role conflicts. And most importantly, the jointly collected information must be compiled, assessed, and synthesized, which is difficult if agencies don't cooperate.

The desire to improve coordination across agencies led the Bush administration to create the new cabinet-level Department of Homeland Security. It included the former customs, naturalization, and immigration agencies now combined into US Citizenship and Immigration Services (USCIS), the newly established Transportation Security Administration, the Federal Emergency Management Agency, the US Coast Guard, the Secret Service, and fifteen other bureaus and departments. Reflecting on the coordination failures leading up to the 9/11 attacks and the subsequent attempt to reorganize the US intelligence and security services, Oliver Williamson remarked in his acceptance speech for the 2009 Nobel Prize in Economics, "The US has a Council of Economic Advisers; I look forward to the day when there's also a Council of Organizational Advisers." Maybe such a council would have foreseen potential problems that had been missed by the National Security Council (itself the inspiration for the Council of Economic Advisers).

REBELS WITH A CAUSE—BUT NO LEADERSHIP

Remember Extinction Rebellion (XR), the environmental group that made a lot of noise in 2019 and 2020? The UK group organized a series of marches that blocked major streets and thoroughfares in London. Despite its militancy, XR enjoyed widespread public support. Its antics even prompted the British parliament to declare a "climate emergency." XR was then hit by two incidents. The first was the Covid pandemic, which made public protests more difficult. The second was civil war.[4]

XR embraces the "bossless," fluid approach of Holacracy, in which individuals self-organize into temporary teams to accomplish particular tasks. As such, XR eschews the traditional hierarchy in favor of self-organizing, partly overlapping "circles." This approach makes sense for an organization that engages in localized, small-scale protest: each circle, or local team, can coordinate its own actions independently of the rest of the organization.

This is the well-known structure of semi-autonomous "cells" that revolutionary movements have often used, particularly in preparation for some kind of large-scale revolution to overturn the established order. But the cell structure and its modern equivalents, such as Holacracy, make it hard to coordinate something on a bigger scale and to agree on major changes to strategy.

When such needs arise, the "invisible" or latent hierarchy usually becomes very visible and the real power-holders step into the limelight: the Lenins, the Maos, the Pol Pots. Extinction Rebellion was no exception. The triggering incident was a debate about tactics: Should XR continue with its militant approach, or should it soften its tone and negotiate with politicians? XR's founders, Gail Bradbrook and Roger Hallam, represented the militant approach, while Farhana Yamin, who headed XR's political team, called for the more pragmatic approach. Ultimately, the fundamental divide between these two positions couldn't be crossed:

> Ms. Yamin's faction was denounced as traitors. They were subjected to a "Conflict and Resolution Circle," which one insider says "was basically a hippie way of saying 'Fuck off.'" That handed more power to Mr. Hallam's group, who thought riskier actions would provoke a heavy-handed response from the state, and thus public sympathy. The group's cooler heads say they spent most of the summer of 2019 fighting madcap ideas. One, claims an insider, was to glue thousands of teenagers to London's Tube carriages at rush hour. A more restrained version led to two activists being pulled from a train roof by angry commuters. A dispute over whether to target Heathrow airport became particularly disruptive.[5]

Part of the problem was that from the beginning XR was a collection of very different groups with different aims and different views of proper tactics. It didn't have an effective way to make collective decisions, and things went off the rails when the original founders tried to assert their authority. As *The Economist* laconically observed: "XR has set up an Actions Council, which will adjudicate on internal battles. It just hasn't got around to meeting yet."[6]

In sum, having too flat an organizational structure made XR unable to act. Because it had no good way of handling its problems of cooperation, these escalated into conflict. And conflict led to members losing motivation and ability to coordinate their actions.

We see this pattern time and again with revolutionary movements, particularly those that lack leadership, clearly defined goals, and a means of coordinating to achieve longer-term goals. The "Arab Spring" protests that started in Tunisia in 2010 and rolled through Yemen, Syria, Bahrain, and Egypt—where Cairo's Tahrir Square protest gathered international headlines—were largely coordinated on the ground, from the bottom up, by activists using Facebook and other social media platforms to share plans. The protests ultimately contributed to the ouster of longtime leaders, including Muammar Gaddafi and Hosni Mubarak. And yet only in Tunisia did a constitutional, democratic government emerge to replace an autocratic state.

Of course, revolutions are complex affairs, and the organizational structure of the revolutionaries is only one factor affecting outcomes. But revolutions are not the only example of what happens when leadership and central coordination are lacking. In early 2021, a group of Reddit users worked together to drive up the share prices of GameStop, AMC, Nokia, and BlackBerry to punish Wall Street hedge funds that had heavily shorted those stocks. The "Reddit Short Squeeze" cost the big funds more than $12 billion and unleashed a torrent of lawsuits and regulatory scrutiny, but led to no fundamental changes to the trading system.[7]

Similarly, the Black Lives Matter movement, which emerged following the 2013 acquittal of George Zimmerman in the Trayvon Martin case and exploded onto the national scene in 2020 after the death of George Floyd in police custody in Minneapolis, has been plagued by internal conflict that arises in part from the lack of a formal structure. BLM is a loosely organized network of local groups led by cofounders Alicia Garza, Patrisse Cullors, and Opal Tometi, who head the Black Lives Matter Global Network Foundation, a legally incorporated 501(c)3 nonprofit connected to the Tides Foundation and affiliated with the Black Lives Matter Political Action Committee and BLM Grassroots, a network of local organizations. In 2021 Cullors stepped down from her role as executive director of the foundation over news reports about her personal wealth; her role with the broader BLM movement is unclear. According to a *Politico* report from December 2020:

> From the beginning, Black Lives Matter was a grassroots effort, born in the streets with no central hierarchy. The idea: to keep power concentrated in the hands of its members, the people.
>
> That's changing. After a summer of protests that made Black Lives Matter a household name, those atop the movement are making a series of moves to alter its power structure: organizing a political action committee, forming corporate partnerships, adding a third organizing arm and demanding an audience with President-elect Joe Biden.
>
> The moves have triggered mutiny in the ranks. Ten local chapters are severing ties with the Black Lives Matter Global Network, as the national leadership is known. They are furious that Patrisse Cullors, its remaining co-founder, assumed the role of executive director of the group and made these decisions without their input. That's a move that, to some, signaled a rebuke of its "leaderful" structure, which gave every member an equal say and kept anyone—including a founder—from overreaching.[8]

Clearly there is tension within BLM between those who want to keep it a bossless organization and those who think more structure is needed, but transitioning from the former to the latter is not an easy task. The sociologist Fabio Rojas has shown how the "black power" movement of the 1960s became institutionalized and formalized in the creation of Black studies departments in universities.[9] It remains to be seen whether BLM can follow a similar path and have lasting influence on public policy.

TOO MUCH DECENTRALIZATION IN COMPANIES

These cases suggest that in political and social movements there can be too much decentralization. Of course, how much is "too much" is not always obvious until the structure fails. The weaknesses in the organization of the US intelligence agencies became visible only in the aftermath of a massive attack, the prevention of which would have required sustained coordinated efforts between multiple agencies. The weakness of XR became clear only when decentralization resulted in the development of deep fault lines in the organization, and this caused internal conflict. BLM's challenges emerged after it became a household name and its budget shot up.

Companies are no different in this respect: they can also be too decentralized. Oticon and Zappos tried radical decentralization but went too far. More generally, the management literature is full of concerns about "silos," groups of people in companies that become insular and disconnected from the rest of the organization. Of course, some independence for operating units can be good, particularly for firms like Berkshire Hathaway that are organized as loose conglomerations of independent businesses. But most firms need a certain amount of coordination throughout the organization.

Consider this description of the problems facing Sears in 2013. Sears had adopted a decentralized structure in hopes of strengthening employee initiative. But this led to individuals and groups looking out mainly for their own interests:

> As some employees had feared, individual business units started to focus solely on their own profitability and stopped caring about the welfare of the company as a whole. According to several former executives, the apparel division cut back on labor to save money, knowing that floor salesmen in other departments would inevitably pick up the slack. Turf wars sprang up over store displays. No one was willing to make sacrifices in pricing to boost store traffic.[10]

Or consider Daimler/Chrysler, the biggest industrial merger ever. The CEO of the merged operation, Jürgen Schrempp, failed to impose common standards across the Chrysler and Daimler units. The whole argument for the merger had been achieving economies of scale, but those economies could only be achieved if common standards were adopted by the units, enabling common-platform manufacturing, a model that allows different car models to share many basic components. The platform approach, of course, can be highly advantageous, but it requires a lot of coordination. Because the merged firm lacked centralization and coordination, it failed to realize the promised economies of scale.

XR, Sears, Daimler/Chrysler, and similar organizations suffered from "coordination failure"—they could have created more value if they had persuaded more individuals and groups to work together. "Coordination" refers here to figuring out what should be done, by whom, when, how, and in what quantities to create value. Production planning and logistics are about such coordination. But so is much else that goes on within and between companies—or for that matter in households, families, and friendships.

The problem is that it is not always obvious how coordination should take place. Zoom back four or five decades. Protests were much more difficult to organize then, as people didn't have access to the digital technology that nowadays makes it quick and inexpensive to coordinate even mass gatherings literally on the spot, as witness the flash mob phenomenon or the Arab Spring protests a decade ago. It is much easier for XR and similar movements to organize events such as blocking the major London thoroughfares than it would have been in, say, the 1950s. Technology allows decentralized groups to organize to exercise what the economist John Kenneth Galbraith called "countervailing power" against large, powerful firms.[11]

Indeed, much of the case for the bossless firm is that the costs of organizing without bosses have dramatically declined. If we can all coordinate in real time via our cell phones and similar devices, why would we need a boss to tell us what to do, when to do it, and at what level? Well, it seems that in spite of easy access to state-of-the-art digital technology, the US intelligence agencies and XR still found it difficult to coordinate. So did Oticon and Zappos. Even though the costs of coordinating in real time may have declined, they certainly still exist. And coordinating a value chain or a large-scale software development effort in real time may be a much more complex undertaking than coordinating a flash mob or a protest among peers (for example, other young people or students) who are united behind a purpose or a cause.

There's another reason why coordination problems are not trivial and may persist in spite of digital technology: human psychology! A manager in production is waiting for colleagues from IT to arrive and reprogram two of the robots that are not correctly performing their operations. IT tells the manager that they are delayed because of scheduling conflicts. The production manager may get annoyed, and as the pressure on him builds, he becomes increasingly irritated. When the IT guys finally arrive, he yells at them, accusing them of tardiness. A coordination issue has caused conflict.

Or imagine that various functions in a company—for example, sales, operations, back office, logistics, and field engineering—have closely collaborated to make the purchase, delivery, and installation of a new premium fiber-optic product a seamless customer experience. The company quickly makes a reputation for handling the process in a superior way, and sales of the new product skyrocket. Management is very pleased and wants to reward the functions involved with extraordinary bonuses (to distribute among the employees). In order to distribute the awards in a fair manner, management asks the functions to report about their roles in the successful process. In response, all of the functions overreport their own effort, not because they are dishonest, but because of human psychology: we tend to systematically exaggerate our contributions to joint efforts. It is easy to see how this creates conflict: while I may unwittingly exaggerate my efforts, others may have an objective assessment of how much I contributed. If they tell me (or I find out that they told the manager) that I contributed less than I thought, I will be upset.

So even people and companies that are entirely honest and have zero intention of cheating may end up disagreeing badly and finding themselves in conflict. Moreover, conflicts have an unfortunate tendency to escalate. An important role for managers is making sure that processes are coordinated to help avoid conflict. Reducing conflict if it does emerge is another key managerial task.

In contrast, independent companies that collaborate may have a hard time reducing conflict once it starts. Taking cases to court often makes things much worse. Recent business history is crammed with incidents like the 2011 breakup of the Volkswagen-Suzuki alliance, an agreement designed to allow Suzuki to use much of Volkswagen's electric and hybrid vehicle technologies, while Suzuki would offer VW its own technologies, as well as access to the Indian market.

Sadly, the partnership quickly unraveled in a storm of disagreements and cultural differences. By October 2011, Suzuki claimed that VW had breached their contract, particularly in failing to hand over the hybrid technology. A month later, the two companies terminated their agreement to work together. When Suzuki demanded that VW return its near 20 percent stake, the German firm refused to do so. The dispute eventually went to an international arbitration court.

The disagreements over the VW-Suzuki contract, which may have reflected culturally based differences and misunderstandings, escalated into full-blown conflict, demonstrating that coordination often gets mixed up with cooperation. A key task for managers, however, is to reduce the conflict potential in such situations by means of planning, defining operating procedures and routines, and communicating.

TOO MUCH DECENTRALIZATION MAY ALSO HARM COOPERATION

Coordination problems are about getting employees to act in the best interest of the company, even if doing something slightly different would provide more personal benefit. For instance, the boss wants me to share client information with another member of the sales team, but I want to be salesperson of the month, so I keep some information to myself. To alleviate this problem the boss might try to monitor me more directly, switch from individual to group sales bonuses, or get rid of the bonus system altogether. But those remedies cause other problems. In such cases there are usually no perfect solutions, only trade-offs.

The more decentralized the firm, the greater the likelihood of these kinds of coordination problems. Worker autonomy and reliance on self-organizing teams can be highly motivating for employees and makes good use of worker-specific knowledge, but one result can be individuals and groups not working well with other individuals and groups. They may not speak the same language: there is an old joke that "PC" means "placebo control" to R&D workers, "preclinical" to the unit that deals with regulatory authorities, "personal computer" to the IT department, and "political correctness" to HR. Of course, workers and teams in different areas of the company have different educational and social backgrounds. But these differences also result from socialization—that is, gradually adopting the ways of thinking of those with whom we routinely interact. Such differences in "framing" can be a source of friction between employees and between units.

Sometimes simple rules make coordination work. In most countries, people drive on the right side of the road. In the United Kingdom and some former British colonies, people drive on the left. Neither system is inherently better or worse, but everyone better observe the same custom on the same roadway! Likewise for other social conventions that are easily stated, communicated, and understood. Red means "stop" and green means "go." Speak so others can hear you, but maintain personal space. Use English (or French, or Mandarin, or Swahili).

In other cases, either more complex, flexible, and subtle rules or norms are needed, or managers need the authority to drive coordination from the top down. As we will see in Chapter 14, successful managers know when to balance the rules-based, hands-off approach to coordination with the discretionary approach. But the mix of centralized exercise of authority and delegation changes over time as the contingencies faced by companies change. Thus, as tends to happen during times of crisis, 2020 saw a host of CEOs taking back control in various ways. Jeff Bezos "took back the wheel" by transferring in 2021 to the position of chairman of the board at Amazon, and Mark Zuckerberg did the same at Facebook (now Meta).[12] As a commentator observed: "CEOs, especially at mega-caps like Amazon, Disney, and Facebook, often delegate much of their tasks to their direct reports, teams, chiefs of staff, much like a government executive. But when things get tough, executives often retrieve the control they've ceded and take matters into their own hands."[13] So, in crises, centralization apparently overrides decentralization and organizations become more hierarchical, in the sense that more decision-making power gets concentrated at the top. Why is that?

Flat and structureless organizations get into trouble when coordination and cooperation problems proliferate. Either no one has the job of keeping these problems in check, or those few managers who do have too much to look after. Mistakes are made, unanticipated bottlenecks emerge, and scheduling conflicts pop up everywhere. Resources are wasted, and the blame game begins. Employees start mistrusting employees in other units (or their own units) and their managers. Feeling demotivated, they slack off. Productivity stalls. The sick day emails become more frequent. Also, as we argue in the next chapter, entrepreneurial and innovative activities may suffer, counterintuitive as this seems. Indeed, by supporting, enabling, and nurturing new products and services, new production methods, and entry into new markets, hierarchy can be good for innovation.

13

HIERARCHY PROMOTES INNOVATION AND ENTREPRENEURSHIP

CLAYTON CHRISTENSEN WAS AN ECONOMICS MAJOR AT BRIGHAM Young University in the early 1970s when he took time off, as is customary for Mormons, for a two-year mission. Christensen was assigned to South Korea, where he became fluent in Korean. He went on to Oxford as a Rhodes Scholar, then worked for Boston Consulting Group and in the Reagan administration after earning an MBA from Harvard. After heading a technology company he cofounded, Christensen entered Harvard Business School's doctoral program and would write a dissertation on the disk drive industry.

Christensen noticed that each successive innovation in disk drives—accompanied by dramatic increases in the amount of data that could be stored on disks—came not from the big, established companies but from smaller, newer firms. Christensen termed this phenomenon "the innovator's dilemma" and argued that the incumbent firms missed opportunities to innovate because they were focused on their best customers, those who demanded the highest level of performance, and failed to notice that simpler, cheaper technologies could deliver more bang for the buck.

Christensen, after joining the Harvard faculty, generalized his idea to a variety of industries and published it in 1997 as *The Innovator's Dilemma: When New Technologies Cause Great Firms to Fail*, which became one of the most famous business books of the last twenty-five years.[1]

Christensen's book popularized the notion of "disruptive" innovation—a new technology or production method that not only brings new products to market but also disrupts the structure of the industry, such that the dominant firms are supplanted by new entrants. (Disruptive innovation is distinguished from "sustaining innovations," which leave the existing structure of the market intact.) The basic point, which has been the subject of much recent controversy, is straightforward: large, established companies are focused on improving their offerings for specific customers—namely, the most demanding, whose business is critical for the company's profitability.[2] These companies thus overlook segments of the market where customers value price or ease of use or simplicity over performance. These segments can be targeted by small entrants offering sufficient functionality at a lower price. The established players tend to ignore these entrants until the latter have moved upmarket and begun delivering performance across different segments, maybe even forcing incumbents to adopt the entrants' offerings. This is disruption. As Christensen puts it:

> Generally, disruptive innovations were technologically straightforward, consisting of off-the-shelf components put together in a product architecture that was often simpler than prior approaches. They offered less of what customers in established markets wanted and so could rarely be initially employed there. They offered a different package of attributes valued only in emerging markets remote from, and unimportant to, the mainstream.[3]

Think of the Model T Ford, which was cheaper and easier to maintain than the other cars on the market in 1908; it filled a niche and was a roaring success, even though the customer could have it in any color he wanted—as long as that was black. The desktop PC was much less powerful and could perform fewer tasks than the mainframe and minicomputers that dominated the business world in the late 1970s and early 1980s, but it was easy to use, much less expensive, and good enough to perform routine office tasks—leading to huge wins for Microsoft, Intel, Dell, Compaq, and other PC hardware and software providers at the expense of DEC, Data General, Wang, and Honeywell. The first digital music players and their MP3 files were much worse than vinyl records at reproducing sound, but you could hold a thousand songs in your pocket, helping the iPod (and its even more transformative successor, the iPhone) and digital music platforms to eventually revolutionize the music industry.

CAN LARGE FIRMS INNOVATE?

Christensen shows how incumbents, by focusing on their currently most profitable customers, often miss opportunities to invest in new technologies, markets, and sectors. Rather than say that incumbents cannot innovate, however, or that all industries are ripe for disruption, he holds that disruption occurs only where certain conditions hold. Nevertheless, in our classes for executives, we have seen that Christensen's theory is widely misunderstood as a general theory of how established firms fail to react to competitive threats from innovation. That's not too surprising, because this more general story is part of management folklore. It is repeated over and over again in the business magazines and by the gurus and consultants. The story goes roughly like this.

Established hierarchical firms are so caught up in their successful past that they lose sight of new and profitable business ideas. They have cadres of middle managers whose main jobs seem to be suppressing new ideas, perhaps via "killer acquisitions" intended to keep the target company from introducing innovations that would threaten the established firm.[4] Job descriptions are narrow so that employees will focus on simple functions and small goals. The established companies lack systems to monitor their internal and external environments and soak up the good ideas that may become successful innovations.

According to this story, big companies produce mediocre innovations or stop innovating at all. Think of the Oakley Thump sunglasses with a built-in MP3 player: fragile, ugly, with poor sound quality, this product started at $400 when launched in 2004. Or the 2002 Smith & Wesson attempt to produce . . . a bike. Remember the bizarrely styled Pontiac Aztec? Razor's exploding Hoverboards? Barnes & Noble's Nook, designed to take on Amazon's Kindle? Or Microsoft's attempted iPod killer, the Zune? And everyone knows the story of Kodak failing to capture the market for digital cameras, a favorite cautionary tale expounded in any MBA strategy or innovation class.

The overall message is that rigid procedures, stifling bureaucracy, meddling middle managers, and executives without vision kill creativity, knowledge-sharing, freedom, and spontaneity, and with them corporate innovation, leaving the scene open for small, agile companies that are typically upstarts with flat hierarchies. Or so they say.

This message that we have all heard many times is another example of building a narrative around some cherry-picked, high-profile examples. It's the mantra of proponents of the bossless company narrative who bash corporate hierarchy for its alleged hostility to entrepreneurship and innovation.

Consider "Unit X," part of a big company dedicated to making "moonshot" attempts to solve humanity's great problems by inventing radical new technologies. Unit X runs on bottom-up management principles and is organized very much like bossless companies such as Valve. It is freewheeling and anarchistic. A manager holds the title of "Head of Getting Moonshots Ready for Contact with the Real World."

The projects that Unit X has been involved in (typically in the initial stages) include storing electricity in molten salt, creating contact lenses for diabetics that track glucose levels, and producing delivery drones. Unit X also considered constructing a giant copper ring around the North Pole in order to produce electricity by exploiting the magnetic field. Although this idea was abandoned, there are other Unit X products that you probably use every day. Have you searched for something on the internet? Have you needed something translated? Then you were using technology that originated in Unit X.

Unit X, as you may have guessed by now, is real: Unit X is Google's "X" division for radical innovation. It represents an important counter to the narrative that big companies can't be innovative. Moreover, many of the world's biggest companies—not just Big Tech—are also highly innovative. Go back almost a century, to 1924, when AT&T and Western Electric founded Bell Labs, their R&D factory for telecom that developed the first transistors, lasers, and photovoltaic cells. Bell Labs held more than seventeen thousand patents and its scientists won nine Nobel Prizes for work carried out there. As Jon Gertner puts it in his 2012 book *The Idea Factory*: "For a long stretch of the twentieth century, Bell Labs was the most innovative scientific organization in the world. It was arguably among the world's most important commercial organizations as well, with countless entrepreneurs building their businesses upon the Labs' foundational innovations."[5]

The top tech companies all have corporate research labs, and Google has many, including Google AI (formerly Google Research), Robotics at Google, and Advanced Technologies and Projects.[6]

Hierarchy, then, can be the friend, not the enemy, of innovation. A recent example is the rapid development of Covid-19 vaccines by Pfizer and Johnson & Johnson, two big players in the pharmaceutical industry, as well as by newcomer Moderna. These vaccines made use of publicly funded research, and of course these companies and many others around the world were directly paid by governments to develop the vaccines. Without the well-oiled innovation machines of the big players, however, the actual development, production, and distribution of the vaccines would probably have been much slower.

But what if big, hierarchical companies became innovative simply by acquiring smaller companies with flatter structures? After all, corporate history is full of examples of more traditional companies acquiring leaner, supposedly more innovative upstart companies in their industries. When biotech began to produce real advances in the mid-1970s and the prospects of biotechnological manufacturing of pharmaceutical products became a distinct possibility, Big Pharma took an interest.

Acquisitions or equity stakes might look like an alternative to innovating. Why would a company develop its own biotech research capabilities when it could just wait for a smaller firm to do it, then buy it up? For example, in 1990 Hoffman-LaRoche (now Roche) acquired a majority stake in Genentech, the pioneer company founded in 1976 by venture capitalist Robert Swanson and biochemist Herbert Boyer. If you look closely, you see that this kind of acquisition wasn't designed just to gain control of a product or technology or to eliminate a competitor, but to access the target company's knowledge and capabilities.

In a 2012 email to Facebook CFO David Ebersman (revealed in an antitrust hearing), CEO Mark Zuckerberg explained his strategy for acquiring newer, smaller companies like Instagram (which subsequently became a Facebook subsidiary):

> I didn't mean to imply that we'd be buying them to prevent them from competing with us in any way. Buying them would give us the people and time to incorporate their innovations into our core products, which is how we'd do the integration rather than actually combining the products. I'm mostly excited about what the companies could do together if we worked to build what they've invented into more people's experiences.[7]

In other words, even if a smaller company is acquired for its innovative products or technologies and is run as a stand-alone business unit (a "greenfield" operation), the acquiring company can still integrate its knowledge and capabilities. That's one of the benefits of hierarchy: authority can be delegated and (limited) autonomy given to subunits, while the responsibility for firmwide coordination and cooperation is retained. Setting up special subunits with unique responsibilities is a feature, not a bug, of hierarchy.

How does hierarchy enable creativity, risk-taking, and innovation? Let's take a closer look.

IS SMALL BEAUTIFUL? AND BIG UGLY?

The brilliant economist and social critic Joseph Schumpeter thought only large, successful firms could afford the R&D necessary to bring new goods and services to market. The bossless company narrative claims just the opposite—that managerial hierarchies stymie innovation. Cheaper, more modular, and more flexible innovation strategies supposedly have little need for hierarchy anyway; as we noted, Clayton Christensen's idea of the "innovator's dilemma" is widely interpreted as a general explanation for how large, dominant incumbents systematically miss innovation opportunities available to smaller, newer entrants.

It is also true that a lot of the research on entrepreneurship, innovation, and established hierarchical firms emphasizes the *difficulties* faced by these firms in being entrepreneurial. One line of research looks at rewards. There is now much more variation in pay between companies and within companies than there was a few decades ago. Still, big companies with salaried employees may find it difficult to replicate the strong incentives of a start-up, where success or failure depends on innovation.

What can go wrong in big companies? Imagine you're a research scientist in the lab of a major pharma company. You get a bright idea on how to use artificial intelligence to sift through a huge class of molecules to find one that could launch drug development directed at a particular disease.

You know that cracking this problem will lead to a big bonus or promotion. There is a lot of talk about a "crisis" in drug discovery and development as the pace of innovation has slowed. (The number of "new molecular entities" approved by the US Food and Drug Administration's Center for Drug Evaluation and Research has steadily declined over the last few decades, though the pace has picked up in the last couple of years.[8]) Big Pharma is very interested in new promising ideas, so you can expect a nice reward if you find a valuable new molecule.

But you also know that breakthrough drugs are worth billions; Pfizer's cholesterol-fighting Lipitor has earned about $150 billion, and the arthritis medicine Humira generated more than $100 billion for AbbVie, with $20 billion coming in just one year (2019). Your bonus, no matter how generous, will be just a tiny fraction of the value you help create. Will it be worth the effort?

Even if your supervisor wants to be generous, managers know that giving some employees very large rewards can make other employees envious. Hierarchies tend to "compress" wages by overpaying low performers and underpaying high performers, relative to what they are worth, to keep everyone happy, especially when workers can easily compare their jobs and pay.[9] This pay system can be demotivating. If an employee feels unappreciated and under-rewarded, they may react by leaving—"spinning off" their own company and taking their knowledge (and perhaps a few key coworkers) with them. By running their own company, they appropriate the profit stream from the idea they first explored at the company they left.

Other research suggests that innovativeness declines because of top managers' cognitive blinders, which make them miss threats in the environment. The Canadian strategy professor Danny Miller captured this point by coining the notion of the "Icarus Paradox."[10] In Greek mythology, Icarus was the son of Daedalus, who built the Labyrinth for King Minos of Crete. (Its function was to contain the monstrous Minotaur, but that is a different story.) To escape from Crete, Daedalus built wings using feathers and wax. That was a great innovation! But Daedalus warned Icarus of the dangers of complacency and hubris. Complacency would lead him to fly too low, where the sea's dampness might clog the wings. Hubris, on the other hand, might encourage Icarus to fly too high and get too close to the sun, which would melt the wax in the wings. Icarus ignored his father's warnings and in his hubris did fly too close to the sun. The wax in the wings melted, and Icarus dropped to his death in the sea. Successful companies similarly fail *because* of their past successes, which engender overconfidence and thus produce hubris as well as complacency.

Everyone knows about Tupperware, the high-quality plastic food containers for keeping leftovers organized in your fridge (and other uses, such as in birdbaths, first aid kits, and so on). Old-timers will remember those pastel-colored retro ads with slogans like "When you lock in freshness, you set yourself free" (aka "The Tupperware Promise"). Tupperware was created after World War II by Earl Tupper when DuPont asked him to explore peacetime uses for plastic. Working at a plastic factory after his landscaping business had been hit by the Great Depression, Tupper had been tinkering with plastic molding machines and working on improving plastic containers. The first commercially viable product was the

Wonderbowl with its "burp seal" (which would be featured in a *Seinfeld* episode as the thing that "locked in freshness").

Initially, Tupperware didn't sell well in stores, so Tupper devised an alternative marketing and sales channel: the Tupperware party. Tupperware parties may seem like part of the gray flannel suit era (early on, the strict dress code for Tupperware ladies included white gloves), yet they are very much a thing of the present. More than half a million such parties are held each year in France (of all places) alone.[11]

Despite its presence in kitchens around the world, Tupperware has been in trouble for decades. Global sales have been declining, and share prices dropped from $90 in 2013 to $3 in 2020.[12] The reasons? Plastic is increasingly seen as a health risk. Some plastics have been shown to have hormone-mimicking properties, and some have been linked to cancer risks. Tupperware has also been under fire from certain parts of the feminist movement that see it as a gendered product that caters to traditional stereotypes about women. The lightweight, practical plastic containers made homemaking easier and helped provide work for many women (the Tupperware sales reps), but they carry a certain stigma. Tupperware managers were so enamored with the product that they failed to see these threats: the Icarus Paradox at work! (Tupperware's various diversification moves—into cosmetics, for instance—do not appear to have been successful.)

Another challenge for successful firms trying to stay ahead of the competition by innovating is that they are run by professional managers, not by the engineers or inventors (those with the deep knowledge), nor even, usually, by the founders (those with the greatest passion and commitment to the core products and services). In a diversified firm, the top executives may know little about the day-to-day operations of the subsidiaries and the details of each market. They are also subject to the whims of investors and stock analysts and beholden to the quarterly earnings report. R&D is a big expense that can hurt the short-term bottom line, even while promising big gains down the road. The discipline of public capital markets can make these managers "myopic," in that they may see only the short-term costs and miss the longer-term potential of innovation. Indeed, one of us (Klein, writing with Professor Robert Wuebker) has provided some evidence that large, diversified firms do less R&D than smaller, more specialized, but otherwise similar competitors.[13]

Thus, it is not really surprising that what we might call the "small firm effect" has a strong grip on the imagination. This is the idea that smaller firms, often start-ups, are disproportionately more entrepreneurial and innovative than larger firms.[14] Pundits and commentators will sometimes point to research that looks at the links between firm size and R&D. The empirical evidence is mixed: under some circumstances, smaller firms have higher average ratios of R&D sales, but the pattern is not consistent.

Many people think that traditionally organized, vertically integrated, heavily diversified firms like GE, the Big Auto companies, the Big Tobacco companies, and so on, may have once served a valuable purpose: they cranked out enormous amounts of mass-produced physical goods for a mass market at low cost. But we now have a knowledge-based economy in which services dominate and customization and specialized products are key. In such an economy, maintaining competitive advantage requires constant innovation, and the traditional hierarchy isn't good at this. Throw into this argument firms like Kodak that failed to discover the next best thing and the case seems compelling: hierarchy is bad for innovation. The best that big companies can do, supposedly, is to try not to kill innovations by maintaining a hands-off approach and letting new ideas emerge from below, as with Oticon's spaghetti organization style, or by setting up an autonomous innovation unit like Google's X. Unfortunately, according to this argument, such approaches are usually unstable. Eventually senior managers become too strongly tempted to intervene and meddle, and then innovation dies.

The kernel of truth in this narrative is that many important recent technological breakthroughs were made by outsiders, either start-ups or firms new to the industry. Apple in its first two decades was the quintessential disruptive start-up. In creating one of the first mainstream and popular personal computers and the first commercially successful graphical user interface, cofounders Steve Jobs and Steve Wozniak and a handful of employees outcompeted large mainframe and minicomputer companies. As iTunes and the iPod revolutionized the music industry and the iPhone revolutionized mobile telephony, Apple of the 2000s exemplified the successful firm moving into new industries that were far removed from its core business.

Think also of some other very different, but extremely influential, innovations: strobe lights, the zipper, the defibrillator, high-resolution digital X-ray, the helicopter, the safety razor, continuous casting, biomagnetic imaging, the hydraulic brake, prestressed concrete, the solid-fuel rocket engine, the optical scanner, and the pacemaker. All came from small firms, many of them start-ups. So this list settles it, right?

Not quite. Many other important innovations came from large firms: containerized shipping (Sea-Land Shipping), laser printing (Xerox), smartphones (Apple), the multidivisional corporate structure (DuPont), the transistor (Bell Labs/ATT), digital cameras (Kodak), protease inhibitors (Merck and Abbott Labs), plasma screens (Fujitsu), hybrid cars (Toyota), the electric guitar (Gibson), Pyrex (Corning), voice recognition (IBM), disposable diapers (Procter & Gamble), alkaline batteries (Union Carbide), electronic hearing aids (Siemens), the ballpoint pen (Eversharp), and the jet engine (Messerschmitt). These game-changers all came from the big incumbents. And they weren't all the work of autonomous units and bottom-up processes (the proverbial "skunkworks" carried out by visionary engineers and scientists); many were championed specifically by top management. Classic examples are Thomas Watson Jr.'s involvement in IBM's development of the 360 system and the very direct involvement of Steve Jobs in many of Apple's innovation initiatives.

These are just stories, right? Can we say anything more systematically? We can. The University of Sussex has long maintained one of the top research programs on the history of innovation. The economist Bruce Tether examined innovation data held by the university to see what kinds of firms produce what kinds of innovations. He found that, while smaller firms produced more innovations per capita than larger ones, the larger firms tended to produce the more valuable innovations. If the goal of innovation programs is quality, not quantity, then large firms are more than holding their own.[15] Another study looked at a large number of radical innovations in the consumer durables and office products categories and found that in the United States more of these innovations came from large firms than from smaller firms; though the reverse was true in western Europe and Japan, the study cast doubt overall on the idea of a general "incumbent's curse."[16]

In sum, the empirical evidence is nuanced. Big, hierarchical firms are sometimes more innovative than smaller, flatter firms, but not always. Context matters.

HOW HIERARCHY HANDLES INNOVATION

If big, successful companies tend to rest on their laurels, are reluctant to disturb their existing product lines and revenue streams, and are less "hungry" than upstart outsiders with nothing to lose, how can they use innovation to stay ahead of the competition?

To answer that question, let's think systematically about innovation and start by noting that innovation comes in many forms. Joseph Schumpeter distinguished five types of innovation: introducing a new good or a new quality of a good (say, the iPhone); introducing a new method of production (Henry Ford's assembly line); opening a new market (Japanese electronics entering the United States and European markets in the 1960s); establishing a new source of supply (global manufacturing moving to China); or reorganizing an industry (the consolidation of oil markets by John D. Rockefeller Jr. or Andrew Carnegie's reorganization of the steel industry).

Schumpeter emphasizes that innovation is a *value* concept—that is, it relates to products or processes that create economic value—and is thus different from invention, an engineering concept that results in a new gadget. In other words, innovation is simply the actual, "practical" implementation of new ideas relating to products, processes, and ways of organizing. When we use the word to talk about what companies do, we mean that the purpose of implementing a new product, process, or way of organizing is to create (and appropriate) more value.

Researchers have made important strides in characterizing different types of innovation. There is Clay Christensen's distinction between sustaining and disruptive innovation. We can also contrast incremental innovation (say, going from the iPhone 12 to the iPhone 13 and its slightly better processor, brighter screen, and greater memory) and systemic innovation (going from flip phones and monochrome BlackBerrys to the first iPhone with its full-screen color display, touch interface, and App Store). Innovations sometimes diffuse very rapidly, starting with a few early adopters and then cascading rapidly until the entire market is penetrated. For example, color TV was introduced in the United States around 1960, and by 1965 about 5 percent of US households had a color TV. By 1975, that number had leaped to nearly 70 percent. Microwave ovens, cell phones, personal computers, and household internet access show similar patterns. By contrast, older innovations like the automobile, the telephone, electricity, and electric refrigeration took much longer to penetrate the majority of US households.

But how do we measure the *amount* of innovation in an industry or society? How do we judge the innovativeness of a given company? Examples such as those cited here seem like cherry-picking. More systematically, we can try to count new product introductions by different types of firms and in different industries, but it's hard to standardize these measures across contexts. Researchers have therefore focused on things we *can* measure, such as R&D expenditures (an input into innovation) and patents (an output of innovation). Unfortunately, these are not perfect measures, and no clear and consistent picture emerges from the data of whether large firms or small firms, established firms or new firms, hierarchical firms or flat firms, invest more in R&D or do more and better patenting. Contrary to popular opinion, when we look across the whole range of companies and industries, there is no clear evidence that larger firms, more established firms, or more hierarchical firms are less innovative, on average, then their smaller, newer, more often bossless competitors.

What does seem to matter is the *organization* of the hierarchy. As one of us (Klein) argued in a paper with management professors Mark Packard and Karen Schnatterly, managers can promote innovation through *sponsorship* (providing resources and "project champions" for innovations developed at lower levels), *autonomy* (giving employees the latitude to experiment and innovate), and *incentives* (rewarding employees for coming up with useful innovations).[17]

Consider W. L. Gore, a company that encourages innovation from the bottom up and has a system characterized by strong incentives, high levels of autonomy, and informal sponsorship. Gore encourages its engineers to experiment by providing "dabble time"—a half-day per week dedicated to the pursuit of ideas of employees' own choosing. The compensation system offers strong incentives for innovation through equity- and innovation-based bonuses.[18]

Apple, by contrast, uses a top-down system for generating innovative ideas and developing new products and services, offers few incentives for innovation and little autonomy, and requires formal sponsorship of innovation projects. Top management evaluates all potential projects, rejecting most. As Steve Jobs once explained, innovation "comes from saying no to 1,000 things to make sure we don't get on the wrong track or try to do too much."[19] Apple tries to encourage a general culture of creativity without providing specific incentives for employee innovation. Despite this hierarchical structure, no one would accuse Apple of not being an innovative company!

Both Gore's bottom-up and Apple's top-down approaches have been very effective. Apple relies more on central coordination because its products and services share common hardware and software components and are part of an integrated "ecosystem." (For example, the iPhone contains proprietary Apple hardware, runs Apple's iOS operating system, connects to Apple's App Store, Apple Music, and Apple TV, and so on.) Gore, by contrast, has a more modular, independent portfolio of projects.

Another interesting finding from the research literature is that R&D drawing heavily on advanced science tends to be concentrated at the top of the corporate hierarchy (such as in a company-level research facility), while R&D in more mundane areas tends to be conducted in labs housed at lower-level divisions of a company.[20] This "hierarchical" approach to R&D tends to be taken in companies that focus on narrow business areas and in companies whose complex technologies may require a hierarchy to keep track of what is going on. This research also finds that more decentralized companies tend to invest less in R&D and to achieve lower R&D productivity.[21]

Centralizing R&D can make it easier to coordinate R&D efforts, leading to higher returns to R&D. Also, it is easier for a company with R&D personnel concentrated in one unit to specialize. One R&D employee or a team of such employees can focus on exploring one line of science or technology, while another team explores a different line. This is more difficult when R&D is spread thin across many units in the company.

An advantage of hierarchy is that it can structure innovation processes appropriately, according to these characteristics. For example, to what extent are highly specialized R&D workers required because the company's R&D relies on advanced scientific discovery? In some cases (as with Gore), top managers may choose to be less directly involved—but they can make that choice.

THE ROLE OF MANAGERS

How much do top managers influence innovation and entrepreneurship, and how does it matter? Consider Intel, the Santa Clara, California, tech company founded in 1968 by Gordon Moore (one of whose claims to fame is Moore's Law—the idea that the number of transistors per chip will double every year) and Robert Noyce (co-inventor of the integrated circuit). The company was managed for a long time by Andy Grove, who turned Intel into the world's largest semiconductor company. Intel is organized into largely autonomous units organized as product divisions. Like many product-based companies, Intel also makes use of a matrix model and cross-functional teams.

One of the world's foremost experts on Intel is the Stanford Business School professor Robert Burgelman, an authority on technology management and strategy. Burgelman has studied the interplay at Intel between management decisions at various levels and the firm's overall strategy.[22] Usually a strategy process goes like this: Top management, assisted by heavyweight consultants and in dialogue with the board of directors and representatives of major stakeholder groups, devises a strategy for the company as a whole. That strategy highlights the central business areas of the company, how the company will strengthen its position in core markets (or, occasionally, how it will leave some of them), and which new business areas the company will grow and how. The strategy is then implemented and executed.

Of course, we know that it doesn't always work out this way. There is often a huge distance between the originally planned strategy, the revised strategy that emerges over time, and what is implemented in the end. All sorts of things happen that weren't anticipated—not just the major, potentially disastrous events that Nassim Taleb calls "black swans" but also mundane changes in consumer demand, competitor reactions, and regulation.[23] In the mid-1980s, Federal Express wanted to add a new layer to its core business area of package delivery. It developed ZapMail, a new internal service for sending documents within FedEx using fax machines. The printed documents would then be delivered to customers, drastically reducing delivery time. Though sound, the reasoning failed to take a critical contingency into account: more and more businesses and individuals were buying fax machines, eliminating the potential market that FedEx had imagined.[24]

Emergent strategy that deviates from intended strategy may also lead to positive outcomes. The 2010 movie about Facebook's origins, *The Social Network*, shows that Zuckerberg's original intended strategy for Facebook (rather, "Facemash")—showcasing various female Harvard students and allowing viewers to vote on their attractiveness—was rather different from the strategy that quickly emerged of developing the site into an open global social network.

Strategies, no matter how carefully designed, are road maps to destinations we have never visited, over territory that has not been carefully explored. Moreover, Burgelman teaches us something even more important: strategy doesn't necessarily come from the top. Sometimes it emerges organically, from the bottom up.

Intel had already created the first commercial microprocessor chip in 1971, but there wasn't much of a market for it. Personal computers barely existed; they were beginning to emerge as hobbyist kits around the mid-1970s and wouldn't take off commercially until the 1980s. Intel's main business areas in the 1970s were SRAM and DRAM memory chips. In the 1990s, Intel changed its main business area to microprocessors, a move in response to the heavy growth of the computer industry, particularly in personal computers. Did this happen because Intel's top management observed that memory chips were becoming commodities and that microprocessors were going to be the high-growth, high-value-added product, and thus they made the strategic decision to switch corporate resources from memory circuits to microprocessors?

According to Burgelman, not really. When he examined the details of Intel's strategic moves in the first part of the 1980s, he found that most new strategic initiatives emerged, not from the upper echelons, but from midlevel managers. Because top managers were too far away from the real action, they continued to consider Intel a memory company, even when Intel's market share in memory was in steep decline. However, Intel had cultivated a strong, decentralized innovation culture that empowered middle management to invest in innovative products without seeking explicit executive consent—in other words, they followed the bottom-up model employed by Gore, not the top-down model favored by Apple. Midlevel managers, observing declining sales of memory circuits, realized that the firm's competences in circuit design and process technology design could be transferred to microprocessors, a market that Intel had already pioneered and had never entirely left. As a consequence, Intel exited the memory business in 1984—a strategic move that came across as almost a fait accompli when top managers realized what was going on!

Burgelman's account features a strong narrative, a surprising outcome, well-known characters, and the underdogs prevailing. It has been extremely influential in our thinking about how strategy and technology are intertwined with managerial decisions. Along with Henry Mintzberg's many influential writings on strategy processes, Burgelman's analysis implies that companies should empower middle managers to design and implement innovation programs and processes, while encouraging top managers to adopt a hands-off approach.

Burgelman's account is not exactly part of the bossless company narrative; after all, some bosses, namely midlevel managers, are useful in this telling. But Burgelman is skeptical about the role of top managers in the creative process and suggests that members of the C-suite, lacking the right knowledge to get involved in innovation processes, should stay out of them and leave the innovating to better-equipped employees. (The bossless company narrative generalizes this model to virtually any function in the company, not just innovation.)

In conducting research with the leading strategy thinker Jay Barney and Jacob Lyngsie, a Danish management professor, one of us (Foss) recently contested this line of thinking.[25] First, we noted how integral the belief in the superiority of bottom-up innovation has become in the bossless company narrative. Second, as part of the general emphasis on diversity in contemporary business discussions, everybody seems to agree that diversity is also good for innovation.

Consider the facility service management giant ISS, a Danish firm. ISS employs around four hundred thousand employees in more than forty countries. Employees have very diverse backgrounds, and many are immigrants. Maarten Van Engeland, who served as CEO of ISS until recently, says that employee diversity in terms of age, gender, and cultural background "pays," based on an analysis of ISS employee surveys linked to data for team performance. The idea is a familiar one: the greater ability (up to a point) of diverse teams to identify and handle problems leads to many innovative improvements, small as well as large.[26]

While much of the discussion has been on issues of racial, gender, and cultural diversity, education is often also invoked, particularly in the case of innovation. Remember all the buzz around fifteen years ago about the "creative class"?[27] The urban planning guru and professor Richard Florida claimed that big vibrant cities with high levels and many types of creative, highly educated professionals and, of course, "bohemians" show particularly high levels of innovation dynamism and development. That was a very pleasing message, particularly for anyone who was a mayor, a well-educated professional, or a high bohemian. Florida sold a lot of books.

But here is the thing: We have both worked as a middle manager in the role of head of a department in a university, a type of organization that is based on a particular kind of creative class, namely academics. We are both also in the business of innovation (thought innovations). Knowledge workers in academia aren't the easiest people to manage. The prima donna syndrome is rampant, and conflicts erupt continuously (because, as Woodrow Wilson, Henry Kissinger, and Wallace Sayre have been variously credited with saying, "academic politics is the most vicious and bitter form of politics, because the stakes are so low").

Universities are based (or, some would say, *were* based) on the idea of diversity and a high degree of autonomy. But they are also messy places. Their outputs are usually not bought and sold in a marketplace. Many key employees have lifetime tenure. In other words, it takes more than having highly creative personnel to create an innovative culture—it takes the right organizational structure and effective management as well.

To find how bottom-up processes and diversity are associated with innovation, Barney, Foss, and Lyngsie's research included an analysis of a big data set with information about employees and firms in Denmark.[28] They found that innovation gets a boost when employees have highly diverse educational backgrounds. This makes sense because differences in education are likely to cause employees to look at the business and what it is doing in different ways. Cognitive diversity can be good for identifying and solving problems and for coming up with innovative solutions. But the boost from educational diversity isn't that big. The same is true with bottom-up initiative: giving lower-level managers the right to engage in innovative activities does boost innovativeness. But when we also consider the influence of top managers on the innovation process, something happens: in companies where there is much diversity and where lower-level managers are encouraged to take initiatives that relate to innovation, the impact on innovation is much bigger when top management is *also* involved in the innovation process—for example, when top managers supply overall ideas and set the direction.

In other words, empowerment, bottom-up initiative, and diversity can be good for innovation and creativity—but they need to be shaped, channeled, and pruned by a managerial hierarchy. From one perspective, this finding isn't surprising. When people are really different—say, in terms of education—they can find it hard to communicate with each other and to coordinate their efforts. Similarly, if there is too much emphasis on bottom-up processes, coordination typically suffers, as we argued in the previous chapter. Thus, innovation calls for management and hierarchy. But there is also a more subtle reason why some higher-level control is needed when innovation processes are characterized by bottom-up initiative and diversity.

The Oticon spaghetti organization became too successful in terms of idea generation—in the sense that it generated significantly more ideas than it could implement. The result may sound like an embarrassment of riches, but it isn't. Specifically, with a lot of ideas to choose from and limited resources, management has to select those ideas it believes in. But employees (say, R&D scientists) are likely to work harder and smarter when they have some assurance that their ideas will be approved and pursued. Say you're told to develop a specific new solution to a quality or reliability problem with the firm's core product. If there is no overall direction and almost anything goes at your company, you're likely to worry that your project will be rejected by management for further development, or that company priorities will change to emphasize scale and discounting over quality and reliability. You may spend a lot of time and effort on a project that gets sidelined or abandoned, perhaps without explanation. Such an outcome would clearly be demotivating.

Therefore, employees like to have some overall direction issued when assigned tasks. Of course, this is what managers, and in particular top managers, do. By establishing the rules of the game—even in the innovation space—by either describing particular areas to pursue or clearly defining innovation paths, managers can give confidence to those considering how much time and effort to invest in innovation.

Even smaller, entrepreneurial firms can benefit from a managerial hierarchy. Recent research examined a large number of German technology start-ups and found that firms with middle managers are more innovative than those with flatter structures, even though the former are more "bureaucratic."[29] The reason is straightforward: by delegating routine tasks to middle managers, founders can focus on innovation and long-term strategy. A well-designed hierarchy is a way of distributing specialized, yet complementary, tasks across a team. Why should everyone do everything?

EXPLOITING AND EXPLORING

Hierarchy also helps us avoid too much innovation. What, you say? How can a firm ever be too innovative? It happens. Oticon, for example, was working on so many novel projects at one point that employees got frustrated. And there is a more general problem with innovation: managers control what they put in, but not what comes out.

Remember that the purpose of the firm (its commercial purpose, anyway) is to create and capture economic value. Innovation is a key to creating and capturing more value in the long run, though it sometimes puts short-term profitability at risk. But remember that managers don't control the *outputs* of innovation; they control the *inputs*. Think of a master baker, someone with extraordinary skill at cake design and considerable knowledge of ingredients and baking techniques. Most of the time her desserts are delicious, but every once in a while even the master baker, just like the home cook, creates a culinary disaster. Maybe an ingredient was bad. Or she made a mistake in measuring or left the cake in the oven a tiny bit too long. Maybe the recipe just wasn't right. Many of us enjoy watching competitive cooking and baking shows on TV just to see that even the experts can make mistakes.

The point is that managers have to decide how much to invest in innovation, which innovation projects to support, how to motivate R&D workers, and how to handle the interdependencies that typically arise between R&D projects (for example, allocating the efforts of R&D workers across projects and sharing results from one project that may be useful in another). Despite their best efforts, managers cannot guarantee that everything will work. Naturally, most firms invest in a diversified portfolio of innovation projects to manage this risk. But they also have to make sure that, in pursuing new and creative products and business models, they don't impair what the company already does well. They have to make sure that current activities aren't disrupted too heavily in pursuit of the new and cool; no matter how attractive the two birds in the bush may be, the one in the hand still matters.

Consider Spotify, the Swedish streaming giant we met in Chapter 5. It excels at listening to customers and executing operations and is engaged in constant improvement, while also taking on major innovation projects. In short, it seems to just be good at *everything* a technology company does! If you think this is an unrealistic model for most companies, we agree. Companies cannot be good at everything, nor should they try to be.

To create value and outperform the competition, you need to be good at managing your current processes and assets, such as production, logistics, marketing, and workforce. For example, the toy producer Lego stresses the need to maintain and develop its current operating model, including improving its value chain organization, responding to demand, and interfacing with its user communities. This ongoing work is necessary to keep the business humming and avoiding unnecessary risk. Lego's top management also has its eye on the long run, however, including developing new markets, for example, in China, and expanding its digital business.[30]

Innovative initiatives require patience, new thinking, and a willingness to deal with deeper uncertainties if they are to become the sources of future value creation. If a company doesn't engage in the fundamental activities of both "exploitation" (the mundane and predictable activities associated with execution) and "exploration" (the forays into the unknown associated with creativity, ideation, and innovation), its future survival is in jeopardy. Maintaining inventory, keeping the books, monitoring the production line, and managing typical employee concerns are exploitation activities, while R&D, new product and market development, restructuring, and long-range planning are exploratory activities that promise high rewards but also come with substantial risks. Some forms of innovation—like coming up with a new version of the iPhone with a faster processor, more memory, a larger display, and a better camera—are exploitation activities. The introduction of the first iPhone, along with the App Store, exclusive wireless deals with carriers in various countries, and other elements of the iOS ecosystem (or, as its detractors call it, "Steve's Walled Garden"), are exploration.

Doing both exploitation and exploration well is difficult, and doing both well at the same time is exceedingly difficult. They require different management approaches, build on different capabilities, and use different resources. Stanford professor Charles O'Reilly and Harvard Business School's Michael Tushman introduced the term "ambidexterity" to describe doing exploitation and exploration simultaneously; they argue that successful ambidextrous organizations put their exploratory activities into separate business units that are integrated into the overall company but structurally independent.[31] Oticon's spaghetti organization model seemed to work, at least in the short term, in making Oticon a more innovative company. But in pursuing exploration, CEO Lars Kolind lost focus on exploitation and, as we noted earlier, the company's innovation pipeline—its queue of promising ideas for new products and services in need of further development—became so long that the rest of the organization couldn't keep pace.

In short, someone needs to make sure the company achieves the right *balance* between exploration and exploitation. Spontaneous, bottom-up processes are great for idea generation, and great projects will often emerge. But messy, unstructured processes are not so good at ensuring that resources and effort are well allocated between creative processes and the more mundane activities of producing and selling.

Ambidextrous companies keep the balance by splitting off a dedicated innovation unit focused exclusively on exploration, while the rest of the firm goes about its routine exploitation activities. This is harder to achieve in smaller firms and firms in which the innovative and routine tasks and projects are highly interdependent and complementary. But even here, a well-designed managerial hierarchy can help achieve that balance.

To be sure, if firms are to innovate and stay ahead of the competition, they need employees who are creative, who take initiative, and who aren't afraid to "roll the dice" with crazy ideas. But innovation is not just a matter of having the right people. Innovators need resources, financial support, encouragement, and a project champion. Lone entrepreneurs and start-up teams get this kind of support from funders, advisers, and partners. (Even without a professional angel investor or venture capital firm, entrepreneurs need someone, if only the "three Fs" of friends, family, and fools.)

In many cases, however, successful innovation happens at existing companies, guided by a managerial hierarchy. That doesn't mean that the process is designed from start to finish, or that managers are telling R&D workers what to do. As with management more generally, the right kind of hierarchy is one that provides structure, process, and guidelines. Managers make organization design choices regarding the physical location of R&D facilities; for example, within the last two decades, large multinational companies have increasingly moved R&D resources to fast-developing markets and countries, such as China, India, and Brazil (though the Covid-19 pandemic made some companies less enthusiastic about China). Relatedly, managers make decisions regarding the centralization and decentralization of R&D: how much and what kind of R&D should be performed in central labs and facilities versus in labs and facilities in the business units. These kind of decisions require doing what managers specialize in—taking the broad, corporate view.

Managers must also establish and enforce the "rules of the game" for innovation: how experimentation and product development will be funded, how key projects will be selected, how employees will be encouraged and rewarded for novelty and creativity, and how interdependencies across projects and programs will be managed.

All this cuts against the claims of the bossless company narrative that hierarchies promote bland conformity to the status quo, stifle innovation and creativity, and keep firms from producing the kinds of breakthroughs that keep them at the top of their industry. As with all such exaggerated claims, the truth is more nuanced. As we have emphasized throughout this book, all ways of organizing business have pros and cons and different models work better or worse under particular conditions. This is as true for innovation and entrepreneurship as for any behavior or outcome. Newer, smaller, flatter firms are sometimes more innovative than older, larger, more hierarchical firms. But in the face of resource constraints, scale advantages, strong interdependencies, and similar factors, hierarchies can promote innovation and entrepreneurial outcomes. As always, the devil is in the details.

14

HIERARCHY IN THE TWENTY-FIRST CENTURY

MANAGERIAL AUTHORITY AND HIERARCHY ARE HERE TO STAY. UNDER the right conditions, they are the best ways to handle the coordination and cooperation problems that beset human interactions. Prices and markets, while fundamental for making economically rational decisions, cannot do the job alone. Companies and the authority and hierarchy they embody complement prices and markets. They allow human intelligence and creativity to flourish on a larger scale. Hierarchy also allows specialists to do their work within a larger structure, giving them predictability and accountability.

Hierarchies do all of this well—extremely well, actually. Whatever you think of the tech giants, there is no denying that they do what they set out to do: giving us new-and-improved tech hardware and software; letting us share news and information, work from home, and entertain ourselves like never before; and selling massive quantities of discounted merchandise, delivered right to our homes. Paradoxically, it is exactly their superior efficiency that makes some economists, lawyers, activists, and politicians uneasy about "superstar" firms such as Microsoft and Google. These companies are thought to have too much economic and even social and cultural power precisely because they have such a massive footprint.

Think of the 2.2 million employees of Walmart, or Amazon's 1.1 million. Some of these mega-companies are economies in their own right, bigger than the economies of some smaller countries—and probably better run. That they have been able to grow to such proportions and stay on top is testament to the efficiency with which their hierarchies handle the basic challenges of coordination and cooperation while supplying new goods and services that the market wants. Hierarchy has demonstrated survival value.

We do not mean to suggest, however, that hierarchy and managerial authority will be left untouched by changes in society—far from it! The last few decades have seen massive changes in values, demographics, technologies, and business practices. Hierarchy, as we have shown throughout this book, comes in different forms and can be tailored to work well in different circumstances. The changes associated with the "new economy"— rapid technological progress, instant communication, value creation based on knowledge rather than physical resources, increased global awareness and global trade, a more educated workforce, changing political boundaries and values—as well as the sometimes surprising resilience of religion, the continuing relevance of ethnicity and local culture, and the rise of political and economic populism, all point to hierarchy playing a different role in meeting the challenges of the twenty-first century.

The key challenge for designing and operating hierarchies is to choose the right mix of two opposing forces. The first is the desire, common to us all, for empowerment and autonomy, which help companies mobilize the creativity of employees and exploit their unique knowledge and capabilities. The other is the fact that environments characterized by rapid change often call for the large-scale managerial exercise of authority, particularly when activities across the company are interdependent and employees alone cannot make the required adjustments. These two forces are often in conflict.

The new economy has presented other increasingly important challenges. Companies need to have clear, fairly enforced policies and procedures that achieve coordination and cooperation while respecting employee desires for empowerment and relative autonomy. Managers have to figure out when employees can handle changes and disturbances themselves and when managerial intervention is called for. Adam Mendler, the CEO of the Los Angeles–based incubator company The Veloz Group, spoke to this in a speech about leadership:

> An important way to cultivate a culture of adaptability within your organization is by decentralizing decision-making. If only the people at the very top of the chain of command are authorized and empowered to make decisions, your organization will lack the necessary flexibility to shift to the currents of change in times of uncertainty. Leaders must empower the people they lead.[1]

This sounds good—if the alternative to "decentralizing decision-making" is completely centralizing it! But Mendler's inspiring words elide the tough issues. What decisions exactly should be decentralized (or delegated)? How much discretion should employees have over the decision areas delegated to them? How are these employees incentivized and evaluated? How do executives make sure that all of these decentralized decisions mesh together? A central lesson of theories and evidence on organizational structure is that *there are no universally "best" solutions to organizational problems, only trade-offs that depend on the contingencies facing the company.* Identifying and acting upon those trade-offs—not decentralizing everything, everywhere—is the key to successful leadership.

The bossless company narrative pretends that these trade-offs don't exist. Only full decentralization or delegation—the "make everyone a boss" shtick—makes companies innovative and adaptable. Of course, even proponents of the narrative don't really believe this. When Covid-19 hit in March 2020 and economies were shut down, few leadership gurus proposed that making everyone a boss would address the challenges that companies suddenly faced. Rather, managers had to figure out how to make their companies survive, by changing their business model, moving to a remote-work environment, and adjusting to massive demand shocks and supply-chain disturbances. Of course, employees and their families made plenty of adjustments too! Indeed, the necessity in many industries to go to a remote-work model required delegating many tasks and decision competences. The point is that these changes had to be coordinated, with key decisions made from the top.

The work of coordination and cooperation in a firm is no easy task. And it won't be easier in the future. So let's examine different forms of hierarchy and show how managerial authority can adapt to the unique features of our day. But first, we need to review these transformative economic and social forces in more detail.

TRANSFORMATIVE FORCES
TECHNOLOGY

Technology has been the driver of the obvious changes to life, work, and society that have taken place since the 1960s. Computing, wireless communication, miniaturization, the internet, robotics, social media, artificial intelligence, and cheap transportation have affected all areas of social and economic life. These changes in recent decades have not killed off the traditional company any more than the sailing ship, the factory system, the steam engine, the railroad, the automobile, the radio, or the transistor did in earlier eras. They have allowed some activities to be spread out among more people and companies, leading to an increase in the number of smaller firms that can perform specialized tasks and share with other firms. But when these tasks aren't modular and strong interdependencies are in play, technological progress can lead to greater consolidation, with big firms taking advantage of scale economies to grow their footprints.

These changes will only get more dramatic in the years ahead, with more sophisticated applications of computing like blockchain technologies, greater use of AI and robotics, increased connectivity, and improvements in medical technology. Some of these technologies allow for new, increasingly widespread ways of dealing with the problems of cooperation and coordination. In the process, authority and hierarchy will change as the basic and ever-present economic forces that influence companies impact firms in new and different ways, mediated by new technology.

The increased use of artificial intelligence, not only in manufacturing and distribution but also in business decision-making, has drawn a lot of attention lately. The rise of robotics and other forms of smart machines, including software, has raised concerns about job loss, privacy, the tax base, and other issues. These concerns have extended into worries about the future of management itself. After all, AI can handle large parts of human resource management, ranging from hiring to performance reviews to real-time monitoring.[2] Does technology make management obsolete?

Not at all! First, managers have been using machines to help run their company for a long time. Managers don't walk the factory floor as they did a hundred years ago. Many managers never set foot on the factory floor but stay in their offices, tracking information and keeping a watchful eye on a data-driven dashboard. To be sure, AI-based automation may represent a more transformative change than the robotics-driven automation phase that started a few decades ago. After all, AI is starting to automate management itself. Will we eventually see the bossless, AI-driven company?

We think not, though clearly machines can do a lot of what humans do. Assembly robots have largely replaced line workers in many manufacturing processes, smart kiosks are replacing waiters and fast-food counter workers, and algorithms do much of our comparison shopping, scheduling, purchasing, and delivery of goods. Nevertheless, there is still a role for human intelligence in the business firm.

Authority often manifests itself as the right and obligation to delegate decision authority to subordinates. Robots and AI can be extremely skilled at performing the tasks assigned to them. But can they assign their own tasks? Can intelligent machines design the policies and procedures guiding the use of intelligent machines? Can code write itself? The ultimate decisions about what to do and how to do it will be made by humans, at least for the foreseeable future. Yes, AI will cause major changes in the organization of companies. It will make some hierarchies flatter. But it will not make companies bossless. The ultimate important decisions are where the buck stops, and those decisions will be handled by humans.

There is always a crucial role for subjective human judgment in business decision-making—when to start a company, how to change it, whether to shut it down, and what kinds of decisions and functions can be assigned to machines. Michael Lewis made a splash with his book *Moneyball*, which extolled the virtues of big data and predictive analytics in baseball. Oakland A's general manager Billy Beane, the first to apply these techniques, was "fighting a war against subjective judgments" by using data instead of intuition. But someone had to decide to use predictive analytics in the first place! An algorithm didn't do that.

"Technology" can also refer to new ways of managing, what some call "management innovations."[3] Think of the introduction of Taylor's scientific management, DuPont's multidivisional hierarchical form, the venture-funded tech start-up, or the Apple-style ecosystem. We could include here management styles or approaches like GM's Six Sigma, the Total Quality Management (TQM) movement, or Toyota's just-in-time inventory control. These management innovations represent important changes in how hierarchies are organized, and their impacts have been equal to, or even greater than, those of the great technological innovations that get most of the attention.

We have discussed in this book more recent management innovations typically linked to the bossless company narrative such as Holacracy and Agile Scrum. Another example is retail giant Overstock's use of internal voting systems to decide company priorities. Companies like Hewlett-Packard and Intel have tried using internal bidding systems to form sales predictions and allocate manufacturing capacity. These approaches are highly structured and formalized but do emphasize empowerment, delegation, and autonomy. Although often lumped together within the bossless company narrative, they are best understood as new technologies for managing activities within hierarchies.

UNCERTAINTY

The radical changes associated with recent advances in digital technology have dramatically increased the uncertainty that companies face. Most companies try to avoid uncertainty, which not only makes it difficult to plan ahead but also stymies the coordination of ongoing activities within the company and between the company and its suppliers and customers.[4] To reduce uncertainty companies strike contracts with other actors in their environment, create operating procedures, and build hierarchies that include managers whose main job is to handle unanticipated disturbances. They also invest heavily in digital tools to collect and synthesize data about the company's inner workings and its relationships with customers and suppliers, such as Enterprise Resource Management (ERP) and Customer Relationship Management (CRM) systems, forecasting tools, digital marketplaces, and decision support dashboards. And yet investment and innovations in these digital technologies can generate *more* uncertainty and complexity.

Think of banking. If you were a major executive in banking only decades ago, your competitor analysis would include other banks. Today you also need to consider telecom firms, "fintech" start-ups, companies developing and using blockchain technologies, and even supermarket chains. Whereas you once competed on interest rates and fees, number of branches, and perhaps customer service, now you also compete on the quality and functionality of your mobile app, your ties to complementary financial products and other services, your commitment to social responsibility or sustainability, and other variables outside the core business of banking.

This is, of course, not entirely new. Profitability has always been threatened by new entrants into an industry and by substitute products. But these forces now act much more swiftly and unpredictably. What has changed in banking is that many more players have become potential competitors because, like existing players, they can exploit mobile wallets.

Banking isn't unique. Industry after industry and value chain after value chain has found its markets and industry redefined by technology. Big retailers like Amazon and Alibaba have moved into logistics, as Walmart did decades ago. In turn, logistics companies are borrowing from upstream manufacturing technologies such as 3-D printing, which allows them to transform their physical inventory into digital inventory. Most of these technological developments are very good for consumers and customers, and they can generate big wins for companies capable of riding the digital waves. But companies need managers who can recognize and act upon changes in their environments as well as manage the processes, structures, key performance indicators (KPIs), and rewards that incentivize employees to respond to these changes. In research carried out by one of us (Foss), those companies that were good at delegating decisions to employees, running companywide knowledge management programs, and incentivizing their employees to share knowledge were found to be very good at absorbing knowledge from the company's external environment and deploying it to serve innovation efforts.[5]

Technology isn't the only cause of uncertainty. Politics, culture, society, and contagious diseases are also part of this story. World politics is a constant source of uncertainty; shifting patterns of liberalization, changes in market access, and the emergence of new players from former less-developed countries—all such developments have an impact on business. In addition, changing demographics, such as the aging of the population (in Europe, for example), influence the consumer preferences businesses strive to meet and also who they can hire. The recent pandemic and the fears of similar "unknown unknowns" begin to make the often-heard claim in the business press that companies have never faced more uncertainty begin to look credible. Every day is like the first day of a new school year!

Managers have always been in the business of managing uncertainty. If procedures can handle change, then why have managers? It is when something extraordinary happens that we need managers the most. A well-structured hierarchy helps firms buffer unanticipated shocks. Moreover, managerial hierarchies work best when they themselves can adapt, shifting roles and responsibilities and moving personnel throughout the hierarchy as needed. This is difficult to do, as such changes can upset the previously established balance between people and groups, resulting in perceived winners and losers. When the firm's key decision-makers largely agree on the changes that need to be made and are satisfied with their place in the hierarchy, organizational structures can adapt smoothly as needed. Where there is disagreement and adaptation will cause some individuals and groups to lose their place in the hierarchy, these adjustments are much harder and may require radical reorganization. As a rule, such changes can only come from and be organized by senior management.

This is particularly the case for a company moving into new business areas. For example, in the face of declining opportunities for future blockbusters, many big pharmaceutical companies are trying to remain competitive by developing new business models that emphasize customer service. CEO surveys have repeatedly indicated that CEOs see business-model innovation as the most important kind of innovation.[6] Business-model innovation often involves making major simultaneous choices in a firm's value proposition, its customer base, and value chain organization. The underlying activities may be highly interdependent; for example, some value propositions work only with some customer segments and can be realized only by deploying specific resources and processes. This kind of adaptation, particularly when it takes the company into uncharted territory, requires close coordination and only elevates the importance of senior manager intuition and foresight. Top management not only has to define the company's direction but must also get involved in day-to-day decision-making that makes the new business model come alive.

PREFERENCES

The right amount of authority and hierarchy also depends on what kind of boss and work environment we prefer. The appeal of the bossless company narrative is easy to understand since it speaks directly to the underlying preferences most of us have for self-direction, independence, control over our lives, feelings of competence, and feeling valued by others.[7] Indeed, these desires may have become more pronounced over the last few decades.

Few people enjoy being micro-managed. If that's what "management" is all about, who needs it? Millennial and Gen Z workers in particular want a different kind of workplace than those their parents and grandparents experienced. Much has been made of generational differences in the workplace, including claims that younger workers are less loyal and more entitled than earlier generations. The reality is more nuanced: millennials and Gen-Zs are no less hardworking than previous generations, but they are more likely to see the workplace as a complex network that cuts across formal units and titles.[8] For example, millennials appear to be more mobile than previous generations and are less sentimental about where exactly they work. Of course, for companies looking to add talent, that's great. But managers must now be more careful in exercising authority: if they perceive the workplace as rigid and overly constraining, younger employees may not stay for long.

THE AUTHORITY DILEMMA

These transformative changes catch managers on the horns of a dilemma. On the one hand, the forces of technology and uncertainty seem to call for a stronger managerial hand. Someone has to synthesize signals about changes in the company's environment, consider how these shifts may influence the company and how the company can continue to create value in the future, and initiate the appropriate changes in response. Although skilled managers will certainly consult all the relevant stakeholders, it is hard to imagine them doing so through radically decentralized decision processes or fully participative, "democratic" decision processes. These two "bossless" approaches are unlikely to account for the long-run, broader picture, and both are likely to be slow and cumbersome. It sounds like centralized managerial authority is needed to steer organizational adaptation.

But we also know that a lot can be said in favor of decentralization and empowerment. Decentralization leads to better use of local knowledge, even beneficial local tinkering and experimentation, and it often increases work motivation. Besides, employees increasingly want to have decision-making competence delegated to them and are more and more capable of backing up this demand. Many employees have gained more bargaining power because more outside options are available to them, and by virtue of their specialist knowledge, they are in higher demand and contribute more to company value creation. These employee characteristics speak against the use of centralized managerial authority.

To break out of this box, we need to rethink managerial authority.

RETHINKING AUTHORITY

As we have seen, there is compelling evidence that many firms are delayering and that more decisions are being delegated to employees. Firms are still hierarchical, but hierarchy is changing its form. There is also evidence that the exercise of authority is changing. In what ways?

Consider that authority has many faces. Authority may mean the right to hire and fire, instruct, supervise, intervene, and sanction—*The Man in the Gray Flannel Suit* kind of authority. The bossless company narrative usually targets these managerial behaviors and roles. But the exercise of managerial authority is also associated with other behaviors: leading, creating structures and processes, forging consensus, aligning behavior around shared goals, and fostering change.

We can call these "Mark I" and "Mark II" authority, respectively.[9] They roughly correspond to the distinction between "management" and "leadership." Although "leadership" can also refer to goal-setting, visioning, exhortation, and encouragement as well as the more formal tasks of creating and enforcing the rules of the game and making big resource allocation and investment decisions, which we consider key to Mark II authority.

Both kinds of authority have roles to play; these roles are distinct, although many discussions of management lump them together. Clearly, the same manager can exercise different roles under different circumstances; in that sense, both Mark I and Mark II authority should be in the manager's tool kit. But it is crucial to understand their differences.

First, as we explain in more detail later, the modern world requires a shift toward Mark II authority and away from Mark I. Most workers don't want or need a manager telling them what to do and when to do it. But managers have to design the system in which empowered, autonomous, educated knowledge workers can flourish. Second, using authority in the wrong way (for example, using Mark I authority to address situations that require Mark II authority) may be disastrous. In this chapter, we provide some guidelines for knowing when to use each kind of authority.

What exactly is authority? In the simplest case, Amy has authority over Ben when Amy can, within limits, instruct Ben to do a job, in exchange for payment. This exercise of authority is clearly useful, as it enables Amy and Ben to avoid discussing and arguing and negotiating every time they work together.

In this traditional view of authority based on the views of Ronald Coase, Oliver Williamson, and Herbert Simon, a boss directs a worker to perform a specific task. The worker accepts this instruction if the task lies within what Simon in his early work called the worker's "zone of acceptance."[10] Note that, even in this traditional view, workers are not powerless but can accept a boss's offer or reject it in favor of another offer (or they can become their own boss). Once an offer is accepted, however, the worker is compelled to follow through.

This view of Mark I authority assumes that the boss can select the appropriate task, knows all the possible ways to perform the task, and can observe the output of the task, so that rewards and punishments can be administered appropriately. In other words, the boss doesn't want to perform the task directly (perhaps because she is too busy with other tasks), but she knows as much about the task as the worker does and she may or may not observe exactly what the worker is doing as he performs it.

In the modern, knowledge-based, networked economy, however, it seems unlikely that bosses will know everything their workers know. A tech CEO may be skilled at finance and marketing or good at strategic planning and human relations, but may not know how to code. Even a sales manager may understand the product but be unfamiliar with an employee's specific sales territory. What is the role of authority in those situations?

Simon later described a second notion of authority (perhaps reflecting a changing view of what kind of authority is important in more modern conditions): the role of the boss is to *decide what decisions should be delegated*.[11] That is, the boss selects a target outcome, decides which workers are best suited to achieve it, chooses how much discretion to give to those workers, *and steps aside*. Authority in this sense is not about choosing specific tasks and making sure those tasks are performed, but about setting goals, writing job descriptions, selecting people, and evaluating results. This is our Mark II authority—not micro-management, but macro-management!

Sales positions are often governed by Mark II authority. The sales manager sets targets and leaves it to the salesperson to figure out the best way to meet them. Or the salesperson gets a base salary plus a sales commission, giving him strong incentives to move product. Within some boundaries, the manager may not care what customers are targeted, what sales techniques are used, how customer loyalty is established. As long as the employee is selling a lot, the firm is happy. Authority here consists of hiring (or firing) the employee, setting the sales target, and establishing the base pay amount and the bonus rate. On the surface, it may appear that the employee has a lot of latitude, since he decides how to spend his time, where to go during the day, and what methods to use. But he is still subject to authority—just not the kind of authority that a line worker, with a supervisor peering over his shoulder, is exposed to!

These arrangements work well when *knowledge is distributed*, that is, the boss knows that workers know things she doesn't know. Of course, no management system is perfect, and exercising authority via the choice of delegation has drawbacks as well. Ironically, some workers may prefer less delegation—not because they enjoy being bossed around, but because they prefer to avoid the risk that comes with performance-based pay (or they may even prefer being told what to do). For example, many writers and journalists continue to be employed by newspapers and magazines where they draw a monthly salary in exchange for working on stories assigned by editors. They could quit and become self-employed freelancers, writing what they like and hosting their work on a subscription-based platform like Substack. Most prefer the security (and benefits) of a regular paycheck, however, even though they have less autonomy and independence.

Another drawback relates to interdependencies. An organizational structure with lots of delegation is more complicated than one based on simple command and control, and managers have to make sure employees are exercising the discretion given to them under Mark II authority in ways that fit together. Moreover, company decision-making may be slower under Mark II authority, especially if workers need to discover solutions by themselves. So, while Mark II authority results in a system that is typically more rewarding for knowledge workers and more motivating than the traditional form of authority, it may not work best in all situations.

Delegated decision-making takes various forms. Executive teams and self-managing work groups often rely on dialogue and consensus. Dialogue can be followed by voting, as in cooperatives. Alternatively, group decisions can be made by decentralizing decisions as much as possible. Such approaches have their advantages. Dialogue and consensus may give employees a sense of empowerment and psychological ownership. Decentralized decision-making allows employees to use their own specialized knowledge without having to consult with their superiors. Some companies take a dual approach: they implement a decentralized structure for certain units or processes in the company, while maintaining a more traditional management hierarchy overall.

WHO HOLDS AUTHORITY AND WHY?

The authority relation is asymmetrical. Amy, a project manager, directs Ben, a software engineer, on a project. Why isn't it the other way around? Why doesn't Ben direct Amy? Or why don't they take turns being the boss?

One way to assign people to roles in a hierarchy is to use the criterion of knowledge. Suppose that Amy knows better than Ben how to handle a particular type of problem—for example, dealing with an unhappy customer. Amy could try to teach Ben what she knows about the unhappy customer—or the installation process, or market conditions—or she could train Ben to figure it all out for himself. But this might take time and effort. Maybe Ben just doesn't get it or isn't very "coachable." In this case, it makes sense for Amy simply to tell Ben how to solve the problem. Having Amy give direction to Ben substitutes for lengthy explanations, education, and self-reflection on Ben's part.

Of course, Ben may find this arrangement demotivating. Amy may overestimate her own knowledge. Indeed, there are plenty of cases in which the employee knows more than the boss! Think of the mechanics, plumbers, and carpenters you have hired. You might have been able to do what they do, particularly after studying a few YouTube videos. Still, chances are you hired them because they actually know better. Of course, this is also often a reason why firms hire certain employees: they have some kind of specialized knowledge that the firm needs, or they are likely to acquire such knowledge during their employment. In such cases, the manager may have no knowledge advantage. Then why should she have the authority?

To answer, we have to recognize first that authority not only comes in different forms but also has different sources. In many cases, authority follows from superior knowledge. Think of Socrates, one of the founders of classic Greek philosophy. He surely held "authority" on account of his wisdom and insight—call it "knowledge-based authority." It cost him his life, as he was forced (by those who held a different kind of authority) to commit suicide for "corrupting" the youth of Athens.

Fast-forward some 2,300 years. Remember drummer Buddy Rich from Chapter 8, one of our examples of a dictatorial leader who embraced a totally no-errors culture with an emphasis on perfection? Despite his reputation for bad behavior, Rich was respected by his band members. He could get away with his dictatorial style and personality because he was a great drummer and bandleader. Although he was the official head of the band (and could hire and fire band members at will), his authority wasn't conferred by his position, but by the respect he commanded from his fellow musicians.

Then there is Martin Luther King Jr., the US civil rights advocate and Baptist minister, who was known for his charisma and for advancing civil rights in a nonviolent way based on his Christian beliefs. King also held authority, but it was different from the kind held by Socrates and Buddy Rich. King's authority was largely informal; he was the pastor of a church and president of the Southern Christian Leadership Conference, but his authority came largely from his preaching, writing, and activism rather than from any formal title.

There is also the kind of authority held by politicians and bureaucrats, even those who lack name recognition, an outsized personality, or personal charisma. Central bankers—former US Federal Reserve chairman Alan Greenspan is the classic example here—can be dull, pedantic, even inscrutable, yet enormously powerful by virtue of their office.

The point that authority comes in different forms and has different sources was explicitly made by Max Weber, a seminal thinker on the subject of authority. Weber distinguished between three kinds of "legitimate authority" (that is, authority that is accepted by both ruler and ruled): traditional authority, which is legitimized by existing cultural patterns; charismatic authority, which comes from the personal charisma that inspires devotion and obedience; and bureaucratic authority, which is based on legal rules. Employment law backs up bureaucatic authority, as it allows employers to demand hard work (for example, employees can be required to work overtime, with appropriate compensation) of high quality (for example, poor customer service is not a legally protected workplace behavior) and to demand loyalty. It also gives employers considerable discretion (for instance, being able to fire employees for suspected theft without conclusive proof). Of course, what Weber called "charismatic authority" is perhaps best associated with what we today would call "leadership."

Okay, now it's getting complicated! There are two basic kinds of authority: (1) directing people to specific actions and (2) designing the framework of rules, values, and overall organizational design that shapes how work is carried out within the company. These two kinds of authority come from different sources. Still, we suggest that there are some systematic connections between them. To engage in Mark I authority you don't need charismatic authority of the kind possessed by Dr. King (though it may help). What Weber called "authority of the office" (that is, the position, not the person) is probably enough. However, if you really want to manage your experts in the Mark I way, you better show them that you know what you are talking about—that you also have what we call knowledge-based authority. Hence, effective leaders of the Mark I type are likely to be company insiders who are also subject-matter experts with deep knowledge of the industry, technology, and product line.

To exercise Mark II authority effectively—designing and implementing the company's overall framework for organizing work—a manager typically needs both knowledge-based and charismatic authority. For example, a key aspect of Mark II authority is dealing with conflict and change, resolving disagreements among subordinates, and possibly

changing the rules of the game if these disagreements become more frequent. Effectively enforcing rules and making new rules requires what
philosophers call "procedural justice": employees have to believe that the
rules are transparent and fair and administered without favoritism. This
requires leaders who are seen as wise, experienced, of high character, and
good at exercising judgment in complex situations. Such leaders are likely
to be generalists, with a variety of experiences, some of which may have
been outside the firm's main industry.[12]

Let's build on these distinctions by describing the conditions under
which the different kinds of authority can be used. We begin by discussing common abuses of authority, with a particular focus on what we call
Mark I authority.

HOW NOT TO USE AUTHORITY

One of us (Foss) studied the implementation and use of Agile software
development practices in one of the world's large telecom firms, which we
will call "Company E," across multiple sites over five years.[13] As explained
in our earlier discussion of Spotify, Agile is an approach to general project
management with its own tools, or labels for tools, such as scrum boards,
sprints, stand-up meetings, and velocity charts. Often praised as an approach that empowers teams and employees, Agile was designed for use
in small, team-based software development projects.

Company E adopted Agile to meet customer needs more effectively
in fast-changing markets—particularly software development and professional services—to reduce software development time, and to reduce
development costs. Top management also saw Agile as a way to become
more innovative and support organizational learning across the many
business units of the company. The managers at Company E thought that
Agile would help them manage the "exploitation-exploration" trade-off.
It would make Company E "ambidextrous" by letting it take better care
of routine activities, they hoped, while also becoming more daring and
innovative.

The approach was rolled out over eight R&D units, encompassing
thousands of programmers and software developers. In some ways what

followed was a successful Agile transformation: some R&D units, for example, reduced their lead time by 60 percent and their maintenance costs by 40 percent.

Contrary to managers' intentions, however, implementing Agile drastically reduced innovation and learning within teams and units and across the company in general. Team members reported that they had less time for reflection, bouncing ideas off each other, and sharing knowledge. The company's innovation performance, as measured by new products and patents, began to decline.

One reason for the decline was that the approach made development teams and developers so focused on meeting the deadlines implied by the Agile "sprints" that their attention to learning dropped dramatically, and they were left with little time and energy for documenting new learning from projects. Moreover, because Agile gives more authority to some middle managers, such as the project leads who closely track project performance, the system left many team members feeling stifled by an overbearing managerial hierarchy rather than "self-managed."

Company E might have had more success with a different assignment of roles and responsibilities, a different leadership style, or other individuals in charge. But clearly Agile per se was not the solution to what the company had felt was an overly rigid, hierarchical, or "bureaucratic" setup. We saw something similar with the Oticon spaghetti organization. Eventually top managers in this highly delayered organization came to be seen by employees as meddling and interfering—an almost unavoidable outcome of the short distance between projects and top management.

It is hard to design hierarchy well, perhaps particularly when employees are empowered and the company is delayered. But this is the challenge that managers are increasingly facing.

ENABLING AUTHORITY

One of the most important ways in which managers exercise authority is in how they delegate it to others. We call this "enabling authority" in subordinates. Managers first need to convince employees that they really do have autonomy over certain decisions and actions, and to trust that managers are not going to take that authority back. And when managers do, on occasion, need to override an employee's decision, they need to proceed carefully, to avoid breaking that trust. Putting employees in situations where leadership is shared, or where it rotates among team members, can be a good way to maintain this trust. Another good way to foster trust is to have explicit and transparent rules and procedures, which convince employees that their authority is real and will not be compromised by opportunistic, micro-managing supervisors.

FOSTERING TRUST

For years, new hires at Nordstrom received its employee "handbook" on a single five-by-eight-inch card: "Rule #1: Use best judgment in all situations. There will be no additional rules." This practice screams the message that this company is trusting you to do the right thing! Research shows that sending relatively vague but trusting signals can be good for motivation and productivity.[14] Conversely, the same research also shows something that has long been suspected: being very specific—that is, micro-managing—harms employee motivation. Clearly there is a sweet spot, an optimum level of delegation.

Trust is necessary because so many things in the workplace go unstated. Expectations change, often without notice. This happens because many aspects of a job can't be anticipated when the relationship begins. What exactly should John Smith, a salesman, be doing to maximize his sales two years from now? Neither John nor his employer knows enough to put this in detail in the job offer or employment contract, so things are left unsaid.

This vagueness can make John feel vulnerable. He may become dependent on the company not only for the paycheck but also for a sense of worth. John's comprehensive knowledge of the company's products, routines, and customers would seem to give him an advantage, as it makes him more productive and a better fit with the workplace overall. But there is a dark side to John's specialized knowledge: the more he knows about his company the harder it is for him to take his skills elsewhere. He has become dependent and less mobile, and that gives his boss more power over him. Such power may be used in ways that are not to John's liking. Obviously, employees care a great deal about such issues. That is why we have sites like glassdoor.com, where employees can learn more about opportunities at other companies.

Under these circumstances, trust is highly important. Organizational psychologists emphasize the importance of "psychological contracts" between employees and management. An employee forms expectations about how she will be treated at work. And likewise, managers form expectations about how the employee will perform her job. Ideally, these expectations should be in sync: the employee expects to put forth effort, be treated with respect, be empowered, and receive recognition, praise, tangible rewards, and opportunities coming her way. In turn, the manager expects the employee to work hard and follow instructions and to reward the employee accordingly. The relation is contractual, but clearly it includes many tacit expectations that are not written down and may not even be verbalized.

For obvious reasons, such expectations may not be in perfect sync: managers or their reports or both may have unrealistic expectations or different conceptions of what constitutes "opportunities" in the workplace, for instance, or of how much overtime employees can be expected to put in. Still, managers will try hard to signal what is expected. And as the parties learn about each other, expectations may get in sync over time, establishing the "psychological contract." Companies that get the "invisible handshake" right reap the benefits—employee efforts and creativity soar, their loyalty and engagement increase, and turnover is reduced. Everyone wins.

Here's the catch: it is very difficult to establish and maintain psychological contracts! Employees report that breaches of psychological contracts are common (while managers, interestingly, are seldom asked about their views).[15] Of course, what is perceived as a "breach" of a contract may simply reflect expectations that were never truly aligned. Or it may result from extraordinary situations arising in which management had to disappoint employee expectations, such as a massive need for employees to work overtime to meet an unexpected surge in demand, or a need to reduce salaries in the event of the opposite happening.

Delegation is an important part of the psychological contract. If John has been told, or led to believe, that he has discretion in how to engage his customers, how to market his wares, and how to allocate his time, then finds that discretion taken away, he will probably feel cheated, the victim of a bait-and-switch. Thus, when managers delegate authority, they need to do so carefully and sincerely if they are to foster the kind of trust that makes a hierarchy work.

DYNAMIC DELEGATION

While nobody likes to have their decisions overruled, it's not so bad if there's an established expectation that decision authority will be moved around as circumstances demand. Consider "extreme action teams," which are made up of specialists who perform urgent and interdependent tasks with highly consequential, but often unpredictable, outcomes. Seal Team Six, which killed Osama bin Laden shortly after 1:00 a.m. on May 2, 2011, was an extreme action team. So are medical teams in extreme emergency centers in hospitals. These teams use "dynamic delegation," an organizational structure under which roles and responsibilities are moved around quickly as needed and sometimes employee decisions are overridden and responsibility is taken away from them.[16]

Dynamic delegation recognizes that teams are composed of members with different experience, knowledge, and seniority, as well as different hierarchical positions. For example, if you check into a hospital emergency room, you may be treated by emergency physicians, who are usually senior specialist doctors; by younger doctors training to be specialists; by "ordinary," nonspecialist doctors; or by interns. You will also meet different kinds of nurses with different positions in the hierarchy, as well as care coordinators, physiotherapists, and pharmacists. Leadership is usually held by the most experienced, most senior emergency-room doctor. She will often delegate many decisions to other team members to avoid becoming overloaded herself. But exactly because of her superior experience and skill, she may also take back her authority over those decisions if things get critical. This is the sense in which delegation is "dynamic."

A recent study finds that dynamic delegation helps extreme action teams perform more reliably, while also providing training and experience for less experienced members. The broader implication is that this kind of "improvisational" process works—but only because it happens within an established hierarchical structure. Moreover, "overruling" may not be perceived as a bad thing when team members think that the person doing the overruling actually knows best. If you are an intern treating a patient in critical condition and the senior physician "overrules" you, saving the patient's life, then you are probably quite happy with being overruled.

Despite such cases, there is little doubt that psychological contracts are often broken by managers engaging in unnecessary and intrusive micromanaging and overruling. Employees may also come to see their position in the workplace and the resources they can use as entitlements. Organizational changes such as restructurings can thus be perceived as breaches of the psychological contract, though the manager would not see it that way! Analyzing data from Spanish manufacturing companies, one of us (Foss) found that such breaches in fact hurt employee productivity.[17] Morale and creativity decline, and employees start to leave.

The ability to establish, maintain, and signal good psychological contracts will be an increasingly important part of the "enabling" exercise of authority. Millennials and Gen Z employees are known for being picky about their employers; this is one reason why mutual understanding and agreement matter so much. But there is a more subtle reason. As work and productive activities increasingly shift from manufacturing to knowledge-intensive services and employees increasingly demand, and are given, voice, influence, and discretion, their efforts and productivity become difficult to observe, measure, and reward. As companies rely on a growing number of specialists, the potential for misunderstandings and errors, and for exercising authority badly, increases as well.

These factors combine with the rising need to manage adaptation to uncertainties in the company's environment to make the manager's job not only more important but more challenging. Interpersonal skills will become even more important in the future.[18]

NURTURING RELATIONS

Building and maintaining good psychological contracts is all about sustaining good relations. Managers thus have to focus not only on how they deal with employees but also on how employees deal with each other, both within their unit, department, or function and across silos. Managing workplace disputes is an obvious example, but proactive coaching, information-sharing, and positioning are also important. Maintaining good relations can also involve deciding what information to keep private (such as salaries) and when to keep employees apart in order to avoid disputes or to discourage employees from comparing their job duties, compensation, or support systems to those of their colleagues.[19] Although employees may prioritize dealing with their bosses, it is often horizontal collaboration with employees at similar levels in the company but in other units that leads to innovation and increased customer value.[20]

FORMALIZATION AND TRANSPARENCY

Surprisingly, highly decentralized organizations need a lot of structure so that work is done well. As we saw in Chapter 10, the technology used in Morning Star's tomato processing plant is simple and well understood. The clearness of each employee's role enables the company's system of internal contracts between employees to work. But at companies where the technology is complex and less well understood and roles are not precisely defined, the "coordination problem" of who does what and when emerges. Employees and unit managers may become disgruntled. Turf wars may erupt.

For example, many IT companies experience a recurrent type of conflict between developers and the employees in charge of security. The Central Intelligence Agency, certainly an IT-intensive organization, allegedly has a sign on the wall next to the door leading to the security department that reads, "THE ANSWER IS NO."[21] While security's intention may simply be to prod developers to double-check their products, it is easy to see how its signaling may make developers wary about approaching the department, leading to lack of cooperation and attempts to bypass security. Thus, coordination problems turn into more poisonous cooperation problems, which may damage internal relations and be hard to repair.

The classic hierarchical instrument of clearly defining roles avoids such problems. Sure, formalization and job descriptions can be constraining and job descriptions can become perceived entitlements that make it difficult to engage in organizational change or that even lead individuals or units (for example, the CIA security department) to overstate their right to control particular organizational decisions. But these tools of hierarchy do have the very distinct advantage of facilitating the flourishing of human effort and creativity by helping managers reduce coordination and cooperation problems. Choosing not to define roles and jobs and formalize processes and procedures is not a good alternative.

In principle, role and task transparency can do the same. If we all know that Paul sings lead and plays the bass, John sings harmony and plays rhythm guitar, George plays lead guitar, and Ringo plays drums, and if all these parts fit together smoothly, the result is great music. Everyone knows his role and how the roles complement each other. Such transparency can work in a small consultancy, a repair shop, or a subunit in a bigger company with just a few employees whose clearly defined roles add up to a coherent whole.

Problems arise when there are conflicts among roles. Who is going to sing lead? Who gets songwriting credit? The larger and more complex the organization, the greater the likelihood of conflict. There are a lot more roles to define and fill. Employees come and go. It's difficult to figure out who is doing what, how well tasks are being performed, and whether changes need to be made. Full transparency in a large organization may lead to information overload. This is partly why larger organizations are typically divided into departments, divisions, branches, project teams, or other subunits, all of which can be managed like smaller units.

Should the activities of one subunit be transparent to another? On the one hand, it might seem better to have each group focus on its own tasks and not be distracted by what's going on in other units. Let Apple's iPhone division focus on making great phones without worrying about how Apple Music or Apple TV is doing. Let the executive team stress about that. On the other hand, some knowledge of the company's overall strategy and performance is necessary for any group to perform well; if Apple is investing more in content creation and integrating media properties with its hardware devices, the teams making these devices might want to design them differently. Finding just the right level of transparency between units is a key management challenge.

EXERCISING AUTHORITY SMARTLY

Every business model, strategy, organizational structure, or management style has its strong and weak points. Exercising authority smartly means figuring out what decisions to delegate, who to put in key positions, and when to intervene, as well as deciding whether the system needs to be revised in response to changing conditions.

Under some contingencies, or conditions, the advantages of delegating a decision or an action may outweigh the costs, but not under other contingencies. Good managers know this intuitively, but that doesn't make it easy to make the call. As we have repeatedly emphasized, getting delegation right is a perennial management challenge. Moreover, besides the "hard" aspects of organizational design, like formal rules, incentives, and monitoring, there are the "softer" parts from psychology and ethics to be considered: employees expect rules to be fair, they take pride in being empowered, they want their jobs and roles to feel significant, and they are subject to the biases and judgment errors (jealousy, overconfidence, motivated reasoning) to which everyone is prone—even managers! Taking all this into account is truly difficult. The management writer Stefan Kühl thinks that organizational design is so complex and fraught with contraction and paradox that the search for optimal delegation is "futile."[22]

This is an exaggeration, but getting delegation right is hard—it's not simply a matter of "empowering workers to be their best," as the bossless company narrative naively suggests. We have shown that companies like Spotify and Valve, which house mostly independent software projects with little need for coordination between them, can leave team size and composition, project requirements, and even some budgets up to the teams. Bottom-up organization—not literally bossless but flat, flexible, and organic—makes sense for these companies. But not for, say, a large manufacturing company that has a portfolio of highly interdependent products featuring shared design and components and that sells bundles of complementary products. For such a company, more centralized control is needed.

The theory of complementarities introduced in Chapter 4 illustrates how organizational structure, technology, and market conditions mesh. So do the individual elements of a firm's organizational model. Giving a line worker bonuses based on the amount produced, or paying a salesperson on commission, gives each employee strong incentives to work hard. But these incentives only make sense if the line worker or salesperson has the ability to hit the target—that is, if they have enough control over what they do and how they do it that the incentive program actually enables them to do better.

Imagine a truck driver being paid by the haul, with a bonus for faster delivery. To get the bonus, the driver studies the available routes, pays careful attention to traffic, and minimizes the number of food stops. But what if the parent company sets the route and does not allow the driver to deviate from it? What if company policy specifies exactly one fifteen-minute break every two hours, no more, no less? This driver won't get the bonus no matter how hard he tries, so why should he bother? He has no control over his actions, so he isn't motivated by an incentive scheme. Likewise, giving the driver control over his route and schedule makes little sense if the company pays only fixed salaries and no performance bonuses. Incentive schemes and delegation go together; neither works without the other.

In deciding what, when, and how to delegate, managers can benefit from a few simple rules that help them focus on the following conditions.[23]

The speed of decision-making. Which is more important: getting a decision exactly right, or deciding quickly and getting it right enough? If time is of the essence—if there is a high degree of decision-making urgency—then the better alternative is often having higher-level managers make the decisions without dialogue and consensus, especially since the timeliness of decisions is a common source of frustration.[24] Of course, decisions made quickly may turn out to be wrong. But if the costs of delay are high enough, then quick decisions are often worth the risk.

One advantage of centralized decision-making under fast-moving conditions is that it cuts through much of the internal politics that slows things down. The introduction and rapid diffusion of the personal computer in the 1980s radically disrupted the existing microcomputer industry. We might expect that the dominant firms, as they struggled to react and adapt, would have been beset with internal conflict as engineers, programmers, salespeople, and executives tried to chart a path forward. And yet, despite the rapidly evolving technology and industry, decision-making in these companies was typically centralized, quick, and accompanied by little in the way of organizational politics (seeking out allies, building coalitions, influencing the internal agenda, and so on).[25] When things move fast, the need to concentrate on what is going on in their environment gives people less time and energy to devote to organizational politics.

Managers and employees will spend less time forming coalitions, exchanging favors, and trying to persuade colleagues to see things their way if they know that, when quick decisions are needed, the "autocratic" boss will decide. The return of Steve Jobs to Apple in 1997 is an apt illustration. In his absence, Apple had become a constellation of fiefdoms. Upon returning, Jobs quickly overhauled the company's tangled product line and switched the focus to a few clearly targeted offerings.

Okay, we're not arguing for dictatorship, simply pointing out that top-down decision-making is often faster than more organic, bottom-up modes of organizing. Does this need for quicker decisions justify the possibility of making bad decisions or having a demotivating effect on employees? That depends on the reason speed is needed, the capability of top managers, and the attitudes and expectations of employees.

Speedy decisions are often made in response to threats, typically a sudden and unexpected drop in company performance. In fact, companies are much more likely to react when they face a negative discrepancy between their current performance and where they would like to be. When they greatly surpass such aspirations, the tendency is to think that they are doing just fine and so they change very little. When there is a threat to a company's existence, decisions become highly consequential. Under these conditions, a decentralized approach is likely to perform less well, as subordinates are less willing to assume responsibility in the face of such risk. This slows down decision-making and may lead to low-quality decisions. Therefore, when faced with threats, senior managers are likely to concentrate and to retain control over key decisions.

Employee knowledge. To paraphrase the question famously asked by Senator Howard Baker during the hearing about the Watergate burglary during the Richard Nixon administration, what do employees know, and when do they know it? Is the most critical knowledge held by senior managers (who know the company's overall strategy), by middle managers (who have a bird's-eye view of their department or division), or by lower-level employees (who know their customers best)? Can knowledge at lower levels of the company be neatly summarized (say, in a customer relationship management database) and made available to higher-level managers so that they are better able to make most of the decisions? It is crucial that managers ask themselves these questions.

The problem is that there is plenty of trouble ahead if management falls into the "digital trap"—the belief that, with new digital tools, all decision-relevant knowledge can be digitized. But much decision-relevant knowledge just cannot be concentrated in this way; it is literally inside the heads of employees, and even if it is conveyable to others, employees may not want to share it. While the new digital tools may assist decision-making at the top, they have their limits, particularly in the face of dispersed knowledge.

In a modern company, the knowledge crucial to success is dispersed across the employees and cannot at all be concentrated at the top management level. It exists in the heads of developers, marketing and sales people, production workers, and so on. This is not, however, a good reason for companies to strive for maximum delegation by "making everyone a boss." Sure, employees closer to the action often do have better knowledge about *local* conditions—say, the characteristics of their key customers or their own sales territories. But reporting systems are supposed to relay some of that local information to top managers, even if the information is often distorted, reporting and decisions are delayed, and reports don't include all relevant information. More important, senior managers are likely to have more information about corporate strategy, overall market conditions, legal or regulatory issues, and other issues that are important and not available to employees.

The Intel example in Chapter 11 shows that this isn't *always* the case. At a critical point in Intel's history, when it transitioned from mainly producing memory chips to mainly producing microprocessors, its middle managers had a better grasp of the right strategic direction than top managers did. Still, Intel's senior managers were often better positioned to grasp the key issues at the company, industry, and economy levels, as CEO Andy Grove demonstrated.

The fundamental task of a company's top decision-makers is to synthesize all information that could have a large effect on the company's current and future performance and make the big decisions on this basis. They can rely on advisers, experts, consultants, and what we earlier called "extreme action teams." But ultimately the buck stops with the CEO. So, while some decisions should be delegated to employees with superior knowledge of local conditions, overall authority—including decisions about what decisions to delegate!—cannot be passed down the line.

What knowledge really matters? The decision to delegate also depends on knowledge that each of us needs to make a right decision. Gaining additional information can sometimes be more bother than it's worth. When I'm looking for a restaurant, I search directories or use dining apps or ask friends until I find a place that seems good enough. I don't spend hours researching every restaurant. I don't need to know everything to make a good decision; I only need to know enough, particularly when the costs of gathering more information are greater than the expected benefit.

Employee feelings of ownership. Employee perceptions also come into play here. When employees feel that they "own" their budgets and decision rights, taking away those decision rights poses particular challenges.

One of us taught a course for many years with complete control over topics, readings, and classroom activities, then moved to another university where the curriculum for that course was controlled by the department to ensure uniformity across instructors. Losing that autonomy led to a lot of frustration and resentment!

The behavioral economics concept of "loss aversion" comes into play here: people tend to value things they had and lost more highly than things they never had—so that moving from a decentralized to a centralized system is going to cause some pain. The gains from centralization must be strong enough to overcome these costs, and managers must be prepared to explain clearly why the changes are needed.

Procedural justice. Procedural justice, the idea that the company consistently applies fair and transparent principles when resolving disputes, is important. If employees believe that the firm's procedures are just, they are more likely to accept managerial intervention, whether that be the occasional overriding of an employee's decision or a centralized system itself. Can managers explain why autonomy must be curtailed? Do employees feel that their concerns about autonomy and responsibility are heard and taken seriously? If so, then choosing not to delegate certain decisions, or to intervene when necessary, is likely to work. If not, employees may become disgruntled.

HIERARCHY FOR TODAY

The need for hierarchy isn't going away, but the form it takes is changing—deciding how things will be done rather than telling people what to do, designing and enforcing the rules of the game rather than making everyone play it in a certain way. The old Taylorite factory and the office full of gray flannel suits, systems characterized by command and control, aren't coming back. The modern economy calls for management that creates processes, rules, procedures, and norms that attract educated and self-motivated workers and organizes people into flexible structures and groups that take advantage of knowledge, talent, and fit. As Haier Group's Zhang Ruimin puts it, "Leaders of other enterprises often define themselves as captains of the ship, but I think I'm more the ship's architect or designer. That's different from a captain's role, in which the route is often fixed and the destination defined."[26]

As we noted earlier, access to digital tools can help managers carry out this modern role of designing, monitoring, guiding, and problem-solving. But the dark side of micro-management beckons, and managers need to resist the tendency to measure everything, to reward only that which can be measured, and to downplay the role of human judgment. They need to use these tools smartly to enhance their ability to delegate, supervise, and lead change where necessary. They don't need to know everything, but only just enough, and they need to consider what their employees want and think is fair in designing structures and systems.

15

THE HIGHLY EXAGGERATED DEATH OF THE MANAGER

ACCORDING TO THE BOSSLESS COMPANY GURU GARY HAMEL, "Management is the least efficient activity in your organization. . . . A hierarchy of managers exacts a hefty tax on any organization."[1] Many organizations have tried to avoid paying this tax by delayering, delegating, streamlining, and democratizing—with varying levels of success.

We have no problem with Holacracy, self-managed teams, internal markets and contracts, and other hallmarks of the near-bossless company being used in a careful and balanced way. There is a lot to learn from these experiences! Our targets have been the breathlessly hyperbolic narratives and the grand, sweeping claims of their universal applicability.

For instance, Hamel and Michele Zanini claim that "the cost of excess bureaucracy in the US economy amounts to more than $3 trillion in lost economic output, or about 17% of GDP."[2] To get this figure, they calculate, from Bureau of Labor Statistics figures, the ratio of managers to employees in the US economy—about 1-to-4.7. They then look at the manager-to-employee ratio of a handful of near-bossless poster companies, including many we have discussed in these pages, such as Morning Star, Gore, and Valve; their estimated manager-to-employee ratio is 1-to-10. From this calculation they conclude that more than half the managers in the US are unnecessary!

The absurdity of this calculation is obvious: every company is different, and no single management model works well for every company in every set of circumstances—not even for these cherry-picked companies outside of a few good years. Hamel and Zanini picked a few extreme outliers and assumed that every company can and should do what those outliers (sometimes) do. It's like observing that people who live in the tropics spend very little on winter clothing and heating equipment, computing how much is spent on those things by people who live in more temperate zones, and concluding that all that additional spending is wasted. We could save so much money if Alaskans lived like Floridians—even while living in Alaska. Sadly, this level of reasoning is par for the course in much of the bossless company literature.

SETTING THE RECORD STRAIGHT

In a way, it's not surprising that the old ways of the workplace appear outmoded. There are no curmudgeon consultants traveling the lecture circuit to extol the benefits of the traditional reporting- and command-based hierarchy. CEOs eagerly embrace the new trends. As the *Economist*'s "Schumpeter" columnist speculated:

> Not only is it in the interest of senior management to promote their role at the expense of the middle manager, it also suits the consultants who work on firms' HR strategy to compliment the people that are paying them. Consultants now concentrate almost exclusively on the idea of leadership; "management" is hardly mentioned. That simple change of emphasis can, after all, double their fee.[3]

In writing this book, we have faced the challenge of criticizing ideas that are seen as hip and avant-garde and taken on the tough assignment of defending—of all things—hierarchy. But as we hope has been made clear, we have not defended traditional hierarchy per se, but the need for managerial authority and its accompanying hierarchy adapted for an age of more mobile, better educated, and more demanding employees, rapid technological change, and specialized knowledge as an important factor of production.

Hierarchy and managerial authority are here to stay. The bossless company narrative, with its emphasis on the withering away of the hierarchy, is hopelessly naive. It falsely characterizes hierarchy as coercive rather than enabling. The few existing bossless companies are outliers, so the experience of radically flat organization is and will remain foreign to most practicing managers. The vast majority of employees will continue to have specific job descriptions, will need to familiarize themselves with rules and procedures manuals (or at last videos detailing them), and will answer to their bosses. Yes, we know that this sounds tedious and dreadful to many people, but this system works—it addresses and solves the fundamental challenges of coordination and cooperation facing every organization and company. And though we all like to poke fun at "bureaucracy" and "The Man," what we are usually criticizing is not the basic idea of bureaucracy or leadership, but what we see as aberrations. Thus, what we want is well-functioning hierarchy. Many of us can intuitively see that a bossless organization won't give us this and in fact is more likely to encounter perils such as lack of coordination and the formation of powerful but non-accountable cliques in the workplace.

Also, many current management practices do not align well with a "bossless" model. As we pointed out, influential approaches like Agile for product development and manufacturing, though team-based, are not exactly bossless. The older and even more influential "lean" manufacturing approach—which seeks to maximize productivity while minimizing waste through the relentless elimination of defects, a balanced activity flow, preventive maintenance, and strong communication—is also very far from being bossless. Although this approach features strong worker involvement and buy-in, it also involves procedures, tight planning, optimized workflows, surveillance, and other features that don't align easily with the freewheeling "make everyone a boss" philosophy. In other words, some of the most influential management approaches of the last decade or so fly in the face of the bossless model of organizing.

We think this seeming contradiction manifests a broader tension between two key trends in modern management thinking: on the one hand, the emphasis on employee involvement; on the other, the emphasis on optimized processes and just-in-time production. The latter may easily overwhelm the former. In daily management, the direct concern with meeting output targets pushes the softer concern with employee management into the background. And the demands of process optimization and quick deliveries easily take us full circle back to something almost like a Taylorite production, with close monitoring of employees, now sometimes with peer pressure added to the watchful attention of the manager.

These tendencies are reinforced by the ongoing digital transformation, that is, the increased reliance on "big data" analytics, artificial intelligence, and similar computerized tools for analysis and decision support. These tools are promoted under the banner of improved, data-driven decision-making. And yet, though digital tools can be used to support decentralization, they can also work in the opposite direction: digitalization can make more powerful tools available to senior managers for gathering and synthesizing information about customers, rivals—and employees! When we collected data through surveys and interviews with top managers, we were surprised to find that the majority expected digitalization to make themselves and their headquarters more powerful—"surprised" because this expectation runs counter to the popular view that digitalization is likely to lead to more employee empowerment and more delegation of decisions to business units.

There is little doubt that digital tools do indeed make a company's top management and headquarters more powerful and capable of exercising more authority. But digitalization is a double-edged sword. It is easy for managers to become overreliant on digital tools. If decisions need to be made swiftly and "conventional" sources and kinds of information are adequate, then relying on digital techniques may cause decision paralysis. In one example reported in our research, a large industrial group was excited by the cool new interactive dashboards of its recently implemented Customer Relationship Management system, which allowed the company to identify key customers in real time, track every single customer interaction, and monitor sales developments. The easy-to-use CRM system was one big invitation to micro-management (as well as delayed decision-making)!

If top managers give in to this temptation, they risk harming the learning, creativity, and innovation that takes place at lower levels and relies on knowledge, intuition, and insights that are imperfectly captured (at best) with digital tools and statistical techniques. Trying to press them into a format suitable for digital transmission can lead to a loss of that knowledge and demotivate employees, who then become less capable of exercising initiative and creativity.

Although talk of "digital tools" and how they may clash with employee initiative and creativity sounds very twenty-first century, the key insight that managers need to think about technology in the context of the "human factor" wouldn't have been foreign to important early management thinkers such as Chester Barnard, who were fully aware of the importance in the workplace of "soft" psychological factors.

Another motivation for writing this book was seeing the bossless company narrative ride roughshod over classic management ideas, as if no one has ever thought seriously about issues such as the pros and cons of centralization and decentralization. We need to rediscover the thinkers, perspectives, and intellectual traditions that developed a robust understanding of the need for hierarchy.

Speaking of the classics from a personal perspective: in K–12 schooling in the United States in the last few decades, we have seen a revival of the "classical education" model, which emphasizes Latin and Greek, the classic Western literary and philosophical texts, and the formal study of logic and rhetoric along with the standard primary- and secondary-school curricula.[4] One of us sent his children to a Classical Christian School. The idea behind this movement is that modern teaching methods and sources are missing subjects, materials, and techniques that have stood the test of time and have value and meaning in the modern age.

We would be delighted if this book contributes to a revival of "classical" management education. Many first-rate minds have thought (if not quite from antiquity) about managerial authority and hierarchy and the roles and functions of managers. Given the ubiquity of management as a function in a modern economy, thinking about management—in particular, what management is and what it is good for—has overwhelming importance. It has been important to us to stress that such thinking dates back a long time and is a very serious intellectual enterprise. We need to think more than twice before discarding a large body of classical management thinking on the nature, role, and value of the managerial hierarchy. And we definitely don't want to reshape or discard a function that has demonstrated tremendous survival value and been examined by thinkers such as the great German sociologist Max Weber, one of the most influential intellectuals of the twentieth century, and the late Oliver Williamson, whose Nobel Prize–winning ideas have inspired many of our arguments (and who was Klein's PhD dissertation adviser). In considering their impact on daily life, the leading management thinkers compare well with the greatest thinkers from other disciplines.

This claim may seem like comparing apples to oranges—management writers aren't developing vaccines or inventing flying cars. But before lives can be saved and before research into saving lives can happen, there must be resources and wealth that enable research and development, production, and distribution. Poor societies are disease-ridden societies. Sound management theory contributes to wealth creation and thus, albeit indirectly, also "saves lives." (The converse is also true, as in the Cold War–era joke about a Soviet May Day parade. Rows of soldiers and tanks marching past the reviewing stand are followed by a group of unassuming people in business suits. "Who are they?" the Soviet premier asks his aide. "Oh, those are the economists. You have no idea how much damage they can do!")

HIERARCHY FOR TODAY

Hierarchy today is different from hierarchy in the days of Henry Ford or even Steve Jobs. Hierarchy has proven over time to be a highly adaptive creature that responds to changes in the preferences and tastes of customers and consumers, changes in technology, and changes in policies and institutions, including global liberalization and large-scale deregulation.

There is also no denying that over the last three to four decades hierarchy has changed its appearance, if not its function. The greater informality in society at large has spilled over into the workplace. The 1960s Manhattan workplace depicted in *Mad Men* had its share of boozing and philandering, but a suit and tie were worn at all times (except when the philandering was successful). Sure, companies nowadays are much more "open" in the sense that the typical company has more collaborative relations with outside parties, often for the purpose of engaging in innovation projects. But those firms are still guided by a managerial hierarchy, even if that hierarchy now emphasizes processes and procedures rather than overt command and control.

Companies have delayered, reducing the number of managerial levels between top and bottom, not to do away with bosses but to give those at the top more influence on what goes on beneath them. Our tools for measuring and rewarding performance have also changed. Annual reviews (or more frequent reviews) with specific KPIs were not widely used until just a few decades ago. But more and better performance management and greater use of rewards hardly indicate bosslessness; on the contrary, they imply that bosses care a lot about performance but are focusing on what employees produce rather than on how much they work. In other words, hierarchy and managerial authority still have their basic features, but their overall appearance has changed.

We are confident that the company of the future will continue to adapt as it always has. There may be lessons to learn from the bossless company narrative about the value of informality and self-management in some company activities, typically those that lie outside operations. Many companies will (continue to) benefit from looser horizontal ways of sharing experience and knowledge in communities of practice, as Spotify clearly does. Managers need to be attentive to the changing characteristics of the workforce as attitudes toward work-life balance change and demand for different specialists increases, along with their bargaining power.

The way authority is exercised in the workplace will surely change, but it needs to be exercised smartly! Talking about an ethos of participation but acting in ways that directly contradict it is a recipe for disaster.

Managerial authority still works, but it needs to be accompanied by strong, credible communication and a commitment to fair process, particularly as bosses become more powerful. Hierarchy is not disappearing, and if it seems to be, that is mainly the effect of delayering, which happens, the data shows, so that top managers can better exercise authority close to operations. As more companies delayer, it will only become even more important to exercise authority smartly. As Mark Twain might have put it, the death of the manager is highly exaggerated.

ACKNOWLEDGMENTS

THIS BOOK REFLECTS YEARS OF THINKING, WRITING, TEACHING, AND arguing about how organizations work, why some perform better than others, and how they are changing. We were both trained as economists, but we do most of our research, writing, and teaching in business strategy, entrepreneurship, and organization studies. Attuned to what F. A. Hayek called the "marvel of the market," we were initially attracted to arguments that companies should try to organize themselves like markets by decentralizing, delegating, and empowering their workers to act like independent agents. About two decades ago, we noticed that the people we met in our MBA and executive MBA classes were similarly attracted to these ideas. One of us was a member of a university committee tasked with examining whether the traditional organizational unit of a university, the department, could be done away with, with all activities being handled by self-organizing teams.

The more we thought about it, however, and the more carefully we looked at the empirical evidence, the more we realized that the flattening hierarchy is largely a myth—hierarchies are not being flattened as much as advertised, and it works only in a few specialized cases. This led us to a deeper appreciation of the classic works in organizational economics from thinkers like Ronald Coase, Herbert Simon, Alfred Chandler, and

Oliver Williamson, who explained how well-structured managerial hierarchies add value. Our debt to these thinkers should be obvious throughout the text of this book.

The two of us have been studying these issues since the early 1990s and have been collaborating for more than twenty years, including two books and many articles, essays, and monographs.[1] Our ideas on the role of hierarchy emerged through several academic articles and essays written with various collaborators; the more popular summaries appear in a 2014 article in *Sloan Management Review* and a 2019 essay in *Aeon*.[2] The positive reception to these two works inspired us to produce a book-length treatment of our arguments.

We are grateful to our many colleagues and research collaborators who have helped us think through these ideas, with particular thanks going to Jay Barney, Teppo Felin, Kirsten Foss, Anna Grandori, Sandra Klein, Christos Kolympiris, Lasse Lien, Joe Mahoney, Anita McGahan, and Todd Zenger. Kirsten Foss and Sandra Klein deserve special thanks for putting up with us personally as well as professionally. We've also benefited from teaching and discussing these ideas with students and colleagues at Copenhagen Business School, Baylor University, the Norwegian School of Economics, Bocconi University, and the University of Missouri. Amanda Mockaitis helped get the final manuscript in shape.

Our editor, John Mahaney, was extremely helpful (and patient) in sharpening our arguments and forcing us to write in clear, accessible prose—not easy for academics, especially when discussing complex and subtle ideas.

NOTES

CHAPTER 1: FIRE ALL THE MANAGERS?

1. Niall Ferguson, *The Square and the Tower: Networks and Power, from the Freemasons to Facebook* (London: Penguin Books, 2018).

2. Gary Hamel, "First, Let's Fire All the Managers," *Harvard Business Review*, December 2011.

3. Gary Hamel and Michele Zanini, *Humanocracy: Creating Organizations as Amazing as the People Inside Them* (Boston: Harvard Business Review Press, 2020).

4. Frederic Laloux, *Reinventing Organizations: A Guide to Creating Organizations Inspired by the Next Stage of Human Consciousness* (Millis, MA: Nelson Parker, 2014).

5. Robert Michels, *Political Parties: A Sociological Study of the Oligarchical Tendencies of Modern Democracy*, translated by Eden Paul and Cedar Paul (New York: Free Press, 1915).

6. Quoted in "RenDanHeYi: The Organizational Model Defining the Future of Work?," *Corporate Rebels*, April 2019, corporate-rebels.com/rendanheyi-forum/.

7. Paul Michelman, "The End of Corporate Culture as We Know It," *Sloan Management Review*, Summer 2017.

8. Ed Zitron, "Say Goodbye to Your Manager," *The Atlantic*, September 17, 2021.

9. For mentions and discussions of these companies, see, for example, Michael J. Mol and Julian M. Birkinshaw, *Giant Steps in Management: Creating Innovations That Change the Way We Work* (Englewood Cliff, NJ: Prentice-Hall, 2008); Nicolai J. Foss, "Selective Intervention and Internal Hybrids: Interpreting and Learning from the Rise and Decline of the Oticon Spaghetti Organization," *Organization Science* 14, no. 3 (2003): 331–349; Hamel, "First, Let's Fire All the Managers"; Phanish Puranam and Dorthe Døjbak Håkonsson, "Valve's Way," *Journal of Organization Design* 4, no. 2 (2015): 2–4; Julian Birkinshaw, "What Lessons Should We Learn from Valve's Innovative Management Model?," *Journal of Organization Design* 3, no. 2 (2014): 8–9; Nicolai J. Foss and Peter G. Klein, "Why Managers Still Matter," *Sloan Management Review*, September 2014, 73–80; and Ulrich Möller and Matthew McCaffrey, "Levels Without Bosses? Entrepreneurship and Valve's Organizational Design," in *The Invisible Hand in Virtual Worlds: The Economic Order of Video Games*, edited by Matthew McCaffrey (Cambridge: Cambridge University Press, 2022), 211–240.

10. Tim Kastelle, "Hierarchy Is Overrated," *Harvard Business Review* blog, November 20, 2013.

11. "In Many Ways, I Believe This Is All Just the Beginning—A (Long Overdue) Interview with the Author of *Reinventing Organizations*, Frederic Laloux," *Medium*, May 7, 2018, medium.com/@fredlaloux/in-many-ways-i-believe-this-is-all-just-the-beginning-a697a33a555b (accessed May 10, 2021).

12. The trend toward flatness may also exacerbate gender inequality and segregation in the workplace. One study finds that firms with flatter hierarchies attract fewer female applicants, mainly because women see such firms offering them fewer opportunities for career advancement, more problems with fit, and greater workloads. See Rueben Hunt, Saerom Lee, and Justin Flake, "The Hidden Cost of Flat Hierarchies on Applicant Pool Diversity: Evidence from Experiments," working paper, Ross School of Business, University of Michigan, March 15, 2022.

13. Alicia Clegg, "Boss-less Business Is No Workers' Paradise," *Financial Times*, September 18, 2019.

14. Douglass C. North, "Institutions," *Journal of Economic Perspectives* 5, no. 1 (1991): 97–112, 97.

CHAPTER 2: WELCOME TO FLATLAND

1. Statista Research Department, "Distribution of Games Released on Steam Between 2004 and 2016, by Release Year," November 30, 2016, www.statista.com/statistics/750099/steam-games-release-annual-distribution/.

2. Eddie Makuch, "Valve Is the Most Desirable Employer in Video Games, Study Finds," GameSpot, August 19, 2014, www.gamespot.com/articles/valve-is-the-most-desirable-employer-in-video-game/1100-6421807/.

3. Many games have in-game economies, meaning that customers can not only pay for various game items but also trade such items with other players. See James Cook, "Greece's New Finance Minister Used to Manage Virtual Economies in Video Games," Insider, February 4, 2015, www.businessinsider.com/yanis-varoufakis-valve-game-economy-greek-finance-2015-2?r=US&IR=T. For Varoufakis's own blog post on the organization of Valve, see "On Spontaneous Order, Valve, the Future of Corporations, Hume, Smith, Marx, and Hayek: A One Hour Chat with Russ Roberts on ECONTALK," February 25, 2013, www.yanisvaroufakis.eu/2013/02/25/on-spontaneous-order-valve-the-future-of-corporations-hume-smith-marx-and-hayek-a-one-hour-chat-with-russ-roberts-on-econtalk/.

4. Alex Hern, "Valve Software: Free Marketeer's Dream, or Nightmare? The First Anti-Cap Software Company," *New Statesman*, August 3, 2012, www.newstatesman.com/blogs/economics/2012/08/valve-software-free-marketeers-dream-or-nightmare (accessed April 21, 2021).

5. Ryan Cooper, "How Capitalism Killed One of the Best Video Game Studios," *The Week*, June 4, 2019, theweek.com/articles/844962/how-capitalism-killed-best-video-game-studios.

6. Cooper says: "There is clearly a lot more money in being an Amazon-style distribution platform than in developing games. What's more, that money is a lot easier to make. First-mover advantage and network effects do most of the work for you" (ibid.). As if moving first and capturing network advantages were easy, obvious, and effortless!

7. Valve Corporation, *Handbook for New Employees* (Bellevue, WA: Valve Press, 2021), 46.

8. Ibid.

9. Frank Cifaldi, "How Valve Hires, How It Fires, and How Much It Pays," Game Developer, February 25, 2013, www.gamedeveloper.com/business/how-valve -hires-how-it-fires-and-how-much-it-pays.

10. Varoufakis, "On Spontaneous Order, Valve, the Future of Corporations."

11. Don Tapscott and Anthony Williams, *Wikinomics: How Mass Collaboration Changes Everything* (New York: Portfolio, 2008); Ori Brafman and Rod A. Beckstrom, *The Starfish and the Spider: The Unstoppable Power of Leaderless Organizations* (London: Penguin, 2006); Clay Shirky, *Here Comes Everybody: The Power of Organizing Without Organizations* (New York: Penguin, 2008); Jacob Bøtter and Lars Kolind, *Unboss* (Copenhagen: Jyllands-Posten, 2012); Gary Hamel and Michele Zanini, *Humanocracy: Creating Organizations as Amazing as the People Inside Them* (Boston: Harvard Business Review Press, 2020).

12. Vivian Giang, "What Kind of Leadership Is Needed in Flat Hierarchies?," *Fast Company*, May 19, 2015, www.fastcompany.com/3046371/what-kind-of-leadership-is -needed-in-flat-hierarchies (accessed December 30, 2021).

13. Justin Bariso, "This Email from Elon Musk to Tesla Employees Describes What Great Communication Looks Like," *Inc.*, August 30, 2017, www.inc.com/justin-bariso /this-email-from-elon-musk-to-tesla-employees-descr.html.

14. "Saving David Brent," *The Economist*, August 15, 2011.

15. Alfred P. Sloan Jr., *My Years with General Motors* (Garden City, NY: Doubleday, 1964).

16. Frederic Laloux, *Reinventing Organizations: A Guide to Creating Organiza- tions Inspired by the Next Stage of Human Consciousness* (Millis, MA: Nelson Parker, 2014).

17. Tom Peters, *Thriving on Chaos: Handbook for a Management Revolution* (New York: Alfred A. Knopf, 1987); Tom Peters, *The Pursuit of Wow! Every Person's Guide to Topsy- Turvy Times* (New York: Vintage, 1994).

18. Edwin A. Abbott, *Flatland: A Romance of Many Dimensions* [1884] (New York: Dover Thrift, 1992).

19. Philippa Warr, "Former Valve Employee: 'It Felt a Lot Like High School,'" *Wired*, July 9, 2013, www.wired.com/2013/07/wireduk-valve-jeri-ellsworth/.

20. André Spicer, "No Bosses, No Managers: The Truth Behind the 'Flat Hierarchy' Facade," *Guardian*, July 30, 2018, www.theguardian.com/commentisfree/2018/jul/30 no-bosses-managers-flat-hierachy-workplace-tech-hollywood.

21. Robert Michels, *Political Parties: A Sociological Study of the Oligarchical Tenden- cies of Modern Democracy*, translated by Eden Paul and Cedar Paul (New York: Free Press, 1915). Norman Cohn's classic *The Pursuit of the Millennium: Revolutionary Mil- lenarians and Mystical Anarchists of the Middle Ages* [1957] (Oxford: Oxford Univer- sity Press, 1970) has interesting illustrations of ostensibly bossless cults that end up worshiping powerful leaders. Woody Allen's 1971 film *Bananas* revolves around this theme.

22. Bradi Heaberlin and Simon DeDeo, "The Evolution of Wikipedia's Norm Net- work," *Future Internet* 8, no. 2 (2016): 14.

CHAPTER 3: BOSSLESSNESS AND OUR CHANGING CULTURE

1. David G. Tarr, "The Steel Crisis in the United States and the European Community: Causes and Adjustments," in *Issues in US-EC Trade Relations*, edited by Robert E. Baldwin, Carl B. Hamilton, and Andre Sapir (Chicago: University of Chicago Press, 1988), 173–198, www.nber.org/system/files/chapters/c5960/c5960.pdf.

2. See Donaldson Brown, vice president, General Motors Corp., "Decentralized Operations and Responsibilities with Coordinated Control," paper presented at the American Management Association convention, New York City, February 1927.

3. Warren Bennis and Philip E. Slater, *The Temporary Society* (New York: Harper & Row, 1968).

4. See, for example, Henry Mintzberg, "Organization Design: Fashion or Fit?," *Harvard Business Review*, January 1981.

5. Alvin Toffler, *Future Shock* (New York: Random House, 1970).

6. Timothy Leary, "Foreword," in *Counterculture Through the Ages: From Abraham to Acid House*, edited by Ken Goffman and Dan Joys (New York: Villard Books, 2004), ix.

7. Virginia Postrel, *The Future and Its Enemies: The Growing Conflict over Creativity, Enterprise, and Progress* (New York: Free Press, 1998).

8. For the story of the ad, see Coca-Cola Company, "Creating 'I'd Like to Buy the World a Coke,'" www.coca-colacompany.com/company/history/creating-id-like-to-buy -the-world-a-coke.

9. Robert M. Grant, "The Future of Management: Where Is Gary Hamel Leading Us?," *Long Range Planning* 41, no. 5 (2008): 469–482, esp. 476.

10. Ibid., 476.

11. See the Esalen website at www.esalen.org/.

12. "Lunch with the FT: Werner Erhard," *Financial Times*, April 28, 2012.

13. James Collins et al., eds., *Harvard Business Review on Change* (Boston: Harvard Business Review Press, 1998).

14. Kenneth Labich and Tim Carvell, "Nike vs. Reebok: A Battle for Hearts, Minds, and Feet," *Fortune*, September 18, 1995.

15. Ibid.

16. Steve Jobs, "'You've Got to Find What You Love,' Jobs Says," Stanford University commencement address delivered June 12, 2005, Stanford News, June 14, 2005, news .stanford.edu/2005/06/14/jobs-061505/.

17. Adam Lashinsky, "How Apple Works: Inside the World's Biggest Startup," *Fortune*, August 25, 2011.

18. Ibid.

19. Ken Wilber, "Foreword," in Frederic Laloux, *Reinventing Organizations: A Guide to Creating Organizations Inspired by the Next Stage of Human Consciousness* (Millis, MA: Nelson Parker, 2014), xvii.

CHAPTER 4: ANTICIPATING FLATLAND

1. The intellectual origins of the bossless company narrative are discussed in Michael Y. Lee and Amy C. Edmondson, "Self-Managing Organizations: Exploring the Limits of Less-Hierarchical Organizing," *Research in Organizational Behavior* 37 (2017): 35–58.

2. Ralph Stayer, "How I Learned to Let My Workers Lead," *Harvard Business Review*, November/December 1990.

3. Tom Peters, "Strategies for Continuous Learning in the Workplace, Part II: The Johnsonville Foods Saga," tompeters!, 1988, tompeters.com/columns/strategies-for-continuous -learning-in-the-workplace-part-ii-the-johnsonville-foods-saga/.

4. Ricardo Semler, "Managing Without Managers," *Harvard Business Review*, September/October 1989.

5. Ricardo Semler, "Out of This World: Doing Things the Semco Way," *Global Business and Organizational Excellence*, July/August 2007, 21.

6. Ibid.

7. Peter A. Maresco and Christopher C. York, "Ricardo Semler: Creating Organizational Change Through Employee Empowered Leadership," Academic Leadership: The Online Journal 3, no. 2 (2005): article 8, scholars.fhsu.edu/alj/vol3/iss2/8.

8. Semler, "Managing Without Managers."

9. Ibid.

10. Ricardo Semler, *The Seven-Day Weekend: Changing the Way Work Works* (New York: Warner Books, 2004), 24.

11. Pim de Morree, "Fixing Work That Sucks: Semco's Step-by-Step Transformation," Corporate Rebels, 2019, corporate-rebels.com/semco/ (accessed April 26, 2021).

12. Reed Hastings and Erin Meyer, *No Rules Rules: Netflix and the Culture of Reinvention* (London: Penguin Press, 2020).

13. Shalini Ramachandran and Joe Flint, "At Netflix, Radical Transparency and Blunt Firings Unsettle the Ranks," *Wall Street Journal*, October 25, 2018.

14. Gary Hamel, "Innovation Democracy: W. L. Gore's Original Management Model," Management Information eXchange, September 23, 2010, www.management exchange.com/story/innovation-democracy-wl-gores-original-management-model.

15. Cited in Ruth Mayhew, "Cons of a Lattice Organizational Structure," *Chron.*, n.d., smallbusiness.chron.com/cons-lattice-organizational-structure-3836.html.

16. Davi Krackhardt and Jeffrey R. Hanson, "Informal Networks: The Company Behind the Chart," *Harvard Business Review*, July/August 1993.

17. Mia Reinholt, Torben Pedersen, and Nicolai J. Foss, "Why a Central Network Position Isn't Enough: The Moderating Roles of Motivation and Ability for Knowledge Sharing in Employee Networks," *Academy of Management Journal* 54 (2011): 1277–1297.

18. Benn Lawson, Kenneth J. Petersen, Paul D. Cousins, and Robert B. Handfield, "Knowledge Sharing in Interorganizational Product Development Teams: The Effect of Formal and Informal Socialization Mechanisms," *Journal of Product Innovation Management* 26, no. 2 (2009): 156–172.

19. Malcolm Gladwell, *The Tipping Point: How Little Things Can Make a Difference* (Boston: Little, Brown, 2000), 186.

20. Tom G. Burns and G. M. Stalker, *The Management of Innovation* (London: Tavistock, 1961).

21. Wesley D. Sine, Hitoshi Mitsuhashi, and David A. Kirsch, "Revisiting Burns and Stalker: Formal Structure and New Venture Performance in Emerging Economic

Sectors," *Academy of Management Journal* 49, no. 1 (2006): 121–132; Arthur Stinchcombe, "Social Structure and Organizations," in *Handbook of Organizations*, edited by James March (Chicago: Rand McNally, 1965), 142–193.

22. Douglas MacGregor, *The Human Side of Enterprise* (New York: McGraw-Hill, 1960); Hamel, "Innovation Democracy."

23. See in particular Gary Hamel and Michele Zanini, *Humanocracy: Creating Organizations as Amazing as the People Inside Them* (Boston: Harvard Business Review Press, 2020).

24. Jay R. Galbraith, *Designing Complex Organizations* (Reading, MA: Addison-Wesley, 1973).

25. John J. Morse and Jay W. Lorsch, "Beyond Theory Y," *Harvard Business Review*, May 1970.

26. A good, if technical, summary of this literature is in Erik Brynjolfsson and Paul Milgrom, "Complementarity in Organizations," in *Handbook of Organizational Economics*, edited by Robert Gibbons and John Roberts (Princeton, NJ: Princeton University Press, 2013), 11–55.

27. Augustin J. Ros, *Profits for All? The Costs and Benefits of Employee Ownership* (Huntington, NY: Nova Science, 2001).

28. Mondragón Corporation, "Co-operative Culture," web.archive.org/web /20101125084323/http://www.mondragon-corporation.com/ENG/Co-operativism /Co-operative-Experience/Co-operative-Culture.aspx.

29. Peter S. Goodman, "Co-ops in Spain's Basque Region Soften Capitalism's Rough Edges," *New York Times*, December 29, 2020.

30. Michael L. Cook and Constantine Iliopoulos, "Ill-Defined Property Rights in Collective Action: The Case of US Agricultural Cooperatives," in *Institutions, Contracts, and Organizations*, edited by Claude Ménard (Aldershot, UK: Edward Elgar, 2000), 335–348.

31. Tom Standage, *The Victorian Internet: The Remarkable Story of the Telegraph and the Nineteenth Century's Online Pioneers* (New York: Walker and Company, 1998).

32. David C. Mowery, "*Plus ca change*: Industrial R&D in the 'Third Industrial Revolution,'" *Industrial and Corporate Change* 18, no. 1 (2009): 1–50.

33. Vivien A. Schmidt, *Democratizing France: The Political and Administrative History of Decentralization* (Cambridge: Cambridge University Press, 2007).

34. Jack Kelly, "Spotify Will Let Employees Work from Anywhere They Do Their Best 'Thinking and Creating,'" *Forbes*, February 12, 2021, www.forbes.com/sites /jackkelly/2021/02/12/spotify-will-let-employees-work-from-anywhere-they-do-their -best-thinking-and-creating/?sh=721b477be046.

35. M. Keith Chen, Peter E. Rossi, Judith A. Chevalier, and Emily Oehlsen, "The Value of Flexible Work: Evidence from Uber Drivers," *Journal of Political Economy* 127, no. 6 (2019): 2735–2794.

36. Barton H. Hamilton, "Does Entrepreneurship Pay? An Empirical Analysis of the Returns to Self-Employment," *Journal of Political Economy* 108, no. 3 (2000): 604–631.

37. Peter Drucker, *The Practice of Management* (New York: Harper & Row, 1954).

CHAPTER 5: OLD WINE IN NEW BOTTLES?

1. James A. Brickley, Clifford W. Smith Jr., and Jerold L. Zimmerman, "Management Fads and Organizational Architecture," *Journal of Applied Corporate Finance* 10, no. 2 (1997): 24–39.

2. Hofstede Insights, "Country Comparison," www.hofstede-insights.com/country -comparison/denmark,finland,norway,sweden/.

3. Published for the English-language market as Jan Carlzon, *The Moment of Truth* (Cambridge, MA: Ballinger, 1987).

4. Arthur Reed, "Carlzon's Out to Raze Pyramids," *Industry Week*, April 28, 1986.

5. Warren Bennis, "Leadership from Inside and Out: We Need Leaders Instead of Managers, Sure, but What Is the Difference? A Doer and a Thinker Try to Explain," *Fortune*, January 18, 1988.

6. Maria Eriksson, Rasmus Fleischer, Anna Johansson, Pelle Snickars, and Patrick Vonderau, *Spotify Teardown: Inside the Black Box of Streaming Music* (Cambridge, MA: MIT Press, 2019).

7. See, for example, Catherine Brown, "Spotify's Organizational Structure for Flexible Growth and Expansion," Rancord Society, updated April 12, 2019, www.rancord .org/spotify-organizational-structure-design-structural-characteristics (accessed April 9, 2021).

8. Brian Dean, "Spotify User Stats," Backlinko, October 14, 2021, backlinko.com/spotify -users; Spotify: For the Record, "About Spotify," newsroom.spotify.com/company-info.

9. Rasmus Fleischer, "Universal Spotification? The Shifting Meaning of 'Spotify' as a Model for the Media Industries," *Popular Communication* 19, no. 1 (2021): 14–25.

10. See, for example, Brown, "Spotify's Organizational Structure."

11. Mark Cruth, "Discover the Spotify Model: What the Most Popular Music Technology Company Can Teach Us About Scaling Agile," Atlassian Agile Coach, www .atlassian.com/agile/agile-at-scale/spotify (accessed December 30, 2021).

12. Gunnar Hedlund, "A Model of Knowledge Management and the N-Form Corporation," *Strategic Management Journal* 15 (1994): 73–90.

13. See Henrik Kniberg and Anders Ivarsson, "Scaling Agile @ Spotify—With Tribes, Squads, Chapters, and Guilds," October 2012, blog.crisp.se/wp-content/uploads /2012/11/SpotifyScaling.pdf (accessed April 21, 2021).

14. Hirotaka Takeuchi and Ikujiro Nonaka, "The New Product Development Game," *Harvard Business Review*, January 1986.

15. Maria Carmela Annosi, Nicolai Foss, Mats Magnusson, and Federica Brunetta, "The Interaction of Control Systems and Stakeholder Networks in Shaping the Identities of Self-Managed Teams," *Organization Studies* 38 (2017): 619–646.

16. See Maria Carmela Annosi, Nicolai Foss, and Antonella Martini, "When Agile Harms Learning and Innovation (and What Can Be Done About It)," *California Management Review* 63 (2020): 61–80.

17. This and many other facts about the US executive market are reported in Carolina Frydman, "Rising Through the Ranks: The Evolution of the Market for Corporate Executives, 1936–2003," *Management Science* 65 (2019): 4951–4976.

18. Mike Davies, "CEO Turnover at Record High; Successors Following Long Serving CEOs Struggling According to PwC's Strategy and Global Study," PwC Global, 2019, www.pwc.com/gx/en/news-room/press-releases/2019/ceo-turnover-record-high.html.

19. Tony Hsieh, *Delivering Happiness: A Path to Profits, Passion, and Purpose* (Boston: Business Plus, 2010).

20. Tony Hsieh, "Why I Sold Zappos," *Inc.*, June 1, 2010, www.inc.com/magazine /20100601/why-i-sold-zappos.html.

21. Tony Hsieh, "How Zappos Infuses Culture Using Core Values," *Harvard Business Review* blog, May 24, 2010, hbr.org/2010/05/how-zappos-infuses-culture-using -core-values (accessed November 13, 2020).

22. Ibid.

23. From the Wikipedia entry on Zappos: "On September 9, 2013, Zappos moved their headquarters from Henderson, Nevada to the former Las Vegas City Hall building in downtown Las Vegas. CEO Tony Hsieh, at the time stated that he wanted 'to be in an area where everyone feels like they can hang out all the time and where there's not a huge distinction between working and playing.' The move was lauded by Las Vegas mayor Oscar Goodman who said 'This move will bring about a critical mass of creative persons to the inner core of Las Vegas in addition to causing a significant shot in the arm for the economy and for new jobs.'" "Zappos," en.wikipedia.org/wiki/Zappos (accessed December 30, 2021).

24. Sam Frampton, "How Zappos Customer Service WOWs Customers to Win," Chattermill, March 13, 2020, chattermill.com/blog/zappos-customer-service/ (accessed December 30, 2021).

25. Roxanne Warren, "10 Things to Know About Zappos Customer Service," Zappos .com, April 17, 2020, www.zappos.com/about/stories/customer-service-things-to-know.

26. Hsieh, "Why I Sold Zappos."

27. Some of these stories are collected at "10 Zappos Stories That Will Change the Way You Look at Customer Service Forever," Infinit-O, 2020, resourcecenter.infinit-o .com/blog/10-zappos-stories-that-will-change-the-way-you-look-at-customer-service -forever/ (accessed December 30, 2021).

28. As reported in Alessia Fabbioni, "Best of Zappos Customer Service Stories," *Medium*, March 7, 2019, medium.com/@alessiafabbioni/best-of-zappos-customer -service-stories-543606d76637.

29. Noah Ashkin and Gianpiero Petriglieri, "Tony Hsieh at Zappos: Structure, Culture, and Change," Insead IN1249-PDF-ENG, August 26, 2016, 6.

30. Alaska Airlines, "Yes THAT Nordstrom Tire Story," October 5, 2015, blog .alaskaair.com/alaska-airlines/nordstrom-tire-story/ (accessed April 21, 2021).

31. Hsieh, "Why I Sold Zappos."

32. Brian J. Robertson, *Holacracy: The Revolutionary Management System That Abolishes Hierarchy* (London: Penguin, 2015).

33. Remember the mathematician Benoit Mandelbrot's "fractals"? Holons are basically fractals.

34. John Bunch, Niko Canner, and Michael Lee, "Beyond the Holacracy Hype: The Overwrought Claims—and Actual Promise—of the Next Generation of Self-Managed Teams," *Harvard Business Review*, July/August 2016, 45.

35. Robertson, *Holacracy*, 22. See "Holacracy Constitution, Version 5.0," www .holacracy.org/constitution/5.

36. Robertson, *Holacracy*, 22.

37. Quoted in Aimee Groth, "Internal Memo: Zappos Is Offering Severance to Employees Who Aren't All in with Holacracy," *Quartz*, March 26, 2013, qz.com/370616 /internal-memo-zappos-is-offering-severance-to-employees-who-arent-all-in-with -holacracy/.

38. Ibid.

39. Aimee Groth, "Zappos Has Quietly Backed Away from Holacracy," *Quartz*, January 29, 2020, qz.com/work/1776841/zappos-has-quietly-backed-away-from-holacracy/.

CHAPTER 6: WHAT THE BOSSLESS COMPANY NARRATIVE GETS RIGHT—AND WHAT IT GETS WRONG

1. See Jacob Bøtter and Lars Kolind, *Unboss* (Copenhagen: Jyllands-Postens Forlag, 2012).

2. Scouts, "Mission, Vision, and Strategy," www.scout.org/vision.

3. Quoted in Joost Minnaar, "How Lars Kolind Created Immense Success by Abolishing Hierarchy (20 Times!)," Corporate Rebels, 2017, corporate-rebels.com/lars-kolind/ (accessed September 15, 2020).

4. John P. Kotter and James L. Heskett, *Corporate Culture and Performance* (New York: Free Press, 1992).

5. That organizational experiment did, however, leave strong traces on the culture. See Nicolai J. Foss and Mathilde Fogh Kirkegaard, "Blended Ambidexterity: Combining Modes of Ambidexterity in William Demant Holding," *Long Range Planning* 53, no. 6 (2020): 102049, doi:10.1016/j.lrp.2020.102049.

6. Oliver E. Williamson, *The Economic Institutions of Capitalism: Firms, Markets, Relational Contracting* (New York: Free Press, 1985), 135.

7. Jerald Greenberg, "Determinants of Perceived Fairness of Performance Evaluations," *Journal of Applied Psychology* 71, no. 2 (1986): 340–342; Robert Folger and Mary A. Konovsky, "Effects of Procedural and Distributive Justice on Reactions to Pay Raise Decisions," *Academy of Management Journal* 32, no. 1 (1989): 115–130.

8. F. A. Hayek, *Law, Legislation, and Liberty*, vol. 1 (Chicago: University of Chicago Press, 1973).

9. Elon Musk, "The Mission of Tesla," Tesla, November 18, 2013, www.tesla.com/blog /mission-tesla (accessed December 15, 2021).

10. Herbert A. Simon, "Organizations and Markets," *Journal of Economic Perspectives* 5, no. 2 (1991): 25–44.

11. Richard N. Langlois, "The Vanishing Hand: The Changing Dynamics of Industrial Capitalism," *Industrial and Corporate Change* 12, no. 2 (2003): 351–385.

12. Heather Boushey and Helen Knudsen, "The Importance of Competition for the American Economy," The White House, July 9, 2021, www.whitehouse.gov/cea/written -materials/2021/07/09/the-importance-of-competition-for-the-american-economy/ (accessed November 23, 2021).

13. Robert D. Atkinson and Filipe Lage de Sousa, "No, Monopoly Has Not Grown," Information Technology and Innovation Foundation, June 7, 2021,

itif.org/publications/2021/06/07/no-monopoly-has-not-grown (accessed November 23, 2021).

14. This is the strategy endorsed in a famous article by the management gurus C. K. Prahalad and Gary Hamel, "The Core Competence of the Corporation," *Harvard Business Review*, May/June 1990.

15. Peter Drucker, *The Practice of Management* (New York: Harper & Row, 1954), 131.

CHAPTER 7: SHOW US THE EVIDENCE!

1. Gary Hamel and Michele Zanini, *Humanocracy: Creating Organizations as Amazing as the People Inside Them* (Boston: Harvard Business Review Press, 2020).

2. Karl R. Popper, "The Critical Approach Versus the Mystique of Leadership," *Human Systems Management* 8 (1989): 259–265, 262.

3. Brooke Macnamara, David Z. Hambrick, and Frederick L. Oswald, "Deliberate Practice and Performance in Music, Games, Sports, Education, and Professions: A Meta-Analysis," *Psychological Science* 25 (2014): 1–11.

4. See, for example, David Autor, "Skills, Education, and the Rise of Earnings Inequality Among the 'Other 99 Percent,'" *Science* 344, no. 6186 (2014): 843–851.

5. David Autor, "Polanyi's Paradox and the Shape of Employment Growth," Working Paper 20485 (Cambridge, MA: National Bureau of Economic Research, 2014).

6. Christopher Lehmann-Haupt, "The Man Who Invented American Efficiency," *New York Times*, August 11, 1997.

7. Cited in Robert Kanigel, *The One Best Way: Frederick Winslow Taylor and the Enigma of Efficiency* (Cambridge, MA: MIT Press, 1997).

8. Jeffrey Vance, *Chaplin: Genius of the Cinema* (New York: Harry N. Abrams, 2003), 229.

9. Henry Mintzberg, "Organization Design: Fashion or Fit?," *Harvard Business Review*, January 1981.

10. National Research Council, *The Changing Nature of Work: Implications for Occupational Analysis* (Washington, DC: National Academies Press, 1999).

11. Daron Acemoglu and David Autor, "Skills, Tasks, and Technologies: Implications for Employment and Earnings," in *Handbook of Labor Economics*, vol. 4B, edited by David Card and Orley Ashenfelter (Amsterdam: North-Holland, 2011), 1043–1171.

12. Enghin Atalay, Phai Phongthiengtham, Sebastian Sotelo, and Daniel Tannenbaum, "The Evolution of Work in the United States," *American Journal of Economics: Applied Economics* 12, no. 2 (2020): 1–34.

13. Richard A. D'Aveni, *Hypercompetition: Managing the Dynamics of Strategic Maneuvering* (New York: Free Press, 1994).

14. Subsequent research found that a number of claims concerning hypercompetition were exaggerated, at least for the decade from the end of the 1970s to the end of the 1980s, which was characterized by decreasing stability of markets and industries. See Gerry McNamara, Paul M. Vaaler, and Cynthia Devers, "Same as It Ever Was: The Search for Evidence of Increasing Hypercompetition," *Strategic Management Journal* 24, no. 3 (2003): 261–278.

15. Haim Mendelsson and Ravindran R. Pillai, "Information Age Organizations, Dynamics, and Performance," *Journal of Economic Behavior and Organization* 38 (1999): 235–281; Nicolai J. Foss and Keld Laursen, "Performance Pay, Delegation, and

Multitasking Under Uncertainty and Innovativeness: an Empirical Investigation," *Journal of Economic Behavior and Organization* 58 (2005): 246–276.

16. Chuck Blakeman, "An Email from Elon Musk Reveals Why Managers Are Always a Bad Idea," *Inc.*, October 30, 2017, www.inc.com/chuck-blakeman/an-email-from-elon -musk-reveals-why-managers-are-always-a-bad-idea.html (accessed May 15, 2021).

17. Friedrich A. Hayek, "The Use of Knowledge in Society," *American Economic Review* 35, no. 4 (1945): 519–530.

18. OECD, "Education at a Glance," 2020, www.oecd.org/education/education -at-a-glance/.

19. Raghuram G. Rajan and Luigi Zingales, "Power in a Theory of the Firm," *Quarterly Journal of Economics* 113, no. 2 (1998): 387–432.

20. Maria Guadalupe and Julie Wulf, "The Flattening Firm and Product Market Competition: The Effect of Trade Liberalization on Corporate Hierarchies," *American Economic Journal: Applied Economics* 2 (2010): 105–127.

21. Kirsten Foss, Nicolai Foss, and José Vasquez, "Tying the Manager's Hands: Credible Commitment and Firm Organization," *Cambridge Journal of Economics* 30 (2006): 797–818.

22. Sandra L. Robinson and Denise M. Rousseau, "Violating the Psychological Contract: Not the Exception but the Norm," *Journal of Organizational Behavior* 15 (1994): 245–259.

23. André Spicer, "No Bosses, No Managers: The Truth Behind the 'Flat Hierarchy' Facade," *Guardian*, July 30, 2018.

CHAPTER 8: MANAGEMENT ISN'T GOING AWAY

1. Adam Lashinsky, *Inside Apple: How America's Most Admired—and Secretive— Company Really Works* (New York: Business Plus, 2012), 69.

2. Ryan Mac, "Jeff Bezos Reveals His No. 1 Leadership Secret," *Forbes*, April 4, 2012.

3. Julie Wulf, "The Flattened Firm: Not as Advertised," *California Management Review* 55, no. 1 (2012): 5–23; Maria Guadalupe, Hongyi Li, and Julie Wulf, "Who Lives in the C-Suite? Organizational Structure and the Division of Labor in Top Management," *Management Science* 60, no. 4 (2014): 824–844.

4. Gardiner Morse, "Management by Fire: A Conversation with Chef Anthony Bourdain," *Harvard Business Review*, July 2002.

5. Listen at your own risk. The level of profanity is quite amazing: "Buddy Rich Bus Tapes REMASTERED Jazz Drummer," posted on YouTube March 13, 2017, www .youtube.com/watch?v=3Ia95oiS5LE&t=175s.

6. Victoria Koehl, "Christian Bale Famously Lost His Temper on the Set of a 'Terminator' Movie," *Showbiz CheatSheet*, December 18, 2020.

CHAPTER 9: WHAT IS A COMPANY ANYWAY?

1. Oliver E. Williamson, *The Economic Institutions of Capitalism: Firms, Markets, Relational Contracting* (New York: Free Press, 1985).

2. G. C. Allen, *The Industrial Development of Birmingham and the Black Country, 1906–1927* (London: Allen and Unwin, 1929), 56–57. We owe this example to our friend and colleague Richard N. Langlois.

3. Adam Smith, *An Enquiry into the Nature and Causes of the Wealth of Nations* (New York: Random House/Modern Library, 1947), 3–5, 7, 11–12.

4. Joel Bakan, *The Corporation: The Pathological Pursuit of Profit and Power* (New York: Free Press, 2007).

5. See the Earth Charter website at earthcharter.org/ (accessed December 31, 2021).

6. Adolf A. Berle and Gardiner C. Means, *The Modern Corporation and Private Property* (New York: Macmillan, 1933).

7. Paul Adler, *The 99 Percent Economy: How Democratic Socialism Can Overcome the Crises of Capitalism* (New York: Oxford University Press, 2019), 5.

8. US House of Representatives, Judiciary Committee, Subcommittee on Antitrust, Commercial, and Administrative Law, Investigation of Competition in Digital Markets: Majority Staff Report and Recommendations, 2020, judiciary.house.gov/uploaded files/competition_in_digital_markets.pdf?utm_campaign=4493-519.

CHAPTER 10: THE WORST FORM OF ORGANIZATION— EXCEPT FOR ALL THE OTHERS

1. Friedrich A. Hayek, "The Use of Knowledge in Society," *American Economic Review* 35, no. 4 (1945): 519–530.

2. Ludwig von Mises, *Bureaucracy* (New Haven, CT: Yale University Press, 1944), 29.

3. Alfred D. Chandler Jr., *Strategy and Structure: Chapters in the History of the Industrial Enterprise* (Cambridge, MA: MIT Press, 1962).

4. This work includes the Pulitzer Prize–winning book *The Visible Hand: The Managerial Revolution in American Business* (Cambridge, MA: Belknap Press of Harvard University Press, 1977). In *Scale and Scope: The Dynamics of Industrial Capitalism* (Cambridge, MA: Harvard University Press, 1990), Chandler compares corporate capitalism across a number of countries.

5. Tarun Khanna and Krishna G. Palepu, *Winning in Emerging Markets: A Road Map for Strategy and Execution* (Boston: Harvard Business Press, 2010).

6. The great French mathematician Émile Borel offered the following example: "Suppose two million Parisians were paired off and set to tossing coins in a game of matching. Each pair plays until the winner on the first toss is again brought to equality with the other player. Assuming one toss per second for each eight hour day, at the end of ten years there would still be, on average, about a hundred odd pairs; and if the players assign the game to their heirs, a dozen or so will still be playing at the end of a thousand years." Quoted in Armen Alchian, "Uncertainty, Evolution, and Economic Theory," *Journal of Political Economy* 58, no. 3 (June 1950): 211–221, 215.

7. See Phil Rosenzweig, *The Halo Effect . . . and Eight Other Business Illusions That Deceive Managers* (New York: Free Press, 2007).

8. Morten Bennedsen, Francisco Pérez-González, and Daniel Wolfenzon, "Do CEOs Matter?," working paper, December 2010, www0.gsb.columbia.edu/mygsb/faculty /research/pubfiles/3177/valueceos.pdf. The death of a spouse or a child has similar effects. In contrast, the death of a board member does not matter to performance. (Nor does the death of the CEO's . . . mother-in-law.)

9. Thomas Quigley and Don Hambrick, "Macrosocietal Changes and Executive Effects on Firm Performance: A New Explanation for the Great Rise in Attributions of CEO Significance, 1950–2009." Working paper, University of Georgia (2011).

10. Steven W. Floyd and Bill Woodridge, "Dinosaurs or Dynamos? Recognizing Middle Management's Strategic Role," *Academy of Management Executive* 8, no. 4 (1994): 47–57, 48.

11. Giuseppe Soda, Marco Tortoriello, and Alessandro Iorio, "Harvesting Value from Brokerage: Individual Strategic Orientation, Structural Holes, and Performance," *Academy of Management Journal* 61, no. 3 (2018): 896–918.

12. K. C. Kellogg, "Brokerage Professions and Implementing Reform in an Age of Experts," *American Sociological Review* 79, no. 5 (2014): 912–941.

13. Herbert A. Simon, "A Formal Theory of the Employment Relationship," *Econometrica* 19 (1951): 293–305.

14. Herbert A. Simon, "The Architecture of Complexity," *Proceedings of the American Philosophical Society* 106 (1962): 467–482.

15. Recent research confirms Simon's ideas; see Henok Mengistu, Joost Huizinga, Jean-Baptiste Mouret, and Jeff Clune, "The Evolutionary Origins of Hierarchy," *PLOS Computational Biology* 12, no. 6 (2016).

16. GitLab, "The 10 Models of Remote and Hybrid Work," about.gitlab.com /company/culture/all-remote/stages/#:~:text=GitLab%20is%20the%20world's%20 largest,in%20more%20than%2065%20countries (accessed December 20, 2021).

17. Richard Langlois's thinking has been influential in this regard; see his "The Vanishing Hand: The Changing Dynamics of Industrial Capitalism," *Industrial and Corporate Change* 12, no. 2 (2003): 351–382.

18. Kif Leswing, "Apple Sued by Fortnite Maker After Kicking the Game out of App Store for Payment Policy Violations," CNBC, August 13, 2020, www.cnbc .com/2020/08/13/apple-kicks-fortnite-out-of-app-store-for-challenging-payment-rules .html (accessed December 31, 2021).

19. Gary Hamel, "First, Let's Fire All the Managers," *Harvard Business Review*, December 2011, 52.

20. Pim de Morree, "Morning Star's Success Story: No Bosses, No Titles, No Structural Hierarchy," *Corporate Rebels*, 2017, corporate-rebels.com/morning-star/ (accessed September 3, 2021).

21. These examples are provided in Francesca Gino, Bradley R. Staats, Brian J. Hall, and Tiffany Y. Chang, "The Morning Star Company: Self-Management at Work," Harvard Business School Case 9-914-013, June 2013.

22. See, for example, Bruce G. Posner, "Right from the Start: Lincoln Electric Co. Compensates Employees Based on Individual Productivity," *Inc.*, August 1, 1988, www .inc.com/magazine/19880801/5934.html (accessed August 2, 2021); and Frank Koller, *Spark: How Old-Fashioned Values Drive a Twenty-First-Century Corporation* (New York: PublicAffairs, 2011).

CHAPTER 11: HIERARCHY ISN'T A DIRTY WORD

1. Hannah Arendt, *Eichmann in Jerusalem: A Report on the Banality of Evil* (New York: Viking Press, 1963).

2. Martin Gurri, *The Revolt of the Public and the Crisis of Authority in the New Millennium* (South San Francisco: Stripe Press, 2018).

3. Gina Perry, *Behind the Shock Machine: The Untold Story of the Notorious Milgram Psychology Experiments* (New York: New Press, 2012).

4. Magnus Henrekson, "In Defense of Good Power," *Quillette*, October 2, 2021.

5. Christopher Boehm, *Hierarchy in the Forest: The Evolution of Egalitarian Behavior* (Cambridge, MA: Harvard University Press, 2001); T. Douglas Price, "Social Inequality at the Origins of Agriculture," in *Foundations of Social Inequality*, edited by T. Douglas Price and Gary M. Feinman (New York: Plenum Press, 1995), 129–151.

6. Francis Fukuyama, *The Origins of Political Order: From Prehuman Times to the French Revolution* (New York: Farrar, Straus and Giroux, 2011), 44 and 54.

7. Jared Diamond, *The World Until Yesterday: What Can We Learn from Traditional Societies?* (New York: Viking, 2012), 11.

8. David Graeber and David Wengrow, "How to Change the Course of Human History (at Least, the Part That's Already Happened)," *Eurozine*, March 2, 2018.

9. Ibid.

10. Caroline F. Zink, Yunxia Tong, Qiang Chen, Danielle S. Bassett, Jason L. Stein, and Andreas Meyer-Lindenberg, "Know Your Place: Neural Processing of Social Hierarchy in Humans," *Neuron* 58, no. 2 (2008): 273–283.

11. Emily M. Zitek and Larissa Z. Tiedens, "The Fluency of Social Hierarchy: The Ease with Which Hierarchical Relationships Are Seen, Remembered, Learned, and Liked," *Journal of Personality and Social Psychology* 102, no. 1 (2012): 98–115.

12. Richard Ronay, Katharine Greenaway, Eric M. Anicich, and Adam D. Galinsky, "The Path to Glory Is Paved with Hierarchy: When Hierarchical Differentiation Increases Group Effectiveness," *Psychological Science* 23, no. 6 (2012): 669–677.

13. Elena Pikulina and Chloe Tergiman, "Preferences for Power," *Journal of Public Economics* 185 (2020).

14. David Pietraszewski, "The Evolution of Leadership: Leadership and Followership as a Solution to the Problem of Creating and Executing Successful Coordination and Cooperation Enterprises," *Leadership Quarterly* 31, no. 2 (2020): art. 101299.

15. Donald B. Egolf and Lloyd E. Corder, "Height Differences of Low and High Job Status, Female and Male Corporate Employees," *Sex Roles* 24 (1991): 365–373.

16. Edward E. Baptist, *The Half Has Never Been Told: Slavery and the Making of American Capitalism* (New York: Basic Books, 2014); Allen L. Olmstead and Paul W. Rhode, *Creating Abundance: Biological Innovation and American Agricultural Development* (New York: Cambridge University Press, 2008).

17. Baptist, *The Half Has Never Been Told*, 131.

18. Edward E. Baptist, "On Slavery and Management," *Publisher's Weekly*, August 3, 2014.

19. Alan L. Olmstead and Paul W. Rhode, "Cotton, Slavery, and the New History of Capitalism," *Explorations in Economic History* 67 (2018): 1–17.

20. Modern discussions include Xavier Freixas, Roger Guesnerie, and Jean Tirole, "Planning Under Incomplete Information and the Ratchet Effect," *Review of Economic Studies* 52 (1985): 173–191; and John M. Litwack, "Coordination, Incentives, and the Ratchet Effect," *Rand Journal of Economics* 24, no. 2 (1993): 271–285.

21. Matthew Desmond, "In Order to Understand the Brutality of American Capitalism, You Have to Start on the Plantation," *New York Times Magazine*, August 14, 2019.

22. The line is spoken by a character in Goethe's 1796 novel, *Wilhelm Meisters Lehrjahre.*

23. Caitlin Rosenthal, *Accounting for Slavery: Masters and Management* (Cambridge, MA: Harvard University Press, 2018).

24. Ibid., xii.

25. Elizabeth Anderson, *Private Government: How Employers Rule Our Lives (and Why We Don't Talk About It)* (Princeton, NJ: Princeton University Press, 2017).

26. Armen A. Alchian and Harold Demsetz, "Production, Information Costs, and Economic Organization," *American Economic Review* 62, no. 5 (1972): 777–795, 777.

27. Henry Hansmann. *The Ownership of Enterprise* (Cambridge, MA: Belknap Press of Harvard University Press, 1996).

28. Sarah Jaffe, *Work Won't Love You Back: How Devotion to Our Jobs Keeps Us Exploited, Exhausted, and Alone* (New York: Bold Type Books, 2021).

29. Caitlin Rosenthal, "Big Data in the Age of the Telegraph," *McKinsey Quarterly,* March 2013.

30. Ibid.

CHAPTER 12: WHY YOU (MAY) NEED MORE HIERARCHY

1. 9/11 Commission, *Final Report of the National Commission on Terrorist Attacks upon the United States* (Washington, DC: US Government Printing Office, 2004), ch. 11.

2. Luis Garicano and Richard A. Posner, "Intelligence Failures: An Organizational Economics Perspective," *Journal of Economic Perspectives* 19, no. 4 (2005): 151–170; see also Garicano and Posner, "What Our Spies Can Learn from Toyota," *Wall Street Journal,* January 12, 2010.

3. Joseph Michael Newhard, "The Stock Market Speaks: How Dr. Alchian Learned to Build the Bomb," *Journal of Corporate Finance* 27 (2014): 116–132.

4. "Extinction Rebellion Shows How Not to Run a Protest Group," *The Economist,* September 10, 2020.

5. Ibid.

6. Ibid.

7. Tatum Sornborger, "The Big Short (Squeeze): A Look at the Reddit Rebellion Through a Legal Lens," *Fordham Journal of Corporate and Financial Law,* February 22, 2021.

8. Maya King, "Black Lives Matter Power Grab Sets off Internal Revolt," *Politico,* December 10, 2020.

9. Fabio Rojas, *From Black Power to Black Studies: How a Radical Social Movement Became an Academic Discipline* (Baltimore: Johns Hopkins University Press, 2010).

10. Mina Kimes, "At Sears, Eddie Lampert's Warring Divisions Model Adds to the Troubles," *Business Week,* July 1, 2013.

11. Kirsten Foss, Nicolai J. Foss, and Peter G. Klein, "Uncovering the Hidden Transaction Costs of Market Power: A Property Rights Approach to Strategic Positioning," *Managerial and Decision Economics* 39, no. 3 (2018): 306–319; Christian Asmussen, Kirsten Foss, Nicolai J. Foss, and Peter G. Klein, "Economizing and Strategizing: How Coalitions and Transaction Costs Shape Value Creation and Appropriation," *Strategic Management Journal* 42, no. 2 (2021): 413–434.

12. Karen Weise, "Bezos Takes Back the Wheel at Amazon," *New York Times*, April 22, 2020; Deepa Seetharaman and Emily Glazer, "Mark Zuckerberg Asserts Control of Facebook, Pushing Aside Dissenters," *Wall Street Journal*, April 28, 2020.

13. Ethan Wolff-Mann, "Why Amazon, Facebook, Disney Saw Their Chiefs Retake Control," *Yahoo!Finance*, May 11, 2020, finance.yahoo.com/news/why-amazon -facebook-disney-saw-their-chiefs-retake-control-142735464.html?guccounter=2 (accessed April 21, 2021).

CHAPTER 13: HIERARCHY PROMOTES INNOVATION AND ENTREPRENEURSHIP

1. Clayton M. Christensen, *The Innovator's Dilemma: When New Technologies Cause Great Firms to Fail* (Boston: Harvard Business School Press, 1997).

2. An early critique of Christensen's theory is Jill Lepore, "The Disruption Machine: What the Gospel of Innovation Gets Wrong," *New Yorker*, June 23, 2014. See also Andrew King and Baljir Baatartogtokh, "How Useful Is the Theory of Disruptive Innovation?," *Sloan Management Review* 57, no. 1 (2015): 77–90.

3. Christensen, *The Innovator's Dilemma*, 15.

4. Colleen Cunningham, Florian Ederer, and Song Ma, "Killer Acquisitions," *Journal of Political Economy* 129, no. 3 (2021): 649–702.

5. Jon Gertner, *The Idea Factory: Bell Labs and the Great Age of American Innovation* (New York: Penguin, 2012), 1.

6. Oliver Franklin-Wallis, "Inside X, Google's Top-Secret Moonshot Factory," *Wired*, February 17, 2020.

7. House Judiciary Antitrust Subcommittee, "Internet Tech Emails," February 27, 2012, tweet ("Mark Zuckerberg and CFO David Ebersman debate acquisition strategy"), twitter.com/TechEmails/status/1400812133580001281 (accessed September 15, 2021).

8. Patricia Van Arnum, "New Drug Approvals in 2020: Which Drugs Made the Mark?," *DCAT Value Chain Insights*, January 20, 2021, www.dcatvci.org/features /new-drugs-approvals-in-2020-which-drugs-made-the-mark.

9. Jackson A. Nickerson and Todd R. Zenger, "Envy, Comparison Costs, and the Economic Theory of the Firm," *Strategic Management Journal* 29 (2008): 1429– 1449.

10. Danny Miller, *The Icarus Paradox: How Exceptional Companies Bring About Their Own Downfall* (New York: HarperBusiness, 1990).

11. Anna Zambelli, "8 Neat Things You Didn't Know About Tupperware," *Good Housekeeping*, September 28, 2015.

12. "Tupperware in Trouble as Slow Sales Hit Maker of Iconic Kitchenware," *Deutsche Presse*, February 25, 2020.

13. Peter G. Klein and Robert Wuebker, "Corporate Diversification and Innovation: Managerial Myopia or Inefficient Internal Capital Markets?," *Managerial and Decision Economics* 41 (2020): 1403–1416.

14. See, for example, Daniel Elfenbein, Barton H. Hamilton, and Todd R. Zenger, "The Small Firm Effect and the Entrepreneurial Spawning of Scientists and Engineers," *Management Science* 56, no. 4 (2010): 659–681.

15. Bruce S. Tether, "Small and Large Firms: Sources of Unequal Innovations?," *Research Policy* 27 (1998): 725–745.

16. Rajesh K. Chandy and Gerard J. Tellis, "The Incumbent's Curse? Incumbency, Size, and Radical Product Innovation," *Journal of Marketing* 64 (2000): 1–17.

17. Peter G. Klein, Mark D. Packard, and Karen Schnatterly, "Collaborating for Innovation: The Role of Organizational Complementarities," in *Oxford Handbook of Collaboration and Entrepreneurship*, edited by Jeffrey J. Reuer and Sharon Matusik (New York: Oxford University Press, 2019), 587–610.

18. Gary Hamel, with Bill Breen, *The Future of Management* (Boston: Harvard Business School Press, 2007).

19. Peter Burrows, "The Seed of Apple's Innovation," *Business Week*, October 11, 2004.

20. Ashish Arora, Sharon Belenzon, and Luis A. Rios, "The Organization of R&D in American Corporations: The Determinants and Consequences of Decentralization," Working Paper 17013 (Cambridge, MA: National Bureau of Economic Research, May 2011).

21. Nicholas S. Argyres and Brian S. Silverman, "R&D, Organization Structure, and the Development of Corporate Technological Knowledge," *Strategic Management Journal* 25 (2004): 929–958.

22. Robert Burgelman, "Fading Memories: A Process Theory of Strategic Business Exit in Dynamic Environments," *Administrative Science Quarterly* 39 (1994): 24–56.

23. Nassim Taleb, *The Black Swan: The Impact of the Highly Improbable* (New York: Random House, 2007).

24. Bridget Fagan, "Lessons from FedEx's ZapMail Service," *Medium*, October 23, 2018, medium.com/@bridgetfagan3/a-lesson-in-failure-zapmail-45a90cb3793e (accessed December 30, 2021).

25. Jay B. Barney, Nicolai J. Foss, and Jacob Lyngsie, "The Role of Senior Management in Opportunity Formation: Direct Involvement or Reactive Selection?," *Strategic Management Journal* 39 (2018): 1325–1334.

26. Alexandra Cummings, "Diversity Adds Millions to the ISS Bottom Line," ISS, docplayer.net/14152956-Diversity-adds-millions-to-the-iss-bottom-line.html (accessed December 30, 2021).

27. Richard Florida, *The Rise of the Creative Class, and How It's Transforming Work, Leisure, and Everyday Life* (New York: Basic Books, 2002); and Richard Florida, *Cities and the Creative Class* (London: Routledge, 2005).

28. Barney, Foss, and Lyngsie, "The Role of Senior Management in Opportunity Formation."

29. Christoph Grimpe, Martin Murmann, and Wolfgang Sofka, "Organizational Design Choices of High-Tech Startups: How Middle Management Drives Innovation Performance," *Strategic Entrepreneurship Journal* 13, no. 3 (2019): 359–378.

30. Lego Group, "Global Growth Ensures Strong 2014 Result for the LEGO Group," February 24, 2015, https://www.lego.com/en-us/aboutus/news/2019/november/2014-result-for-the-lego-group/.

31. Charles A. O'Reilly III and Michael L. Tushman, "The Ambidextrous Organization," *Harvard Business Review*, April 2004.

CHAPTER 14: HIERARCHY IN THE TWENTY-FIRST CENTURY

1. Young Entrepreneur Council, "14 Solutions for Building a Culture of Adaptability in the Workplace," BuiltIn, August 2, 2020, builtin.com/founders-entrepreneurship/14-practical-solutions-building-culture-adaptability (accessed December 30, 2021).

2. Bernard Marr, "10 Business Functions That Are Ready to Use Artificial Intelligence," *Forbes*, March 30, 2020.

3. Julian Birkinshaw, Gary Hamel, and Michael J. Mol, "Management Innovation," *Academy of Management Review* 33, no. 4 (2008): 825–845.

4. This point is developed in Richard Cyert and James G. March, *A Behavioral Theory of the Firm* (Englewood Cliffs, NJ: Prentice-Hall, 1963).

5. Nicolai Foss, Keld Laursen, and Torben Pedersen, "Linking Customer Interaction and Innovation: The Mediating Role of New Organizational Practices," *Organization Science* 22 (2011): 980–999.

6. IBM Institute for Business Value, "Plotting the Platform Payoff," Global C-Suite Study, 19th ed., IBM Corporation, May 2018, www.ibm.com/downloads/cas/NJYY0ZVG.

7. Edward L. Deci and Richard M. Ryan, "Self-Determination Theory," in *Handbook of Theories of Social Psychology*, vol. 1, edited by Paul A. M. Van Lange, Arie W. Kruglanski, and E. Tory Higgins (Newbury Park, CA: Sage Publications, 2012), 416–436.

8. Jennifer J. Deal and Alec Levenson, *What Millennials Want from Work: How to Maximize Engagement in Today's Workforce* (New York: McGraw-Hill, 2016).

9. The terminology is from Kirsten Foss and Nicolai J. Foss, "Managerial Authority When Knowledge Is Distributed," in *Knowledge Governance: Perspectives from Different Disciplines*, edited by Nicolai Foss and Snejina Michailova (Oxford: Oxford University Press, 2009), 108–137.

10. Herbert Simon, *Administrative Behavior* (New York: Simon & Schuster, 1947).

11. Herbert A. Simon, "Organizations and Markets," *Journal of Economic Perspectives* 5, no. 2 (1991): 25–44.

12. Carola Frydman and Dirk Jenter, "CEO Compensation," *Annual Review of Financial Economics* 2 (2010): 75–102.

13. Maria Carmela Annosi, Nicolai Foss, Mats Magnusson, and Federica Brunetta, "The Interaction of Control Systems and Stakeholder Networks in Shaping the Identities of Self-Managed Teams," *Organization Studies* 38 (2017): 619–646; Maria Carmela Annosi, Nicolai J. Foss, and Daniela Martini, "When Agile Harms Learning and Innovation (and What Can Be Done About It)," *California Management Review* 63 (2020): 61–80.

14. Eileen Y. Chou, Nir Halevy, Adam D. Galinsky, and J. Keith Murnighan, "The Goldilocks Contract: The Synergistic Benefits of Combining Structure and Autonomy for Persistence, Creativity, and Cooperation," *Journal of Personality and Social Psychology* 113, no. 3 (2017): 393–412.

15. Sandra L. Robinson and Denise M. Rousseau, "Violating the Psychological Contract: Not the Exception but the Norm," *Journal of Organizational Behavior* 15 (1994): 245–259.

16. Katherine Klein, Jonathan C. Ziegert, Andrew P. Knight, and Yan Xiao, "Dynamic Delegation: Shared, Hierarchical, and Deindividualized Leadership in Extreme Action Teams," *Administrative Science Quarterly* 51, no. 4 (2006): 590–621.

17. Kirsten Foss, Nicolai Foss, and José Vasquez, "Tying the Manager's Hands: Credible Commitment and Firm Organization," *Cambridge Journal of Economics* 30 (2006): 797–818.

18. Some recent research analyzed a data set of job descriptions for executive positions to show how skills requirements are changing. The researchers used an algorithm to sift through these descriptions and identify salient job aspects. They found a general and increasing relevance of social skills in top managerial occupations. See Stephen Hansen, Tejas Ramdas, Raffaella Sadun, and Joe Fuller, "The Demand for Executive Skills," Working Paper 28959 (Cambridge, MA: National Bureau of Economic Research, June 2021).

19. Jack A. Nickerson and Todd R. Zenger, "Envy, Comparison Costs, and the Economic Theory of the Firm," *Strategic Management Journal* 29, no. 3 (2008): 1429–1449.

20. Amy C. Edmondson, Sujin Jang, and Tiziana Casciaro, "Cross-Silo Leadership," *Harvard Business Review*, May/June 2019.

21. Dan Tynan, "IT Turf Wars: The Most Common Feuds in Tech," *Infoworld*, February 14, 2021.

22. Stefan Kühl, *Sisyphus in Management: The Futile Search for the Optimal Organizational Structure* (Princeton, NJ: Organizational Dialogue Press, 2020).

23. The following is based on Nicolai J. Foss and Peter G. Klein, "Why Managers Still Matter," *Sloan Management Review*, September 2014, 73–80.

24. McKinsey & Company, "Decision Making in the Age of Urgency: A Survey," April 30, 2019, www.mckinsey.com/business-functions/organization/our-insights/decision-making-in-the-age-of-urgency (accessed July 26, 2021).

25. Kathleen M. Eisenhardt and L. J. Bourgeois III, "Politics of Strategic Decision Making in High-Velocity Environments: Toward a Midrange Theory," *Academy of Management Journal* 31 (1988): 737–770.

26. "Shattering the Status Quo: A Conversation with Haier's Zhang Ruimin," *McKinsey Quarterly*, July 27, 2001.

CHAPTER 15: THE HIGHLY EXAGGERATED DEATH OF THE MANAGER

1. Gary Hamel, "First, Let's Fire All the Managers," *Harvard Business Review*, December 2011, 50.

2. Gary Hamel and Michele Zanini, "Excess Management Is Costing the US $3 Trillion per Year," *Harvard Business Review* blog, September 5, 2016, hbr.org/2016/09/excess-management-is-costing-the-us-3-trillion-per-year (accessed December 31, 2021). See Phillip Nell, Nicolai J. Foss, Peter G. Klein, and Jan Schmidt, "Avoiding Digitalization Traps: Tools for Top Managers," *Business Horizons* 64, no. 2 (2021): 163–169.

3. "Saving David Brent," *The Economist*, August 15, 2011.

4. Stanley Fish, "A Classical Education: Back to the Future," *New York Times*, June 7, 2010. According to the US Department of Education, enrollment at members of the US Association of Classical and Christian Schools nearly doubled between 2006 and 2020.

ACKNOWLEDGMENTS

1. The interested reader—we are sure there are at least two or three out there—can find our intellectual biographies in the following sources: Nicolai J. Foss, "Introduction: Knowledge, Economics Organization, and Property Rights," in Nicolai J. Foss, *Knowledge, Economics Organization, and Property Rights: Selected Essays of Nicolai J. Foss* (Aldershot, UK: Edward Elgar, 2009); Peter G. Klein, "Introduction," in Peter G. Klein, *The Capitalist and the Entrepreneur: Essays on Organizations and Markets* (Auburn, AL: Mises Institute, 2009); Nicolai J. Foss, "Judgment, the Theory of the Firm, and the Economics of Institutions: My Contributions to the Entrepreneurship Field," and Peter G. Klein, "My Contributions to Entrepreneurship Theory," in *The Routledge Companion to the Makers of Modern Entrepreneurship*, edited by David B. Audretsch and Erik E. Lehmann (London: Routledge, 2017), 146–153.

2. Nicolai J. Foss and Peter G. Klein, "Why Managers Still Matter," *Sloan Management Review*, September 2014, 73–80; Nicolai J. Foss and Peter G. Klein, "No Boss? No Thanks," *Aeon*, January 14, 2019.

INDEX

Nicolai J. Foss is a professor of strategy at the Copenhagen Business School and one of the most cited European management scholars. He has authored many articles published in management research journals and is a prolific contributor to policy and business debate as a newspaper columnist and contributor to practitioner-oriented magazines.

Peter G. Klein is W. W. Caruth Endowed Chair and Professor of Entrepreneurship at Baylor University's Hankamer School of Business and Carl Menger Research Fellow at the Mises Institute. He was a senior economist at the US Council of Economic Advisers in the Clinton administration and is author or editor of six books and numerous articles, chapters, and reviews.